우루과이라운드

서비스 협상 2

_____

우루과이라운드

서비스 협상 2

한국학술정보

| 머리말

    우루과이라운드는 국제적 교역 질서를 수립하려는 다각적 무역 교섭으로서, 각국의 보호무역 추세를 보다 완화하고 다자무역체제를 강화하기 위해 출범되었다. 1986년 9월 개시가 선언되었으며, 15개 분야의 교섭을 1990년 말까지 진행하기로 했다. 그러나 각 분야의 중간 교섭이 이루어진 1989년 이후에도 농산물, 지적소유권, 서비스무역, 섬유, 긴급수입제한 등 많은 분야에서 대립하며 1992년이 돼서야 타결에 이를 수 있었다. 한국은 특히 농산물 분야에서 기존 수입 제한 품목 대부분을 개방해야 했기에 큰 경쟁력 하락을 겪었고, 관세와 기술 장벽 완화, 보조금 및 수입 규제 정책의 변화로 제조업 수출입에도 많은 변화가 있었다.

    본 총서는 우루과이라운드 협상이 막바지에 다다랐던 1991~1992년 사이 외교부에서 작성한 관련 자료를 담고 있다. 관련 협상의 치열했던 후반기 동향과 관계부처회의, 무역협상위원회 회의, 실무대책회의, 규범 및 제도, 투자회의, 특히나 가장 많은 논란이 있었던 농산물과 서비스 분야 협상 등의 자료를 포함해 총 28권으로 구성되었다. 전체 분량은 약 1만 3천여 쪽에 이른다.

2024년 3월
한국학술정보(주)

| 일러두기

· 본 총서에 실린 자료는 2022년 4월과 2023년 4월에 각각 공개한 외교문서 4,827권, 76만여 쪽 가운데 일부를 발췌한 것이다.

· 각 권의 제목과 순서는 공개된 원본을 최대한 반영하였으나, 주제에 따라 일부는 적절히 변경하였다.

· 원본 자료는 A4 판형에 맞게 축소하거나 원본 비율을 유지한 채 A4 페이지 안에 삽입하였다. 또한 현재 시점에선 공개되지 않아 '공란'이란 표기만 있는 페이지 역시 그대로 실었다.

· 외교부가 공개한 문서 각 권의 첫 페이지에는 '정리 보존 문서 목록'이란 이름으로 기록물 종류, 일자, 명칭, 간단한 내용 등의 정보가 수록되어 있으며, 이를 기준으로 0001번부터 번호가 매겨져 있다. 이는 삭제하지 않고 총서에 그대로 수록하였다.

· 보고서 내용에 관한 더 자세한 정보가 필요하다면, 외교부가 온라인상에 제공하는 『대한민국 외교사료요약집』 1991년과 1992년 자료를 참조할 수 있다.

| 차례

머리말 4

일러두기 5

UR(우루과이라운드).GNS(서비스협상그룹) 회의, 1991. 전5권(V.3 6-8월) 7

UR(우루과이라운드).GNS(서비스협상그룹) 회의, 1991. 전5권(V.4 9-10월) (1) 259

0001

기 안 용 지

분류기호 문서번호	통기 20644- 25611	(전화 : 720 - 2188)	시 행 상 특별취급	
보존기간	영구. 준영구 10. 5. 3. 1.	장		관
수 신 처 보존기간				
시행일자	1991. 6. 5.			

보 조 기 관	국 장	전결	협 조 기 관		문 서 통 제 1991. 6. 07
	심의관				
	과 장				
기안책임자		조 현			발 송 인

경 수 참	유 신 조	경제기획원장관 대조실장	발 신 명 의		반송승 1991. 6. 07

제 목	UR 서비스 협상 관련 조약 검토

대 : 통조삼 10502-320

갓트 사무국으로 부터의 서비스교역 관련 수평적 국제 협정

자료 요청과 관련, 당부가 검토한 우호·통상·항해 조약에 관한 자료를

별첨 송부합니다.

첨 부 : 상기 검토 자료 1부.   끝.

0002

UR/서비스협상관련조약 검토

1991.5.28.

I. 우호.통상.항해조약

1. 조약체결현황

   o 체결국(1개국): 미국(56.11.28.서명, 57.11.7.발효)

   - 참고: 중화민국, 이란 등과는 우호조약을 체결

     (통상.항해에 관한 조약은 아님)

2. 조약적용대상 서비스업종 및 예외업종(한.미간 조약 제7조)

   o 모든 서비스업종에 대하여 적용하되, 운수, 통신, 공익사업,
   은행업무 등에 관하여는 내국민대우 적용유보

3. 조약과 서비스업종과의 관련형식

   o 한.미간 조약은 기본적으로 상품무역과 서비스무역을 구별하지
   않고 무역활동과 투자활동등 모든 영업활동을 포괄적으로
   규율함.

4. 조약상 의무 또는 약속의 성격, 범위, 정의(한.미간 조약 제7조 및
   제22조)

   가. 성격: 내국민대우 및 최혜국대우

   나. 범위(제7조)

   o 내국민대우

   - 운수, 통신, 공익사업, 은행업등을 제외한 기타 서비스업
     활동에 관하여 타방체약국 국민.회사등에 내국민대우 부여
     (한.미간 조약 제7조 1, 2항은 운수, 통신, 공익사업, 은행업무,
     천연자원개발등을 제외한 모든 종류의 상업, 공업, 금융업 및
     기타 영리활동(실업활동)에 관하여 내국민대우를 부여하도록
     규정)

0003

/

- 따라서, 상기 활동을 위하여 내국인과 동일조건하에 외국인의
  지점, 대리점, 사무소 기타 사업수행시설 설치.유지 및 회사
  설립 및 지배.경영가능

  ○ 최혜국대우
  - 모든 서비스업종에 관하여 타방체약국 국민.회사등에 최혜국대우
    부여(한.미간 조약 제7조 4항은 모든 종류의 상업, 공업, 금융업
    및 기타 영리활동(실업활동)에 관하여 여하한 경우에도 최혜국
    대우를 부여하도록 규정)

다. 정의(제22조)
  ○ 내국민대우
    일방체약국의 영역내에서 부여되는 대우로서 당해 체약국의 국민,
    회사, 생산품, 선박 또는 기타의 대상에게 그 사정에 따라 같은
    상황하에서 그 영역내에서 부여되는 대우보다 불리하지 않은
    대우

  ○ 최혜국대우
    일방체약국의 영역내에서 부여되는 대우로서 어느 제3국의 국민,
    회사, 생산품, 선박 또는 기타의 대상에게 그 사정에 따라 같은
    상황하에서 그 영역내에서 부여되는 대우보다 불리하지 않은 대우

5. 조약의 실제시행에 있어서 당사국이 비당사국에 비하여 특별한 대우를
   받는 관행 및 조치의 내용(상공부등 시행부서 검토사항)

6. 관련조치가 조약상 의무자체의 조건(유효기간 만료등) 또는 당사국의
   조치로 무효화 될 수 있는지 여부(상공부등 시행부처 검토사항)

0004

2

o 참고사항 :

  - 한.미간 조약의 유효기간은 10년이며 종료통고가 없는 한
    자동연장 가능

  - 한.미간 조약상 의무보다 유리한 대우를 부여하는 우대조치는
    당해국의 조치로 철회할 수 있으나 조약상 규정에 따라 부여한
    대우는 조약이 유효한 이상 철회불가

II. 사법 및 행정적 지원에 관한 조약

  o 서비스교역과 관련된 사법 및 행정적 지원에 관한 조약은 없음. 끝.

3

0005

외   무   부

종   별 :

번   호 : GVW-1040   일   시 : 91 0605 1100

수   신 : 장관(봉기,수신처참조)

발   신 : 주제네바대사

제   목 : UR/GNS 회의(5)

6.3(월) 속개된 표제회의는 분쟁해결에 대하여 논의하였는바 주요내용 하기보고함.

1. 회의개요

- 강력하고   효율적인   다자간   분쟁해결   체제가마련되어야   한다는   데에는
참가국간견해가일치하였으나   GATT   분쟁해결   절차를   사용하는문제,   개별결정의
분쟁해결   의뢰여부,NON-VIOLATION   CASE,   상품,   서비스간   교차보복등에대하여
선.개도국간 의견이대립되었음2. 주요회의 내용

가. UR 협상결과 도출될 GATT 분쟁해결절차의 수용여부

- 선진국   및   아국,홍콩,싱가폴,헝가리등은   GATT40   년간의   경험을   활용할
필요성등을 들어UR 협상결과 도출될 GATT 분쟁해결 절차(TNC/W/35 P.289-305) 를
대부분 그대로 서비스 분야에원용할 수 있음을 주장한 반면

- 인도,이집트,브라질등은   상품과   서비스는   서로특성이   있으므로
서비스협정에별도의   충분한규정이   담아져야   하며   GATT   절차를   검토할   용의는있으나
이를 그대로수용할 수는 없다고 함.

- 특히, 아국,싱가폴,헝가리등은 상품과 서비스의분쟁해결 메카니즘은 별도로 하고
오직 절차적인것만 GATT UR 협상결과를 원용할 것을주장함.

나. 개별 결정의 분쟁해결 의뢰 및 국내 구제절차 소진 여부

- 서비스협정은   체약국   정부간의   권리,   의무를규정하는   것이지   개인의   권리를
보호하는   것이아니기   때문에   외국은행   설립인가,비자발급등에   관한   개별결정을
곧바로다자간분쟁해결에 의뢰할수는 없으며 국내구제절차가최대한 활용되어야 한다는
데에는 대체로견해가 일치함.

0 그러나 EC 는 국내절차가 수년씩 걸리는것은곤란하기 때문에 이에대한 시한
결정이 필요하다고함.

| 통상국 | 차관 | 1차보 | 2차보 | 경제국 | 법무부 | 문화부 | 교통부 | 체신부 |
| 교육부 | 경기원 | 재무부 | 상공부 | 건설부 | 노동부 | 과기처 | 해항청 | 공보처 |

91.06.06   07:43 DF

외신 1과 통제관

0006

0 이에대하여 인도,파키스탄은 시한을 설정하는것은 서로다른 국내법체계를 조화하는 것이라고반대함.

0 한편, 캐나다는 국내에 이의제기 절차(APPEAL SYSTEM) 가 없거나 주요정책과는관계없는사안으로서 매우 드물게 일어나는 개별사례는분쟁해결에 의뢰할수 있어야 할것이라고함(아국동조)

다. NON-VIOLATION CASES

- 협정상의 의무에 위배되지는 않으나어떤조치로 인하여 상대국의 이익이 침해된경우가서비스분야에 특별히 중요하다는 점에 많은나라의견해가 일치하였으며 이를 보다 명확하게 규정하기위하여 많은 토의가 필요하다는 점이 지적됨

0 말련, 태국, 싱가폴등은 동 규정으로 인하여정부의 일반적인 경제정책 운용까지도 제한받을수있다는 점을 들어 유보적 입장을표시하였으나

0 EC, 캐나다는 일반적인 정책이 아니라 구체적조치로 인하여 상대국 이익이 침해된 경우를의미하여 NON-VIOLATION MEASURES 는 이를 철회할필요가 없으며 오직 보상문제만 제기된다는점에서 VIOLATION CASE 와 분명히 구별된다고반박함.

라. 교차보복

- 아국,유고,헝가리 및 기타 개도국들은 GATT 와GATS 는 서로 다른 법적 규정이라는 점을 들어상품과 서비스간 교차보복에 반대하였으나(서비스분야간 교차보복은 허용)

- 대부분의 선진국들은 보복은 최후의구제수단으로서 거의 발동되지 않는다는 점,서비스에 한정할 경우 보복이 불가능할수 있다는점을 들어 상품과 서비스간 교차보복 허용(특히미국이 강한 입장)을 주장함

0 특히, 캐나다, 스위스,스웨덴,뉴질랜드등은일차적으로 같은 서비스분야, 그다음에 서비스분야간,상품-서비스간 교차보복의 계층구조를 주장함

- 또한 보복의 방법과 관련 HOST COUNTRY 에기설치된 회사,이미 입국한 서비스 공급자의 폐쇄,철수를 요구하기는 법률적으로 곤란할 것이라는점이 지적됨(ACQUIRED RIGHTS)

마. PANEL 구성

- PANELIST 에 분야별 전문가를 참여시키는문제에 대하여 대부분의 나라가 긍정적 입장을표명하였으나

0 동전문가의 역할에 관해서는 선진국들은정식 PANELIST 로 참여할 것을

지지한반면말련, 멕시코등은 자문역할에 한정하여야 하다고함.

　바. 피해와 보상, 보복간의 비례성

　- 모든 나라가 보상 및 보복 규모는 피해규모에비례적이어야 한다고함

　사. 타 국제협정과의 관계

　- 캐나다는 GATS 하의 분쟁해결 결과가 모든 타국제협정에 우선해야 한다고 한반면 EC,인도등은 유보입장을 표명함

　아. 일방조치 자제에 대한 약속

　- 많은 나라가 GATT/ 분쟁해결 협상그룹초안과 같이 일방적 조치자제에 대한 약속이있어야 한다고 지적함.끝

　수신처:경기원, 재무부, 법무부,교육부, 상공부, 건설부,노동부, 교통부,체신부,문화부, 공보처,과기처,항만청

　(대사 박수길-국장)

외 무 부

종 별 :

번 호 : GVW-1039 　　　　　　　　　　　일 시 : 91 0605 1100

수 신 : 장관(봉기, 수신처참조)

발 신 : 주 제네바 대사

제 목 : UR/GNS 회의(6)

6.4(화) 속개된 표제회의 내용을 하기 보고함.

1. 회의 개요

- 용어의 정의(제 34조)

0 인도, 말련등 주로 개도국으로 부터 협정 대상정부조치 (MEASURE) 의 범위, 상업적 주재의범위, 외국 서비스 공급자의 정의등에 대한 문제제기가 있었음.

0 금일 토의 내용을 바탕으로 사무국에서 추가작업하여 적당한 시기에 재논의키로 함.(인도는 제1조 서비스 무역의 정의가 선결되어야 제 34조에대한 논의가 가능하다는 입장)

- 양허 협상 절차

0 각국의 OFFER 제출 시한(확정 시한은 아니며TARGET DATE 임)을 정하여야 한다는데 대체적으로합의가 형성되었으며, 많은 나라가 여름휴가전까지를 목표 일자로 삼아야 한다고언급하였음.

2. 주요 회의 내용

가. 용어의 정의

- MEASURE 의 범위(제 34조 A 항)

0 인도 및 말련은 정부의 모든 행위가 협정대상이 될수는 없으므로 ' IMMEDIATE GENERALAPPLICATION' 이라는 제한 조건을 추가하여야 한다고하는 한편 DECISION 의 범위에 사법적 결정도포함되는지 질의한바 갓트 법률국은 행정결정만 포함된다고 함.

- 서비스 공급의 정의(B 항)

0 인도, 이집트, 말려등은 ' PRODUCTION' 은 부자문제이기 때문에 써비스 무역 협정의 범위를넘어서는 것이며, 제 1조에 대한 합의가선행되어야 한다고 함.

- 서비스 공급에 영향을 미치는 조치(C 항)

통상국	차관		2차보	보사부	문화부	교통부	체신부	교육부
경기원	상공부	건설부	노동부	과기처	해항정	공보처		

PAGE 1 　　　　　　　　　　　　　　　　　　　　91.06.06　　07:22 DF

외신 1과 통제관

0009

0 인도는 I) 항의 ' PURCHASE' 라는 용어와관련 서비스 협정이 수출봉제도 대상으로 하는지문제를 제기함. 또한 III) 항의 ' COMMERCIALPRESENCE OF NATURAL PERSONS' 에 과연 자연인의일시적 주재가 포함되고 있는지 문제를 제기함.

0 멕시코는 II) 항에 ' INFORMATION NETWORK ANDRESERVATION SYSTEM' 을 추가 할것을 주장하였으며

0 스웨덴은 II) 항의 '공중전기봉신망'을보다 넓은 개넘인 ' COMMUNICATION SYSTEM' 으로대체할 것을 주장하였으며, III) 항에 외국에설립된 서비스 공급기업이 제 3국에 다시 제 2차자회사를 설립하는 경우도 포함되어야 한다고 함.

- 외국 서비스 공급자의 정의(E-II 항, F 항 : 서비스의 원산지)

0 인도 및 말련은 외국인이 소유권 또는운영권을 가지나 주재국 법률에 의하여 설립된서비스 공급 기업이 외국기업인지, 국내 기업인지문제를 제기함. (특히 소유지분이 분산되어 있는경우)

0 일본 역시 이와 관련 동 조문의 보완 필요성을지적하였으나, EC 는 동 조문이서비스 공급기업의 국적을 정하기 위한 것은 아니라고함. (법률국도 동 조항의 보완필요성에 동의함.)

0 헝가리는 E-II) 항에 사기업이 아닌 정부가주재국에 기업을 설립하는 경우가 누락되었다고지적함.

- 상업적 주재의 범위(H 항)

0 인도는 영국적 부자의 제외를 주장하였으며,오지리, 브라질등은 ' OTHERWISE'라는 표현이 너무광범위하다고 지적함.

나. 양허 협상 절차

- 0 FFER 제출 시한 설정

0 말련을 제외한 대부분의 나라가 OFFER 제출시한 (INDICATIVE DATE) 를 설정하는데 지지의사를표명하였으며, 호주, 미국, 캐나다등은 하기 휴가전을제시하였음.

0 한편, 멕시코, 헝가리, 알젠틴, 이집트등은 이미OFFER 를 제출한 나라도 추후수정판, 추가판등을내야 하는 점을 고려할때 동 시한이 확정시한이되어서는 안되며목표 시한(TARGET DATE) 이 되어야한다는 점을 강조함.

- R/0 협상 과정의 공개성

0 사무국 문서 5항의 각국의 REAUEST 배부와관련 대부분의 나라가 지지의사를

PAGE 2

0010

16   우루과이라운드 서비스 협상 2

표명하고 최대한공개성이 보장되어야 한다고 하였으나

    0 미국과 일본은 REQUEST LIST 배부 목적을이해할수 없다고 하고 이를 통해 특정국가의상업적 이익이 침해될 수 있다고 반대의사를표명함.

    0 미국은 또한 3항의 '다자간의 주기적 검토 및평가'도 이해할수 없다고 함.

    - 의장은 차기회의 이전까지 각국과 비공식협의를 하여 다음 사항에 대한 타협안을마련하겠다고 함.

    0 양허 협상 절차

    0 실질적 양허 협상 지침

    0 양허 협상 관련 시간 계획

    3. 표제회의는 사무국이 작성 금일 오후 배부한 'SCHEDULING 에 관한 대안'에 대하여 6.5(수)DAVID HAWES(호주대사) 주재로 비공식 협의를가진뒤 6.6(목) 속개할 예정임. 끝

    수신처:경기원, 법무부, 교육부, 상공부, 건설부, 노동부, 보사부, 교봉부, 체신부, 문화부, 공보처, 과기처, 항만청

    (대사 박수길-국장)

외 무 부

종 별 :

번 호 : GVW-1059　　　　　　　　　　일 시 : 91 0606 1800

수 신 : 장 관(봉기, 경기원, 재무부, 법무부, 교육부, 상공부, 건설부, 노동부, 교통부,

발 신 : 주 제네바 대사　　　　　　　　　체신부, 문화부, 공보처, 과기처, 항만청)

제 목 : UR/GNS 비공식 협의

1. 6.4.(화) 캐나다 대표부에서 개최된 아국, 이집트, 유고등 일부 국가와의 비공식 오찬 협의에서 캐나다가 배부한 노동력 이동부속서, 일시적 인력이동에 관한 다자간 공통 약속, 자유화 약속에 관한 COMMON APPROACH 를 별첨 (FAX) 송부함.

2. 상기 문서에 대한 당관 검토 의견은 아래와같음.

가. 노동력 이동 부속서

- 대체적으로 아국 입장에 적합한 것으로 판단됨.

0 1항-3항 A) 는 TNC/W/35 상의 초안과 같음

0 3항 B) 및 4항은 인력 수입 당사국의 규제권한, 노사문제의 분리등을 규정한 것으로서 아국입장에 적합한 것으로 판단됨.

0 5항은 주재국의 최저 임금, 사회보장법등의 적용을 규정한 것으로서 일응 타당한 것으로 판단되나 아국인력의 해외진출, 해외인력의 아국 유입시장. 단점을 재 검토할 필요가 있음

나. 일시적 인력 이동에 관한 다자간 공통약속

- 다음과 같은 이유에서 동접근방식에 대한 긍정적 검토가 필요한 것으로 판단됨

0 현실적으로 각분야별로 구체적인 인력이동범위에 관한 협상을 하기가 번거로움

0 지금까지 제출된 각국 OFFER 에 나타난바와 같이 넓은 범위의 인력이동에 관한 약속을 하기가 어려움

0 아국의 실리 차원에서도 아국 인력시장 상황이 급격히 변하고 있을뿐만 아니라, 특정인력의 부족시 아국의 판단하에 동 인력을 수입하는 것은 적절하나 넓은 범위의 인력 (예: SKILLED WORKER까지)을 서비스협정하에 양허할 경우 BINDING 되어 아국 인력시장 상황 변동, 인력 유입에 따른 각종 사회문제 발생등에도 불구하고 동범주의 인력입국을 계속 허용할 수 밖에 없게된다는 점

통상국	2차보	법무부	문화부	교통부	체신부	교육부	경기원	재무부
상공부	건설부	노동부	과기처	해항청	공보처	1차보		

PAGE 1　　　　　　　　　　　　　　　　　　91.06.07　　08:45 WG

외신 1과 통제관 0012

다. 자유화 약속에 관한 COMMON APPORACH

- 공통 자유하 대상 서비스 분야를 어떻게 설정하느냐에 따라 달라질 것이나 일반적으로 급진적인 대안이라고 평가할 수 있음

0 국내 규제제도가 부적할하거나 아예 발달되어있지 않은 서비스 분야가 많은 개도국으로서는 참여하기에 어려울 것으로 예상됨

0 개도국이 참여한다 하더라도, 국제교역상 가치가별로 없거나 정부 차원에서 규제할 필요가 없는 분야등 일부서비스에 한정될 수 밖에 없을것으로 판단됨

첨부: 캐나다 작성 비공식 문서 1부. (GVW(F)-0193).끝

(대사 박수길-국장)

Annex on the Temporary Movement of Natural Persons Providing Services

1. The provisions of the Agreement relate to temporary movement of natural persons performing particular services in respect of which access commitments have been undertaken. They do not apply to individual job seekers and do not concern, and should not affect, national laws and regulations or international agreements and arrangements regarding citizenship or immigration.

2. Parties may negotiate market access commitments applying to natural persons providing specified services for a temporary period of time. Once such a market access commitment is inscribed in a Party's schedule, all natural persons covered by the commitment shall be allowed to provide the service.

3. a) Benefits from any scheduled commitments shall not be frustrated through the application of national laws or regulations relating to the entry, stay and work on a temporary basis of natural persons.

   b) Nothing in the Agreement or its annexes shall prevent a Party from adopting and enforcing such measures relating to the temporary movement of natural persons providing services as it considers necessary to protect the integrity of, and the orderly movement of natural persons across, its international borders.

4. Nothing in the Agreement or its annexes shall be construed as permitting the temporary movement of natural persons performing particular services in respect of which access commitments have been undertaken where the intent or effect of such movement is to interfere with or otherwise affect the outcome of any labour/management dispute or negotiation.

5. Parties may require that relevant domestic regulations (e.g. minimum wage requirements, social security regulations, health and safety standards, etc.), applicable in the country, province or state where the work is being carried out, be respected by natural persons providing services.

0014

3-1

not yet fully worked out. They would, of course, apply as from the date of entry into force of the GATS.]

Each party to the GATS shall impose no limitations or conditions on market access or national treatment in the sectors and sub-sectors listed at Annex A ("listed services"), in respect of:

    (i) the cross-border provision of a listed service from another party;

    (ii) its consumers of a listed service of another party;

    (iii) the purchase of its listed services by consumers of another party;

May   1991

Common Liberalization Commitments
on the Temporary Movement of Natural Persons Providing Services

The following categories of services providers, who provide services covered by the Agreement, shall be permitted temporary entry into Parties to the Agreement for purposes of providing services, without being required to submit to job validation or equivalent procedures:

    - service sellers
    - the following intra-corporate transferees:
    managers, executives and specialists.

All other entry requirements of Parties continue to apply.

Definitions for the categories are set out below.

Definitions

Service Sellers:

    are representatives of business carrying on activities in a party seeking temporary entry to another party for the purpose of selling or negotiating for the sale of services, or entering into agreements to sell services for that business, where those representatives will not be engaged in making direct sales to the general public.

    length of temporary entry - less than 90 days

Intra-corporate transferees:

    are people who have been employed by their firm for a period of not less than one year and who seek temporary entry in order to render services to the same employer or a subsidiary or affiliate thereof. More specifically:

    managers - are persons within an organization who direct the organization, or department or subdivision of the organization, supervise and control the work of other supervisory, professional or managerial employees, have the authority to hire and fire or recommend hiring, firing, or other personnel actions (such as promotion or leave authorizations) and exercise discretionary authority over day-to-day operations at a senior level.

    executives - are persons within an organization who primarily direct the management of the organization or establish goals and policies for the organization or a major component or function of the organization, exercise wide latitude in decision-making, and receive only general supervision or direction from higher-level executives, the board of directors, or stockholders of the business. (Executives would not directly perform takes related to the actual provision of the service, or services of the organization.)

    specialists - are persons within an organization who possess knowledge at an advanced level of expertise and who possess proprietary knowledge of the organization's product, service, research equipment, techniques, or management. (Specialists would include but not be limited to, members of accredited professions.)

0015

COMMON APPROACH TO LIBERALIZATION COMMITMENTS FOR SELECTED SECTORS,* SUB-SECTORS AND TRANSACTIONS**

[Note: The commitments under these dispositions would be an integral part of the GATS and thus subject to its provisions, as well as the agreed arrangements for dealing with national rules of general application, "head note" provisions and other matters not yet fully worked out. They would, of course, apply as from the date of entry into force of the GATS.]

Each party to the GATS shall impose no limitations or conditions on market access or national treatment[1] in the sectors and sub-sectors listed at Annex A ("listed services"), in respect of:

(i) the cross-border provision of a listed service from another party;

(ii) its consumers of a listed service of another party;

(iii) the purchase of its listed services by consumers of another party;

(iv) the initial establishment[2] in its territory by a juridical person, of another party, which provides listed services.

Interpretative Notes:

1. Parties may nevertheless impose notification requirements on non-nationals where these are required by transparent legislation.

2. In this paper, "initial establishment" is limited to the new implantation of a juridical person through incorporation, the creation of wholly or partially-owned subsidiaries, partnerships, branches or representative offices.

* The financial services sector would be subject to the provisions of a financial services annex, as proposed in MTN.TNC/W/50.

** The temporary movement of service providers would be dealt with by means of a separate set of common liberalization commitments

GU너(재)-0113 3-3   0016

외 무 부

종 별 :

번 호 : GVW-1058   일 시 : 91 0606 1800

수 신 : 장 관(봉기, 경기원, 재무부, 법무부, 상공부, 교육부, 문화부, 건설부 `

발 신 : 주 제네바대사 (보사부, 노동부, 교통부, 체신부, 과기처, 공보처, 항만청.)

제 목 : UR/GNS 회의(7)

   6.5(수) 오후 DAVID HAWES 대사 주재로 개최된 주요국 비공식 협의는 SCHEDULING에 관한 사무국 문서중 국내 규제와 시장접근 제한 조치구분 문제에 대하여 논의하였는바, 주요 내용 하기보고함.

   1. 차별적 조치와 무차별적인 수량제한은 분명히 SCHEDULE 등재 대상이라는데 별 이의가 없었으며, 아국을 포함한 대부분의 나라가 내.외국인간 무차별적인 질적 규제(거주요건, 국적요건, 독점등)도 무역제한 효과가 있으므로 기재되어야 한다는 입장을 견지함.

   0 또한 등재 대상 규제 조치를 규정하는 방법으로서 아국, 스웨덴, 스위스, 유고, 뉴질랜드등이 ILLUSTRATIVE LIST 작성을 지지함.

   2. 이에 반하여 인도, 말련, 멕시코 등은내.외국인간 무차별적 조치는 SCHEDULE등재 대상이 아니라는 입장을 취하였으며,

   0 일본은 객관적 기준에 기초한 규제 조치도 어느정도는 무역에 영향을 미친다는 점을 지적하고 NATIONAL SCHEDULE 은 TRANSPARENCY 목적을 위한것이 아니고 구속효과가 있는 자유화 약속을 기재하는 것인 만큼 보다 조심스럽게 접근 해야한다는 견해를 표명함(독점 및 수량제한은 스케쥴 기재 대상으로 인정) 끝

   첨부: SCHEDULING 에관한 사무국문서 1부

   (GVW(F)-192)

   (대사 박수길-국장)

통상국	법무부	보사부	문화부	교통부	체신부	교육부	경기원	재무부
상공부	건설부	노동부	과기처	해항정	공보처	2차보	1차보	

PAGE 1   91.06.07   08:44 CT

외신 1과 통제관

0017

4.6.91

GUW(서) - 이172   10606/800
             " GUW-1058 첨부,

<u>SCHEDULING OF COMMITMENTS</u>

<u>OPTIONS</u>

As a result of discussions in the GNS (27-28 May 1991) carried out on the basis of an informal note prepared by the secretariat (dated 21 May 1991), the secretariat was requested to identify options as to how the questions relating to the scheduling of commitments could be addressed.

The present note identifies a number of options with respect to the scheduling of commitments that either emerged from the discussions or follow from the questions posed in the secretariat note.

The secretariat has not attempted to be exhaustive in identifying all options, and stands ready to modify this informal note if some important options have not been identified or if participants are of the view that the note should be otherwise modified.

<u>Article VI</u>

Article VI:2 acknowledges that in sectors where parties have undertaken commitments, Parties may require that services or service providers of other Parties meet certain regulations, standards or qualifications. In this respect, Article VI:2 addresses the question of which of these measures should be inscribed in the Party's schedule.

According to Article VI:2, such regulations, standards and qualifications should not be applied in a manner which constitutes a means of discrimination with respect to services or service providers of other Parties, shall be administered in a reasonable, objective and impartial manner, shall be based on objective criteria, and shall not be more burdensome than necessary.

If these conditions <u>are not satisfied</u>, then the relevant measures <u>should be</u> scheduled.

If these conditions <u>are satisfied</u> then the relevant measures <u>need not</u> be scheduled.

If the conditions <u>are satisfied but the size of the market is restricted</u>, then the following options may be considered relevant with respect to measures restricting the size of the market:

A. Such measures <u>are not</u> considered to be restrictions on international trade and therefore are not scheduled;

B. Such measures <u>are</u> considered to be restrictions on international trade and therefore are to be scheduled;

C. Only <u>some</u> of these measures <u>are</u> considered to be restrictions on trade and therefore are required to be scheduled.

In the case of options A or C, the following question is relevant for those measures which are not scheduled:

- is the transparency provision contained in Article III adequate for indicating the existence of such measures, or,

- should a special procedure be adopted for indicating the existence of such measures?

Further, if option C was adopted, it would be necessary to make clear which of the measures should be scheduled. This could be done, for example, on the basis of an illustrative list of measures which participants considered appropriate for scheduling.

It would also appear that further consideration may have to be given to clarifying the meaning of some of the terminology used in Article VI:2 (e.g. what is meant by objective criteria).

0019

7-MISC2

4-2

Articles XVI and XVII

If option A above was the preferred option, Parties would only inscribe in their schedules measures which accord to foreign suppliers, treatment less favourable than that accorded to domestic suppliers.

The following options appear relevant:

(i) A distinction between measures falling under Article XVI and those falling under Article XVII could be based on limitations and conditions that apply at the point of entry to the market, and conditions and qualifications that apply at the stage of operation after entry.

(ii) The distinction between national treatment and market access could be eliminated, and all limitations, conditions or qualifications with respect to the foreign supplier inscribed in one column.

If, however, either option B or C was adopted, then measures which relate to both domestic and foreign services or service suppliers could be inscribed under Article XVI and a distinction between the scheduling of commitments under Articles XVI and XVII would be necessary.

The options listed below are intended to cover both options B and C, bearing in mind that under option C only measures considered to be restrictions to trade would be listed.

(i) A scheduling under Article XVI of non-discriminatory measures which apply both to domestic and foreign services or service suppliers, and under Article XVII only those discriminatory measures affecting entry and operation which apply to foreign services and service suppliers would be scheduled;

- 4 -

(ii) A scheduling under Article XVI of measures (whether or not discriminatory) that apply at the point of entry to the market and under Article XVII of discriminatory measures that apply at the stage of operation after entry.

Modes of Delivery

(i) The current scheduling format is maintained; all four modes of supply are scheduled in each instance.

(ii) The current scheduling format is abandoned; individual modes of delivery are not scheduled in each instance and it is assumed that no restrictions exist unless otherwise specified.

(iii) Individual modes of delivery are scheduled only when considered appropriate. Thus, if an individual mode is not relevant for the delivery of a service, or if no limitations or conditions are applied to, it would not be necessary to schedule that mode of delivery.

In any of the above cases, a measure may be mode specific and apply horizontally, thereby affecting the totality of the country's offer.

Cross-border Trade

The following options would appear relevant:

- no movement of personnel is involved;

- movement of personnel in order to supply a service must be included;

- if the movement of personnel is involved, the duration of stay should determine if the trade is cross-border trade or not.

7-MISC2

0021

외 무 부

종 별 :

번 호 : GVW-1070   일 시 : 91 0608 1100

수 신 : 장관(통기,경기원,재무부,법무부,상공부,교육부, 건설부, 보사부, 노동부, 교통부, 체신부, 과기처, 공보처, 해항청 7)

발 신 : 주 제네바 대사

제 목 : UR/GNS 회의(8)

6.6 (목) 종료된 표제회의 내용을 하기 보고함.

1. 회의 개요

- DAVIDE HAWES 대사로 부터 SCHEDULING 에 관한 비공식 협의 내용 설명과 이에대한 일부 국가의 논평이 있었음.

- 오후에 속개된 회의에서는 차기회의 의제를 결정하고 하기 휴가전까지의 작업과제를 예시하고 회의를 종료하였음.

2. 회의 내용

가. 스케쥴 작성 방법

- HAWES 대사는 국내 규제 (제 6조)와 시장접근제한 (제 16조) 간의 구분 문제에집중한 전일의 협의 내용을 국가간 합의 사항이 아니라 관찰내용이라는 전제하에 다음과 같이 보고함.

0 모든 차별 조치는 스케쥴에 기재되어야 함.

0 FRAMEWORK 제 6조 2항의 기준(무차별적이고 객관적이며 필요이상의 부담을 초래하지 않는 기준의 합리적이고 공평한 운영)에 합당한 조치라하더라도 모든 수량제한 조치는 기재되어야 하며, 일부질적인 규제도 기재되어야 함.

0 그러나 모든 국내 규제를 다 기재할수는 없으므로적절한 균형을 찾아야 함.

0 또한 향후 분쟁해결 대상이 될것인지와관련하여 BINDING 목적의 기재와 정보제공목적의 기재를 분명히 구분하여야 함.

0 FRAMEWORK 조문의 추가 보완이 필요함.

0 많은 국가가 사무국에 스케쥴 대상 조치에 관한ILLUSTRATIVE LIST 작성을 요청하였으며, 사무국문서 대안중 OPTION C를 지지하였음.

- 캐나다는 시장접근 규모를 제한 하는 모든형태의 양적 규제도 기재되어야 하며,

통상국 상공부	2차보 건설부	법무부 노동부	보사부 과기처	고통부 해항정	체신부 공보처	교육부	경기원	재무부

PAGE 1   91.06.08 22:11 BX

외신 1과 통제관

0022

무차별적 질적 규제는 어떤 기준에 합치하지 않은경우에는 기재되어야 하나 동 기준 이 불확실한 바이를 해결하는 두가지 방법을 아래와 같이 제시함.

(1) 스케쥴 기재 대상 조치에 대한 개방향(OPEN-ENDED) 의 ILLUSTRATIVE LIST 에대하여합의하는 방법

(2) 토의 또는 협상을 통하여 협정 규정을 자세하고 정확하게 규정하는 방법

- 이에 대하여 일본 및 개도국들은 다음과 같은 이유로 ILLUSTRATIVE LIST 가 개방형이 되어서는안된다고 반박함.

O ILLUSTRATIVE LIST 에 없기 때문에 스케쥴에 등재되지 않은 규제 조치에 대하여 NON-VIOLATIONCASE 로 분쟁해결에 제소될 위험이 있음.

O 따라서 스케쥴 기재 대상 조치는 명확하게 한정적인 POSITIVE LIST 로 열거되어야 함.

- 한편 헝가리는 스케쥴 기재 대상 조치를 다음과같이 예시함.

(1) 양적 규제(독점 및 QUOTA 포함)

(2) 국적 요건

(3) 구체적 기준이 없는 당국의 자유재량에 의한결정

(4) 지리적 기준에 의한 요건(거주요건)

(5) 특정 단체.협회등에 대한 가입 강제

- EC 는 상기 ILLUSTRATIVE LIST 의 법적 지위에대하여 다음과 같이 의문을 제기한바 의장은 추후 고려 대상이라고 답변함.

O 협정 부속서 인지

O EXPLANATORY NOTE 인지

O 향후 분쟁해결시 PANEL 의 참고 자료로 사용할것인지

나. 향후 협상 일정

- 6.24주 회의 의제

O INITIAL COMMITMENT 에 관한 추가 작업(각국OFFER 평가에 관한 고려, 양허 협상 절차적기준, 실질적 양허 협상 지침)

O 자유화 약속의 기재 방법

O 노동력 이동

O FRAMEWORK 제 1조 (정의 및 범위)

- 하기 휴가전까지의 작업 과제(동문제는 향후협상 진전에 따라 달라질 것이기

PAGE 2

대문에 명확하고 자세하게 제시되지 않았음.)

　　O MFN: MFN 원칙을 형해화 하지 않는 가운데 각국의 어려움을 해결하는 방안

　　O 통신 및 금융부속서

　　O 각국 OFFER 의 개선을 위한 양자간,복수국간 협상(미국은 동 협상 실시를 위한 시간계획 설정을 요청하였으나 의장 및 타국가로 부터 반응이 없었음)

　　O FRAMEWORK 제 1부 - 제 4부 (특히 제 4조, 5조, 11조,12조, 23조).

　　- 한편 의장은 다음사항에 대한 각국의 자료협조를 요청함.

　　O 수평적 협정에 관한 자료 (6.15 까지) ∨

　　O 사무국 작성 서비스 분야 분류표에 대한 서면논평(6.15 까지) ∨

　　O 스케쥴 기재 대상 무차별적 규제 조치 목록 (6.17까지) 끝 ∨

　　(대사 박수길-국장)

경 제 기 획 원

봉조삼 10502-ㅈ약3   503-9149   1991. 6. 7.

수신 수신처참조

제목 UR대책 서비스분야 실무소위원회 개최봉보

1. UR협상그룹 개편에 따라 재구성된 서비스분야 실무소위원회(봉조삼 10502-322, 5.17 참조) 를 다음과 같이 개최코자 하니 참석하여 주시기 바랍니다.

2. 금번 회의에서는 ① Framework 협상 및 9개분야별 부속서협상, 아국의 양허계획표 검토와 관련된 대책을 논의하고 ② 6.15까지 GATT에 제출토록되어 있는 아국의 수평적 협정 및 GATT 서비스업종분류안에 대하여 중점 논의할 계획이니 동대책에 대하여 관계부처에서 이제까지 검토한 내용을 지참하여 참석하여 주시기 바랍니다.

다   음

가. 일   시: '91.6.12(수)   15:00-18:00

나. 장   소: 경제기획원 대회의실 (1동 727호)

다. 의   제

① UR/서비스 협상동향 및 주요쟁점 점검

② 수평적협정 및 업종분류에 대한 검토의견 GATT제출(안)

라. 참석범위: 경제기획원 제2협력관 (회의주재)

"   봉상조정3과장, 산업3과장

공정거래위원회 제도개선과장, 외무부 봉상기구과장,

내무부 지적과장, 재무부 국제금융과장,

법무부 국제법무심의관실 검사, 입국심사과장,

교육부 교육협력과장, 문화부 영화진흥과장,

상공부 유통산업과장, 보건사회부 국제협력과장,

0025

16885

건설부 해외협력과장,   교통부 국제협력과장,

노동부 고용관리과장,   체신부 통신협력과장,

과기처 기술협력2과장, 환경처 정책조정과장,

공보처 광고정책과장,   항만청 진흥과장,

특허청 지도과장,   KIEP 박태호박사, 김태준박사,

K D I 김지홍박사, KOTRA 국제경제과장,

김&장법률사무소 신희택 변호사.   끝.

경 제 기 획 원 장 관

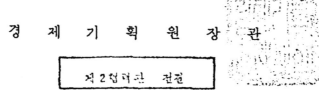

제 2 협력관 전결

수신처: 외무부장관, 내무부장관, 재무부장관, 법무부장관, 교육부장관,
문화부장관, 상공부장관, 보건사회부장관, 건설부장관, 교통부장관,
노동부장관, 체신부장관, 과학기술처장관, 환경처장관, 공보처장관,
항만청장, 대외경제정책연구원장, 한국개발연구원장, 대한무역협회장,
김&장법률사무소장.

0026

경 제 기 획 원

봉조삼 10502- 446   503-9149   1991. 6. 18.

수신 수신처참조

제목 UR대책 서비스분야 실무소위원회 결과통보

  '91.6.12일 개최된 표제회의결과를 별첨과 같이 통보하오니 각부처
(및 기관)는 UR/서비스협상 대책추진에 만전을 기해 주시기 바랍니다.

별첨: UR대책 서비스실무소위 결과 1부.   끝.

경 제 기 획 원

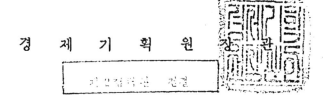

수신처: 외무부장관, 내무부장관, 재무부장관, 법무부장관, 교육부장관,
         문화부장관, 상공부장관, 보건사회부장관, 건설부장관, 교통부장관,
         노동부장관, 체신부장관, 과학기술처장관, 환경처장관, 공보처장관,
         특허청장, 항만청장, 대외경제정책연구원장, 한국개발연구원장,
         대한무역진흥공사장, 김&장법률사무소장.

                          18716   0027

<添 附>

UR對策 서비스分野 實務小委員會 結果

Ⅰ. 會議槪要

- 日 時: '91.6.12, 15:00-18:00

- 場 所: 과천청사 1동 8층 대회의실

- 參席者: EPB 제2협력관 (회의주재),
  15개부처 과장 또는 담당사무관, KOTRA, KIEP, KDI,
  김&장법률사무소의 전문가등 27명

- 會議議題

  ○ UR/서비스協商의 最近進展狀況과 향후 對應方向에 대한 討議

  ○ 分野別 協商對策 推進狀況 점검

  ○ 讓許協商에 필요한 各種資料의 作成現況 점검

0028

Ⅱ. 決定事項

> 다음과 같은 事項을 決定하고 各部處別로 對策을 樹立. 推進하기로 決定

- 서비스一般協定의 Framework 및 分野別 附屬書의 爭點事項에 대한 我國 立場 再確認
  - ○ 다만 勞動力移動(제1조 및 부속서), MFN일탈(제3조 및 부속서), 開途國優待條項(제4조), 支給 및 移轉(제11조), 紛爭解決節次(제23조), 用語의 定義(제34조) 등 既存立場의 보완이 必要한 分野에 대해서는 別途日程을 정하여 關係部處會議를 開催하여 我國立場을 再調整 ✓

- 本格的인 讓許協商이 시작되기 전까지 我國 Offer List의 修正. 補完 및 UR協商 後續對策案을 마련 (7월말까지)
  - ○ Scheduling 方法에 대한 協商結果, 相對國의 Offer List의 自由化 水準, 流通, 金融分野의 追加的인 開放計劃反映 여부 등을 고려

- GATT事務局이 요청한 다음 세가지 種類의 資料를 6.17까지 GATT에 提出
  - ○ 我國이 締結한 水平的 協定의 MFN일탈문제, 서비스분야 分類의 改定案에 대한 檢討意見, 讓許表에 등재할 無差別的인 規制措置 목록
  - ○ 關係部處의 의견을 취합하여 EPB가 綜合案을 작성하고 異見이 있을 경우 關係部處 會議를 開催 ✓

- 協商에 필요한 各種 資料의 조속한 提出
  - ○ 相對國 Offer List의 分析內容(5.22) 및 Request List(2.28)
  - ○ 我國 Offer List에서 除外한 分野의 協商對策(2.10)
  - ○ 業種別 勞動力移動範圍(2.28) 및 業種別 對策資料 (5.16)
  - ○ 제2차 韓美 兩者協議 結果 檢討(5.10)
  - * ( )은 당초 자료제출 예정일

0029

Ⅲ. 주요 논의사항

(EPB 제2협력관) : 4.25 TNC會議以後 다시 本格的으로 再開되고 있는
   UR/서비스협상에 대비하여 關係部處間의 유기적인 協調를 強調

(EPB 담당사무관): 會議資料 報告

(외무부 통상기구과장): 分野別 附屬書등에 대한 協商에 關係部處의
   參與가 必要하다고 言及

✓ (재무부 담당사무관): 金融分野의 協商進行狀況 설명

(교육부 담당사무관): 아직 讓許協商對象이 구체화되지 않았지만 가상적
   인 시나리오를 설정하여 內部的인 準備를 하고 있다고 說明

(상공부 유통산업과장): '91.3월 發表한 "流通市場開放計劃"에 대하여
   업계로부터 반발을 겪고 있는등 어려움을 언급하고 Franchising의
   槪念이 包括的이라고 한다면(미국의 주장) Franchising의 開放
   要求에 대해서는 關係部處의 別途檢討가 필요하다고 주장

(보사부 국제협력과장): 病院關係問題가 가장 중요하다고 보고있으며
   현재 實務局에서 檢討中에 있는바, 6월말이나 7월초에는 결과가
   나올 것으로 기대한다고 언급하고 병원설립과 관련된 필수인력의
   範圍에 대해서 문의

0030

(노동부 담당사무관): 韓國標準職業分類表에 열거된 직종중에서 勞動部
　　　가 생각하는 필수인력의 범위를 발췌하여 지난 '91.2월 各部處에
　　　通報했음을 알리고 이를 바탕으로 하여 各部處가 各業種別로
　　　具體的인 勞動力 移動範圍를 설정할 것을 촉구

(과기처 담당사무관): 技術用役育成法을 立法豫告하는등 엔지니어링
　　　産業界의 競爭力 强化方案을 추진중에 있다고 언급하고 서비스
　　　協商進行狀況이 부진해 짐에 따라 民間業界의 關心이 낮아지고
　　　있는 실정을 소개

(내무부 지적과장): 外國人 土地取得 制限事項을 설명

(법무부 담당사무관): 입국비자 發給關聯制度를 설명하고 各部處가
　　　分野別로 필수적인 勞動力移動 範圍를 설정할 것을 촉구

(문화부 담당사무관): 視聽覺서비스 分野의 協商進行狀況을 설명하고
　　　日本映畵의 國內流入에 대한 對應方向을 紹介

(건설부 해외협력과장): 勞動力移動分野에 대한 아국입장의 조속한 정립
　　　必要性을 强調하고 Framework에 대한 協商에도 關係部處의 參與가
　　　필요한 점을 지적하고 제네바 현지대표부와 關係部處間의 원활한
　　　立場調整 必要性을 主張

(교통부 국제협력과장): 運送 및 觀光分野의 協商進行狀況을 설명하고
　　　향후 分野別 附屬書 協商에 적극 참여할 계획임을 언급

0031

(체신부 담당사무관): 通信分野의 協商進行狀況을 설명하고 '90년도에 對內競爭促進 方案을 도입한 결과 建設分野와 마찬가지로 현재는 相對國市場에 進出할 可能性도 갖고 있다고 언급

(환경처 담당사무관): Offer시 業種分類는 최대한 세부화되는 것이 바람직하다고 提議 ？

(KDI 김지홍박사): 雙務協商과 多者間協商을 연계시킬 필요성을 강조하고 '90년대 중반의 韓國經濟의 位置를 감안하여 海外市場에 積極的으로 進出한다는 전제하에서 Offer하는 것이 必要하다고 지적

(KIEP 박태호박사): 豫想보다 빨리 讓許協商이 進行될 가능성에 대비해야 한다고 지적하고 쿼타등 數量規制를 통하여 漸進的 自由化를 추진하는 方案등을 提議 ✓

(KOTRA 관계자): 相對國에 대한 Request List 作成時 KOTRA가 기작성한 資料를 參考할 것을 언급

(신희택 변호사): 開放分野에 대한 行政指導가 不可能하므로 規制가 필요한 분야는 法的根據를 마련해야 한다는 지적을 하고 外國業體와의 제휴 또는 경쟁사이에서 입장을 정하지 못하고 있는 國內業界에 대해서 정부가 일정한 기간의 開放留豫期間을 확보하고 지원책을 마련하는등 國內業體 育成에 대한 확실한 方向 提示가 필요할 것이라고 언급

0032

발 신 전 보

분류번호	보존기간

번   호 : WGV-0803   910619 2007 FN   종별 :

수   신 : 주   제네바   대사. 총영사

발   신 : 장 관 (통기)

제   목 : UR/GNS 협상

대 : GVW-1070

1. 대호 GNS 협상그룹 의장이 요청한 1) 수평적 협정에 관한 자료,
2) 사무국 작성 서비스분야 분류표에 대한 평가, 3) 스케쥴 기재 대상 무차별적
규제조치 목록을 별첨(FAX) 송부하니 갓트 사무국에 제출 바람.

2. 상기 자료에는 촉박한 자료준비 시한과 일부 민감한 분야에 대한
상세 자료 제출 타당성 여부의 추가 검토 필요성에 따라 기초적인 내용만을
포함시키고, 수정 권리 유보 및 필요시 추가자료 제출 가능성을 언급 하였는 바,
다른 나라들의 자료 제출 동향을 파악 보고 바람.

첨 부(FAX) : 상기 자료 9매.   끝.

WGV(F) - 152

(통상국장 김 삼훈)

보 안 통 제	

앙고재	91년6월19일	통기과	기안자 성명 조현		과 장	심의관	국 장 전결		차 관	장 관		외신과통제

0033

WGV(F) - ~~0803~~ 10619 20 10

韓國으로부터의 提案

천박본

'91.6.19.

WGV-0803 910619 2007 FN

〈水平的協定의 締結現況〉

- 韓國은 이중과세방지협정, 投資保障 및 增進協定, 貿易 및 通商協定, 비자협정등을 체결해오고 있음.

    ○ 이중과세방지협정('70-'91)은 日本, 태국, 西獨등 38개국과 체결해오고 있으며 批准書交換 다음해부터 5년경과후 상대방의 통고에 의해 終了可能

    ○ 投資保障 및 增進協定('60-'91)은 美國, 스위스, 튜니지아등 27개국과 체결해오고 있으며 유효기간은 10년 또는 20년임.

    ○ 貿易 및 通商協定('62-'89)은 브라질, 이탈리아, 獨逸등 21개국가와 체결해오고 있으며, 협정유효기간은 2년-5년 이며 同 유효기간 이후에도 이의제기가 없을경우 계속유효

    ○ 비자免除協定('67-'91)은 태국, 필리핀, 터키등 40개국과 체결해오고 있으며 同 協定은 別途 終了通告가 없으면 계속해서 유효
    . 美國 및 日本과는 복수비자협정을 체결하여 운용중

- 또한 韓國은 美國과 '56년 友好通商航海條約을 체결하였으며 유효기간은 10년이고 別途 終了通告가 없는한 自動延長하기로 되어 있으며 勞動協定은 特別히 締結한 것이 없는 狀態

- 현재 韓國은 同 水平的協定들의 施行過程에서의 유효성과 GATS에 서명국의 MFN適用問題를 檢討中에 있으며 檢討結果가 얻어지는대로 GATT事務局에 提出할 計劃

9-1

0034

〈서비스分野의 分類表 改定案에 대한 檢討意見〉

- 各國의 讓許表는 최대한 GATT分類表에 따라 작성해야 하나
  各業種의 包括範圍에 대한 最終判斷基準은 國內法 및 國內
  分類體系에 따라서 결정

- GATT가 새로작성한 分類表에는 CPC와 附合되지 않는 업종이
  다수있는바 同業種에 대한 定義 및 具體的인 包括範圍의 設定
  이 必要

  ① 事業서비스(1)의 컴퓨터 및 관련서비스중 소프트웨어
     履行서비스(b)의 이행의 정의

  ② 事業서비스(1)의 기타 事業서비스(F)中 Franchising(b)의
     定義

  ③ 事業서비스(1)의 기타 事業서비스(F)중 裝備維持 및 보수
     (n)에 컴퓨터의 維持, 보수가 포함되지 않는다면 컴퓨터
     및 關聯서비스(B)에 追加할 必要

  ④ 通信서비스(2)의 電氣通信서비스(C)중 j,k,m,n과 事業
     서비스(1)의 컴퓨터 및 關聯서비스(B)중 c,d와의 區分
     (c: 정보처리서비스, d: 데이타베이스 서비스, j: 온라인
     정보 및 데이타베이스 정정, k: 전자자료교환, m: 코드
     전환, n: 온라인 정보 및 자료처리)

  ⑤ 통신서비스(2)의 視聽覺서비스(D)中 Sound recording(d)에
     음반원판제작과 복제생산이 포함되는지 여부

9-2

0035

⑥ 建設(3)의 建設關聯엔지니어링 서비스(A와B)와 사업서비스
   (1)의 專門職業서비스(A)중 d,e,f,g와의 區分
   (A: 프로젝트디자인, 계획, 계약, 관리, 감리, 감독등,
    B: 사업성 검토, d: 건축서비스, e: 엔지니어링서비스,
    f: 복합엔지니어링서비스, g: 도시계획 및 조경건축서비스)

⑦ 環境서비스(6)와 專業서비스(1)의 기타 事業서비스(F)중
   下水 및 廢棄物處理, 衛生 및 類似서비스(s)와의 구분
   (s: 하수 및 폐기물 처리, 위생 및 유사서비스)

9-3   0036

〈讓許表에 등재해야할 無差別的 規制措置〉

- 讓許表는 相對國 서비스공급자에게 市場進出 與否에 대한 豫測
  可能性을 주고 明瞭해야 하므로 비록 內.外國人間에 無差別的
  인 規制措置라 하더라도 서비스交易을 實質的으로 제약하는
  規制措置는 讓許表에 등재해야 함.

  o 이런차원에서 韓國은 Offer List 작성시 다음과 같은
    無差別的인 規制制度를 포괄하였음.

    ① 免許(license), 許可(permission), 認可(approval)등
       재량적인 行政規制(discretionary measures)
    ② 事務室(또는 매장)의 面積 및 數
    ③ 外國人投資指針 (특히 외국인 지분율제한)

- 또한 5月會議에서 論議된 다음과 같은 無差別的 規制措置에
  대해서도 追加的인 檢討가 필요하다고 생각

    ④ 學力要件 (educational requirement)
    ⑤ 居住要件 (residence)
    ⑥ 國籍要件 (nationality)
    ⑦ 獨占 (monopoly)
    ⑧ 서비스供給者 숫자(number of service supplier), 免許의
       숫자(number of license)등
    ⑨ 資格取得要件 (qualification)

9-4

0037

Communication from the Republic of Korea

June 19, 1991

<Current status of horizontal agreements>

Korea has concluded Double Taxation Avoidance Treaties, Investment Protection and Promotion Treaties, Trade Agreements, and Visa Waiver Arrangements.

During the period of 1970-1991, Korea has entered into Double Taxation Avoidance Treaties with 38 countries including Japan, Thailand and (West) Germany, terminable by either party upon sending of notice any time after the initial 5-year period.

During the period of 1960-1991, Korea has entered into Investment Protection and Promotion Treaties with 27 countries including the United States, Switzerland and Tunisia, with treaties to be effective over a 10 to 20 year time horizon.

During the 1962-1989 period, Korea has concluded Trade Agreements with 21 countries including Brazil, Italy and (West) Germany, with the average effective period of agreements at two to five years. The effective term, however, will be indefinitely extended as long as there is no objection.

During the period of 1967-1991, Korea has concluded Visa Waiver Arrangements with 40 countries including Thailand, Philippines and Turkey, with arrangements in effect for an indefinite period until an termination notice is issued. Korea's Multiple Visa Arrangements with Japan and the United States are currently in effect.

9-5

Also Korea and the United States concluded the Friendship Agreement on Commerce and Navigation (FCN) in 1956 with the initial effective term set at 10 years but with the understanding that the effective term will be automatically extended unless a termination notice is issued. But Korea has not yet signed a major Labor Agreement.

At the moment, Korea is examining the specific effectiveness of these horizontal agreements arising from the implementation process and the possiblity of extending them to contracting parties of GATS on the basis of MFN. Korea will submit the results of its review at a later period.

9-6

0039

<Comments on the Revised Classification List>

Although the Parties should make their National Schedules adhering to the revised list as much as possible, the actual coverage of sectors or sub-sectors in the National Schedule should be determined by domestic laws and the domestic classification system.

The revised list is mainly based on the Central Product Classification (CPC). Sectors in the list which are not matched with CPC need to be clarified or defined.

① The meaning of "Implementation" of b classified in Computer and Related Services of Business Services is to be defined.
[b: Software implementation services]

② Franchising classified in Other Business Services of Business Services is to be defined.

③ Unless the maintenance and repair of computing machinery includes in n classified in Other Business Services of Business Services, the maintenance and repair of computing machinery needs to be added to Computer and Related Services.
[n: Maintenance and repair of equipment]

④ The differences between j, k, m & n classified in Telecommunication Services of Communication Services and c & d classified in Computer and Related Services of Business Services are to be clarified.
[c: Data processing services, d: Data base services, j: On-line information and data base retrieval, k: Electronic data interchange (EDI), m: Code and protocol conversion, n: On-line information and/or data processing (incl. transaction processing)]

9-7

0040

⑤ Whether Sound Recording classified in Audiovisual Services of
Communication Services includes the production and duplication of
original disk needs to be confirmed.

⑥ The differences between d, e, f & g classified in Professional Services
of Business Services and A & B of Construction and Related
Engineering Services are to be clarified.
[A: Project design, planning, contracting, management, supervision and
 inspection (see also business and professional services), B: Feasibility
 studies, d: Architectural services, e: Engineering services,
 f: Integrated engineering services, g: Urban planning and landscape
 architectural services]

⑦ The difference between Environmental Services and s classified in
Other Business Services of Business Services is to be clarified.
[s: Sewage and refuse disposal, sanitation and similar services]

9-8

<Non-discriminatory measures subject to scheduling>

Non-discriminatory measures which substantially restrict service trade should be scheduled, since national schedules should be predictable and transparent.

In this regard, Korea has scheduled the following non-discriminatory measures in its initial offer list:

o Discretionary measures including license, permission, approval system, etc.

o Size and number of office or shop

o Foreign investment guideline, especially restriction of foreign equity participation.

Also, Korea will consider the following measures which   .... ued at the last GNS meeting, subject to further review.

o Number of service provider or license

o Educational requirement

o Residence

o Nationality

o Monopoly

o Qualification

9-9

0042

외 무 부

종 별 :

번 호 : GVW-1134   일 시 : 91 0619 1800

수 신 : 장 관(통기,경기원,재무부,상공부,체신부)

발 신 : 주 제네바 대사

제 목 : UR/GNS 비공식 협의

6.19(수) 오전 JARAMILLO GNS 의장 주재로 개최된 주요국 비공식 협의 내용을 하기보고함.

1. 금융,통신분야 AD HOC 회의

- 다음과 같이 금융.통신분야 부속서에 관한 ADHOC 회의를 개최키로 합의하였음.

0 일시: 7.10(수) 금융, 7.12(금): 통신

0 성격: GNS 관할하의 AD HOC 회의로 하되 의장은 분야별 전문가와 GNS 의장(JARAMILLO또는 DAVID HAWES 대사) 이 공동 주재함.

2. 양허 협상의 절차적 기준

- 지난 GNS 회의에서 기토의된 바 있는 사무국 작성 초안(5.29자) 에 다음 사항을 반영, 재작성하여 6.24. 주간 GNS 회의에서 논의키로 하였음.

0 1항: 원안대로 유지하되 OFFER 제출시한(확정시한이 아닌 목표 일자)을 공란으로 삽입하여 GNS 회의에서 결정함(목표일자는 7월말이 유력함)

0 3항: 다자간협의, 검토, 평가의 의미를 보다 명백히 함.

0 5항: REQUEST 제출시한을 공란으로 삽입하여 GNS 회의에서 결정함.

각국의 REQUEST LIST 는 상업적 정보의 공개를 방지하기 위하여 당사국외의 다른 참가국에 배부하지않고 사무국이 요약하여 가국에 배부함.(미국의 제의에 별 이견없이 합의함)

3. 양허 협상의 실질적 기준

- TNC/W/35 에 첨부된 초안을 가지고 GNS회의에서 협상하기로 함.끝

(대사 박수길-국장)

통상국   2차보   체신부   경기원   재무부   상공부

외 무 부

종 별 :

번 호 : GVW-1154

일 시 : 91 0620 1900

수 신 : 장 관(봉기,경기원)

발 신 : 주 제네바 대사

제 목 : UR/GNS 협상

대: WGV-0803

대호 다른 나라들의 자료 제출 동향을 하기보고함.

1. 수평적 협정

- 제출국가 (6개국): 콜롬비아, 스위스, 홍콩, 호주,EC, 아국

(노르웨이, 캐나다, 오지리, 미국등 제출 예정)

- 제출 형태: 스위스 및 홍콩은 아국과 같이 대략적인 체결 현황만 제출하였으며, 기타 국가는 사무국 작성 문서에 따라 상세한 내용을 기재

- 사무국의 작업 계획: 각국 제출 자료는 보안을 유지하는 가운데 요약 형태로 배경문서를 작성할 예정이라함. 이와 관련 사무국은 아국이 체결한 협정의 내용을 밝히지 않더라도 체약국 명단제공을 요청하였음.

2. 서비스 분야 분류표

- 제출국가 (12개국): 칠레, 멕시코, 스위스, 스웨덴, 호주, 홍콩, 미국, EC, 싱가폴, 캐나다, 오지리, 아국

3. 무차별적 조치

- 제출국가(3개국): 미국, 헝가리, 아국

- 제출 내용: 자세한 내용은 알수 없으나 아국안과 유사한 것으로 판단됨. 끝

(대사 박수길-국장)

통상국   2차보   경기원

91.06.21   09:35 WG

외신 1과 통제관

0044

주 제 네 바 대 표 부

제네 (경) 20644-566   1991. 6. 21

수 신 : 외무부장관

참 조 : 통상국장, 경제기획원장관 (대외경제조정실장)

제 목 : UR/GNS 협상자료 송부

    갓트사무국에서 작성한 각국 offer 평가에 관한 배경문서를 별첨

송부합니다.

첨부 : 갓트사무국 작성 배경문서   1부.   끝.

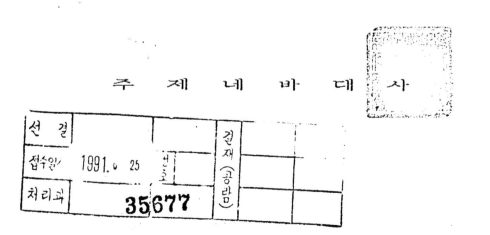

0045

20.6.91

EVALUATING OFFERS AND CONCESSIONS IN THE SERVICES CONTEXT

1.   This informal note should be viewed as an "issues" paper in the sense that its purpose is to raise considerations that participants may wish to address when evaluating offers from a national perspective, and in so doing provide a basis for discussion. As participating countries will presumably wish to compare national offers with those of other participants, the comparability of offers across countries is also addressed. The intention of the paper is not to be exhaustive in the sense of identifying all the issues that need to be addressed, nor is its intention to provide definitive answers to the questions it raises.

2.   The note has five parts.   The _first_ reviews the salient characteristics of the traditional techniques used in GATT tariff and non-tariff barrier negotiations, the objective being to assess the extent to which such procedures are relevant for evaluating offers in services trade and if such procedures may be adapted to apply in the context of services. The _second_ part discusses the implications of the lack of quantitative information for trade in services when evaluating offers.   In the light of the data availability, the _third_ part of the note discusses the feasibility of designing quantitative indicators to compare offers, using the _level_ of market access as a criterion, while the _fourth_ part of the note discuses _changes_ in the level of market access as a criterion for evaluating offers.   The _final_ part of the note contains concluding remarks.

3.   It should be noted at the outset that it is unlikely that any single indicator that can be used with currently available statistics is likely to be considered generally acceptable in terms of quantifying offers. Qualitative criteria are likely to play a complementary role, especially if participating countries wish to take into account the degree to which

0046

A2-OFFERS

- 3 -

offers imply a reduction in market access restrictions relative to the status quo.

I. Techniques Used in Tariff and Non-tariff Negotiations

4. In past tariff negotiations on merchandise trade, offers tended to be quantified by using readily available data on the current bilateral value of trade flows and the matching vector of tariffs. A central element in merchandise trade negotiations has also been the identification of the principal suppliers of specific products. The value of an offer has frequently been measured as the product of the proposed change in the tariff affecting a specific product and the value of imports of that product in a particular year.[1] While negotiations have focused mostly on changes in the level of tariff as opposed to the tariff itself (e.g. the magnitude of the proposed/desired cut in the average level of tariffs), an alternative measure is the reduction in the dispersion across tariffs.

5. The procedures adopted in tariff negotiations do not normally centre on the implications of tariff reductions for changes in economic welfare, nor are they based on the extent to which trade flows are likely to change as a result of the offered changes in tariff schedules.[2] Instead, the approaches followed in tariff negotiations can be characterized as providing negotiators with a focal point; that is, something tangible enabling parties to set objectives, evaluate the position of others, assess

---

[1] Note that this procedure gives a zero weight to countries that have prohibitive barriers to trade in certain products.

[2] This would require a multicountry, multicommodity general equilibrium approach that is capable of taking into account intersectoral linkages (and thus effective rates of protection), use recent and credible estimates of demand, supply and substitution elasticities, and incorporate all relevant government policies, not just tariffs. Even this only provides an indication of the general equilibrium effect induced by what is offered. Dynamic effects, such as induced shifts in comparative advantage, are not taken into account.

0047

A2-OFFERS

negotiating progress and identify acceptable compromises with respect to a particular yardstick. In the case of tariff liberalization, the focal point is normally a measure that takes into account the relative size of trade and the tariffs; it is simple to calculate using readily available data. In fact, the choice of the focal point frequently used in past negotiations (i.e. changes in trade-weighted tariff levels) appears to have been driven largely by data availability.

6. A number of analogies exist between negotiations on services and previous GATT negotiations on non-tariff measures. Some of the considerations that are relevant for services trade are not wholly new - having arisen also in the context of negotiations on "difficult-to-quantify" non-tariff measures. Some of the code negotiations during the Tokyo Round did not take a principal supplier and/or change in barriers to trade approach. The focus was rather on specific measures or rules, the implementation of which was assumed to increase market access. Alternatively, the focus was on easily quantifiable variables, such as the value of past procurement for various government entities. This measure provided a focal point for the government procurement code discussions; it is unrelated to trade per se. If a quantifiable approach is to be adopted in the evaluation of offers in the context of the services negotiations, then a quantifiable counterpart to the more traditional trade liberalizing negotiations "focal point" may have to be found.

II. Data Availability on Trade and Production of Services

7. Trade statistics for services are inaccurate, incomplete and not readily comparable across countries. Of the data that do exist, they neglect the sales of foreign-owned firms that have established a commercial presence, are incomplete with respect to cross-border flows of services, are highly aggregated and are not available on an origin and destination basis. This makes it impossible to identify principal suppliers, and the lack of estimates of the ad valorem equivalent of existing restrictions to services trade does not permit a calculation and comparison of levels and

0048

A2-OFFERS

changes in levels of trade restriction. Indeed, there is to date, no generally accepted definition of what constitutes a barrier to trade in services. Hence, even if service trade statistics were available and comparable across countries[3], the complexities associated with identifying and quantifying barriers to trade in services would still preclude the development of a quantifiable focal point equivalent to those used for merchandise trade.

8.   The only source of comprehensive, comparable data are the production statistics found in the national accounts (i.e. GDP statistics). Such data, measure the importance of different sectors in total services output. The data can measure the total contribution of services to GDP or the total of a subset of sectors (e.g. non-government services plus construction). They also provide a measure of the importance of individual countries in total global output. Thus, the data can be used for both intra- and inter-country comparisons. Two possibilities exist, the first being to use value-added data and the second to employ gross output figures. Gross output data, which include the value of all the intermediate products that are used by an industry, are arguably a better indicator of the relative size of different sectors than value-added data. However, the number of countries reporting value-added data for service industries substantially exceed those that report gross output. The procedure described below can be applied using either measure.[4]

9.   The lack of data similar to that for merchandise trade and the complexities associated with identifying and quantifying barriers to

---

[3]Even if perfect trade data existed, it could be argued that their usefulness is limited given that they cover only a subset of the modes of delivery identified in the national offers. The Secretariat document Availability of Statistics on Services (MTN.GNS/W/94) illustrates the incompleteness of existing trade data.

[4]It is possible to estimate gross output data by multiplying value added figures by average gross output/value added ratios calculated from data reported by those countries that collect both series.

0049

A2-OFFERS

services trade are not necessarily insurmountable problems in devising a focal point. In fact, in some instances, trade data may not be helpful, for example, which countries are principal suppliers at any given point in time may not be relevant and this may change over time. A focus on existing principal suppliers may neglect those countries that currently do not export (or import) significant amounts of a service but have the potential for doing so. Also, it may neglect small countries for which a specific activity might be of great importance.

10. As the value of an offer in a negotiating context is not necessarily a monetary measure - being more a yardstick - it may be possible to use readily available services-related data to find an alternative focal point.

III. Possible Quantitative Evaluation

11. From a national point of view, the problem is the following: can a quantifiable measure be constructed allowing a country to evaluate its own offer and to compare it to that of other participants? In what follows one possible procedure is outlined that would draw on currently available data. This procedure requires, however, subjective judgement on a number of important issues and illustrates the kinds of problems that must be resolved if a non-arbitary quantitative measure is to be developed.[5] Unambiguous solutions to some of the problems encountered are almost impossible, and in practice it will not be feasible - nor desirable - to exclude qualitative variables from an evaluation procedure. The proposed measure assumes initially that the evaluation criterion used is the level of market access that is implied by an offer. Difficulties that arise if the change in market access is used as a (perhaps complementary) criterion are discussed in the next section.

---

[5] An example of which would be counting the number of sectors offered and comparing this to the number of sectors on the reference list.

7

12. In making their offers, participants have adopted a "hybrid" of the positive and negative list approach; it is a positive list approach to the extent that all sectors on which participants are willing to consider making concessions are listed. Four modes of delivery are distinguished per sector. For each mode, limitations, qualifications and conditions on market access and national treatment are identified. This approach defines the basis for identifying the components that are relevant in evaluating offers. The components discussed in this section include: determining the total value of output of the offered sectors as a proportion of total service sector output or GDP; discounting the sectoral offers in the light of limitations, qualifications and conditions placed on market access and national treatment for each mode of delivery; and determining which sectors are most important in relation to individual participants' interests.

A. Output in offered sectors as a proportion of total output

13. A first step in arriving at a quantitative measure might be to determine the total value of output in the relevant sector as a proportion of total service output or GDP. To ensure that offers are comparable, it would, of course, have to be understood among participating countries as to what comprises the negotiable universe of service sectors, i.e. the denominator of any "coverage ratio." Also, while it is not necessary for countries agree on a common nomenclature to implement the procedure, this would greatly facilitate cross-country comparisons.

14. Countries differ substantially in terms of the degree of disaggregation of their national accounts data, so it may not be possible to determine the relative importance of all sectors offered. If this is a problem, a number of benchmark economies could be constructed for the purposes of calculation. For example, countries could be grouped depending on their per capita income levels, with offers of countries with insufficiently detailed data being weighted by the sectoral composition of the appropriate benchmark economy. In this way the data from those

0051

A2-OFFERS

countries with the most disaggregated and up to date figures can be used[6] to provide one form of focal point for purposes of negotiations, even for countries for which GDP data are insufficiently disaggregated. To the extent that the necessary data is available, it could be provided by each country as part of its offer list.

15. The sectoral share measure is at best a starting point, as it does not take into account the extent to which there are limitations, qualifications and conditions on national treatment and market access. However, it can be regarded as the maximum value of the offer (implying no limitations, qualifications and conditions on national treatment and market access). To the extent that limitations, qualifications and conditions are maintained, the actual offer will be less than this upper bound. The implicit assumption, therefore, is that the potential value of the offer is not necessarily related to the restrictiveness of the measure applied in the sector, and the focus is on the absolute level of market access, not on the change in restrictiveness.

16. Despite its obvious shortcomings, an advantage of this procedure is that the share of total output is neutral with respect to factors such as geographic location, endowments, levels of development, etc., which result in significantly different economic structures and sectoral compositions. If country A offers only 5 per cent of it's service sector in GDP terms, while country B offers 15 per cent, one can say that, given the caveats mentioned above, in a relative sense, B has offered three times as much as A. Also, this procedure allows countries a substantial amount of flexibility concerning the choice of the sectors to be included, and ensures that in evaluating offers, the size of a country's economy is taken

---

[6]While GDP data for 138 countries are reported in the GATT database, most countries report figures at a high level of aggregation (i.e. five service sectors). However, more detailed data are available for a subset of countries, and these might be used to construct the "benchmark" country tables.

0052

A2-OFFERS

- 9 -

into account. Another advantage is that focusing on the share of output on which market access is offered gives credit to countries that presently do not impose any barriers in certain sectors and therefore is not biased against countries with more liberal or open regimes.[7]

B. Discounting offers in view of limitations, qualifications and conditions

17. Offers of market access and national treatment may have limitations, qualifications and conditions attached. For countries to be able to compare the value of offers it is necessary to discount offers on sectors where such measures are maintained. Possible limitations, qualifications and conditions on national treatment and market access combined with the existence of four modes of delivery implies eight possibilities for reducing the value of an offer below the maximum (i.e. the upper bound).

(i) Modes of supply

18. To evaluate offers it is necessary to determine the relative importance of modes of supply on a sector-by-sector basis, taking into account the complementarities that may exist between various modes. This requires a set of weights to be determined which can then be used in calculating the "effective" value of the offer in instances where restrictions are maintained on certain modes of supply. In principle, the weights will be determined by a mix of technical and economic factors. It is possible that only a subset of modes will be technically feasible. Also, which of these modes is used, or preferred, by suppliers will depend

---

[7]As noted earlier, "value" in this connection should not be taken to imply a monetary measure. In any event, countries will attach differing importance to any given service sector, whatever its relative weight in total output.

0053

A2-OFFERS

on economic and other factors (costs, need for physical presence, reliability, etc.).

19. Of the four modes of supply, each mode will presumably be of varying significance for different services sectors; some may be irrelevant because of technological or other factors. For example, offering zero restrictions on cross-border delivery or consumer movement in the context of retail banking services is of limited value, as retail banking services usually require a commercial presence. A commercial presence in retail banking may in turn require movement of personnel (management, technical support staff for data processing and information technology, etc.). If there are no restrictions on commercial presence, but there are restrictions on movement of the required personnel, market access may be severely limited. Equivalently, there may be no limitations on movement of personnel, there being instead restrictions on parts of the market (e.g. no deposit taking allowed). Again, the value of the offer will be reduced.

20. Establishing these weights on a sector-by-sector basis is clearly difficult. One practical procedure upon which a country could rely is sector-specific sample surveys. Even then it would probably be impossible to distinguish between domestic and international transactions.[8] While labour-intensive and time consuming, the survey approach is rather straightforward. Thus, the problem here is not so much a conceptual one as one of time and resources. It should be noted, however, that the results of the survey would apply at a specific point in time. Over time, technological and regulatory developments will alter the relevance of the various modes.

---

[8] An alternative might be to investigate patterns of trade and establishment for countries that maintain very liberal trade and investment regimes. However, this is not very useful given the high level of aggregation of existing data.

0054

A2-OFFERS

(ii) <u>Limitations and conditions on market access and national treatment</u>

21. Assuming that a set of weights can be determined for the modes of delivery, a further requirement is to establish how such sectoral weights should be adjusted to reflect the implications of the limitations, qualifications and conditions on national treatment and market access. It would appear necessary to determine the relative restrictiveness of the conditions imposed on national treatment and market access.

22. This might be done by constructing a scale of 0 to 3, for example, with 0 implying that the combined measures affecting market access and national treatment have no real restrictive effect, 1 signifying a minor impact, 3 a major impact, and 2 somewhere in between. By adopting such a procedure, the degree of subjectivity is limited but certainly not removed. Prohibitions and "zero" restrictions should be relatively easy to identify. In the case of non-prohibitive restrictions, it may be possible to allocate measures into two groups. Any scale with more than four elements may, however, be more difficult to implement.

23. While such an approach will have a large subjective element to it, this is also the situation for non-tariff measures in merchandise trade. Compilations of non-tariff measures frequently involve subjective evaluations as to the restrictiveness of various measures (e.g. a global quota compared to liberal licensing. As noted, similar compilations might be made with respect to various conditions on national treatment and market access.

C. <u>Determining relative ranking of sectors</u>

24. The foregoing discussion assumed that the relative importance of a sector could be proxied by its share in total output. While this may be the case in many instances, it will at times not adequately reflect

country-specific preferences. For example, although production data may indicate that the gross output of the transportation industry is five times that of financial services, and that therefore unrestricted access to transportation markets in a country is of greater quantitative significance than unrestricted access to financial markets, this does not necessarily mean that such access is more important for any given country. For the importing country, liberalization in financial services may be more sensitive than transport, while an exporting country may have much greater competitive advantage in the provision of financial services as opposed to transport services.

25. Thus, in the final analysis, the value of an offer for any given country can only be determined by the evaluating country itself, and is, to a large extent, an inherently subjective matter. In terms of applying the foregoing approach to the ongoing negotiations on offers, this implies that each country would have to determine two additional set of weights; one in terms of the sectors it is willing to offer and one for the sectors on which it wants to make requests.

IV. Possible Evaluation Based on Changes in Restrictions

26. Up to this point the focus has been on quantitative evaluation procedures that use the level of market access implied by an offer as a criterion. An alternative - perhaps a complementary - procedure is to take into account the extent to which countries offer to reduce existing restrictions. Some may argue that offers embodying significant rollback, (i.e. increased openness relative to the status quo), are of greater significance than offers that only imply a standstill.

27. Determining the relative value of standstill as compared to rollback commitments will presumably depend on a number of factors. For any sector in any given country, it follows that a rollback offer for a particular sector will be of greater significance than a standstill offer. Furthermore, the value of the offer will increase with the extent of

A2-OFFERS 0056

rollback offered. It is not the case, however, that rollback will always be more significant than standstill. For example, if there are few or no limitations, qualifications and conditions on national treatment and market access, a binding of the status quo is likely to be of greater value than a minimal rollback in a restricted and unimportant sector. Of course, much depends on whether the country offering to bind a relatively liberal regime may, at some time in the future, be likely to impose restrictions. If this probability is considered to be low, the value of the standstill may be limited, so that a rollback offer may be considered of more value. In general, all that can be said is that rollback in any sector in any country will, other things being equal, be preferred by trading partners to standstill.

28. In making cross-sector evaluations of offers, the larger an offered sector relative to total services output, the more significant the offer. And, the greater the rollback, the better the offer. Again, however, relative rankings may not always be easy to determine. Standstill of a relatively open regime for a relatively large sector might be given greater weight than an offer of rollback for a relatively small sector.

29. An implication of this is that even if the criterion of an evaluation procedure is the change in access to a particular market relative to the status quo, some kind of quantitative measures of the importance of a sector to a particular country are likely to remain necessary. Finally, assuming that for any given sector, offers of rollback are considered to be of greater value than standstill, a question that is likely to emerge is that of a benchmark year. If countries are to be given credit for recent unilateral liberalization of market access, it will be necessary to define the term "recent."

30. In principle, the extent of rollback incorporated in an offer may be (part of) a focal point for purposes of negotiations. An example would be the relative magnitude (in GDP terms or service sector output) of the sectors in which rollback is offered as compared to sectors with only a standstill. Again, however, qualitative elements will have to be

0057

A2-OFFERS

introduced, as account should be taken of the relative openness of each sector and the degree to which each rollback offer increases the possibility to compete in the sector concerned.

V. Concluding Remarks

31. It could be argued that what is required for the purposes of evaluating offers is a focal point or yardstick against which to compare different offers. One possible focal point is the value of offered sectors as a proportion of the total contribution of services to GDP. If such an approach were to be pursued, data on the gross output of the sectors offered, both with and without restrictions, should be provided by countries as part of their offer list.

32. It appears obvious that the approach sketched out above would not be easy to implement. Nonetheless, it is perhaps the most straightforward methodology for quantifying offers, where quantification is understood to consist of the use of a simple yardstick. The yardstick approach, however, should not be confused with measures of economic value. Other possible procedures - especially those with a more "economic" focus - would be much more difficult to quantify as they are subject to substantially greater data requirements. For example, an approach relying on computable general equilibrium techniques to simulate the effect of liberalization using actual data on trade and production of sufficient disaggregation are currently not feasible. Even if it were to be feasible, reasonable people can easily disagree on the appropriateness and effects of the assumptions underlying the models used.

33. Any evaluation procedure must, by the nature of the subject matter, have important qualitative elements; the factors that need to be taken into account are frequently not measurable. This would remain true even if perfect data on trade and production were to exist. The reason is that in certain circumstances it may not be obvious how to rank different offers for even the same sector. An example pertains to the relative weight that

A2-OFFERS   0058

should be given to offers incorporating rollback as opposed to those consisting of standstill. One implication of the discussion is that although it is possible to design evaluation procedures, implementation can, in the final analysis, only be undertaken by countries themselves due to the many non-quantifiable considerations.

34. A final remark may be in order. This note has focused on possible evaluation procedures and focal points for services negotiations. It was emphasized that this does not imply a method for calculating the economic value of offers and concessions, but rather a negotiating tool. Thus, the yardstick chosen is unlikely to be of any relevance insofar as determining the value of concessions in the context of possible compensation or retaliation associated with future dispute settlement cases, discussions concerning renegotiation of schedules or withdrawal of concessions due to emergency safeguard protection.

0059

A2-OFFERS

기 안 용 지

분류기호 문서번호	통기 20644-	(전화 : 720 - 2188)		시 행 상 특별취급		
보존기간	영구. 준영구 10. 5. 3. 1.	차 관		장 관		
수 신 처 보존기간		전결				
시행일자	1991. 6.21.					
보조 기관	국 장		협 조 기 관	제2차관보	문 서 통 제	
	심의관					
	과 장					
	기안책임자	조 현			발 송 인	
경 유 수 신 참 조		건 의	발신명의			

제 목   UR/서비스 협상 정부대표 임명

91.6.24(월)-28(금)간 제네바에서 개최되는 UR/서비스 협상에

참가할 정부대표단을 "정부대표 및 특별사절의 임명과 권한에 관한

법률"에 의거, 아래와 같이 임명할 것을 건의하오니 재가하여 주시기

바랍니다.

- 아   래 -

/뒷면 계속/   0060

1. 회 의 명 : UR/서비스 협상

2. 회의기간 및 장소 : 91.6.24(월)-28(금), 제네바

3. 정부대표

    ○ 본부대표

        - 경제기획원 대조실 제2협력관   이윤재

        - 경제기획원 통상조정3과 사무관   김용준

        - 경제기획원 통상조정3과 사무관   유윤선

    ○ 자   문 : 대외경제정책연구원 연구위원 박태호

4. 출장기간 : 91.6.22-30 (8박9일)

5. 소요경비 : 경제기획원 및 KIEP 소관예산

6. 훈   령 : 별 첨.   끝.

    0

    0

0061

UR/서비스 협상(91.6.24-28) 훈령

1. 회의 의제

   o 양허표(National Schedule) 작성 방안 검토

   o 노동력의 이동문제를 포함한 서비스 교역의 범위에 대한 토의

   o 양허협상의 지침 및 절차 검토

   o 각국 Offer의 평가시 고려해야할 사항에 대한 토의

2. 훈 령

   o UR/서비스 협상의 양허표 작성 방법, 서비스 교역의 범위에 대한
     논의에 아래 각제별 대응 방안에 따라 적극 참여하고 관련 정보를
     수집할 것

   o 양허협상의 지침 및 절차 검토, 각국의 Offer 평가시 고려사항에
     관한 협의에도 적극 참여하고 관련 정보를 수집, 향후 아국의
     Offer 개정 및 상대국에 대한 Request list 작성에 대비할 것

3. 각 의제별 대응 방향

   가. 양허표 작성방법

      o 내.외국인간에 무차별적인 규제조치라 하더라도 서비스 교역에
        실질적인 장벽이 되는 경우에는 양허표에 등재하는 방향으로 대처

        - 아국은 Offer List에 인.허가등 규제사항을 기재하여 GATT에
          기제출

                                                    0062

나. 서비스 교역의 범위

o 노동력의 이동문제에 대해서는 <u>각국의 세부적인 입장을 명확히</u>
  <u>파악</u>하여 협상 마무리 단계에서 아국의 입장을 본격적으로
  조정하는데 활용

  - 아국의 종전 입장은 Key-personnel 및 숙련 노동인력까지
    노동력 이동범위에 포함시키자는 입장 이었으나 현재 노동부등
    관계부처의 이견등으로 입장 조정의 필요성 발생

o 외국인 투자에 대해서는 동 서비스 공급형태를 서비스 교역의
  범위에 포함시키는 것은 불가피하나 <u>노동력의 이동문제에 대한</u>
  <u>협상과의 연계 필요성을 인정</u>

  - 현재 선진국들은 "외국인 투자(Foreign investment)" 대신
    "상업적 주재(Commercial presence)" 용어를 사용하여 외국인
    투자를 서비스 교역의 범위에 포함시키는 문제의 우회적인
    해결을 도모

다. 양허협상의 지침 및 절차

o 양허협상의 지침에 대해서는 아직 각국의 입장이 공식적 제시되지
  않은 상태이므로 금번 회의 기간중 <u>주요국의 입장 및 배경을</u>
  <u>파악</u>하여 향후 대응작업에 활용

  - 다만 각개별 국가들의 발전수준이 고려된 신축적인 지침을
    마련하는 것과 또한 모든 국가에게 공통적으로 적용될
    객관적인 기준을 마련하는 것과의 조화 필요성을 주장

0063

o 양허협상 절차에 대해서는 금년말이나 내년초에 UR 협상이
  종료되는 것을 전제로 구체적인 목표 일정(target date)이
  설정되도록 노력

  - 또한 양허협상 과정에 GATT 사무국이 적극적인 역할을 할
    수 있는 여지가 마련되어 양허협상이 전적으로 쌍무적인
    협상에 의해서 비공개적으로 진행되는 것을 방지

라. 각국 Offer의 평가시 고려해야할 요소

o 아직 GATT 사무국의 배경 문서가 제시되지 않은 상태이므로
  현지 협상에서 적의 대처

o 다만 각국 Offer의 내용을 가능한 객관적으로 평가할 수 있는
  다자적인 기준이 마련되어 협상력이 강한 국가에 의한 일방적인
  평가를 제지할 수 있도록 노력.   끝.

0064

경 제 기 획 원

봉조삼 10502-<del>↘↗</del>   503-9149   1991. 6. 19.

수신 외무부장관 (통상기구과)

제목 '91년도 제2차 UR/서비스협상 회의참석

1. 스위스 제네바에서 개최되는 '91년도 제2차 UR/서비스 협상회의 (6.24-28)에 참석할 본부대표단(자문역포함)을 다음과 같이 송부하니 협조해 주기 바랍니다.

다   음

가. 출장자

소 속	직 위	성 명
경제기획원 대외경제조정실	제2협력관	이 윤 재
"	통상조정3과 사무관	김 용 준
"	"	유 윤 선
대외경제정책연구원 (자문역)	연 구 위 원	박 태 호

나. 출장기간: '91.6.22-6.30 (8박 9일)

다. 경비부담: 당원 및 KIEP

첨부: 1. 출장일정 1부.

2. 협상대책자료 1부(별도송부).   끝.

경 제 기 획 원

0065

출 장 일 정

'91. 6. 22(토) 12:40 서울 발 (KE 907)

17:55 런던 착

20:00 런던 발 (SR 837)

22:30 제네바착

6. 24(월) ┐

~   UR/서비스협상회의 참석

6. 28(금) ┘

6. 29(토) 10:50 제네바 발 (SR 1855)

12:15 프랑크푸르트 착

6. 30(일) 14:20 프랑크푸르트 발 (KE 916)

09:50 서울착

0066

기 안 용 지

분류기호 문서번호	통기 20644-28872	(전화: 720 - 2188)	시 행 상 특별취급	
보존기간	영구. 준영구 10. 5. 3. 1.	장 관		
수 신 처 보존기간				
시행일자	1991. 6.21.			

보조기관	국 장	전 결	협조기관		문 서 통 제
	심의관	대 결			
	과 장				
기안책임자		조 현			

경유 수신 참조	경제기획원장관	발신명의	

제 목	UR/서비스 협상 정부대표 임명 통보

1. 91.6.24(월)-28(금)간 제네바에서 개최되는 UR/서비스 협상에

참가할 정부대표단이 "정부대표 및 특별사절의 임명과 권한에 관한

법률"에 의거 아래와 같이 임명 되었음을 통보합니다.

- 아   래 -

가. 회 의 명 : UR/서비스 협상

/뒷면 계속/   0067

나. 회의기간 및 장소 : 91.6.24(월)-28(금), 제네바

다. 정부대표

   ㅇ 본부대표

      - 경제기획원 대조실 제2협력관   이윤재

      - 경제기획원 통상조정3과 사무관   김용준

      - 경제기획원 통상조정3과 사무관   유윤선

   ㅇ 자 문 : 대외경제정책연구원 연구위원 박태호

라. 출장기간 : 91.6.22-30 (8박9일)

마. 소요경비 : 경제기획원 및 KIEP 소관예산

2. 상세 출장 결과 보고서는 본부대표단 귀국후 2주일이내

당부로 송부하여 주시기 바랍니다.   끝.

0068

발 신 전 보

	분류번호	보존기간

번   호 : WGV-0808   910621 1818 DN 종별 : 암호송신

수   신 : 주   제네바   대사. 총영사

발   신 : 장 . 관   (통기)

제   목 : UR/GNS 협상

　　91.6.24-28간 개최되는 표제 협상에 참가할 본부대표단이 아래 임명 되었으니
귀관 관계관과 함께 참석 조치바람.

1. 본부대표.

　　o 경제기획원 대조실 제2협력관　　　　　　이윤재
　　o 경제기획원 통상조정3과 사무관　　　　　김용준
　　o 경제기획원 통상조정3과 사무관　　　　　유윤선
　　o 대외경제정책연구원 연구위원　　　　　　박태호(자문)

2. 훈령 (상세 의제별 대응 방향은 본부대표가 지참)

　　o UR/서비스 협상의 양허표 작성 방법, 서비스 교역의 범위에 대한 논의에
　　　각 의제별
　　　~~아래 각제별~~ 대응 방안에 따라 적극 참여하고 관련 정보를 수집할 것

　　o 양허협상의 지침 및 절차 검토, 각국의 Offer 평가시 고려사항에 관한
　　　협의에도 적극 참여하고 관련 정보를 수집, 향후 아국의 Offer 개정 및
　　　상대국에 대한 Request list 작성에 대비할 것.　　　　　끝.

　　　　　　　　　　　　　　　　　　　　(통상국장 김 삼 훈) 안
　　　　　　　　　　　　　　　　　　　　　　　　　　　　　통 제

양고재	91년 월 21일	통기과	기안자 성명 조현	과 장	심의관	국 장 전결		차 관	장 관

외신과통제

0069

GWW (h)- 0215   *r-62& 1530*

" GVW-1124첨부,

MULTILATERAL TRADE NEGOTIATIONS

THE URUGUAY ROUND

RESTRICTED

MTN.TNC/W/85

24 June 1991

Special distribution

Trade Negotiations Committee

COMMUNICATION FROM THE CHAIRMAN OF THE TRADE NEGOTIATIONS COMMITTEE

Please find attached the letters which I have received for distribution to all participants from the Chairman of the Group of Negotiations on Services (MTN.GNS/W/117), the Chairman of the Negotiating Group on Agriculture (MTN.GNG/AG/W/1), and the Chairman of the Negotiating Group on Market Access (MTN.GNG/MA/W/1).

MTN.GNS/W/117
24 June 1991
Special Distribution

Original: English

Dear Mr. Dunkel,

As you requested, I am setting out below the present
situation in the Group of Negotiations on Services and
stating how the negotiations might be significantly
advanced between now and the end of July. This
assessment is in accordance with my concluding remarks at
the last meeting of the Group.

Negotiations on trade in services are proceeding on
the basis of a draft text sent to Ministers in Brussels
and on the assumption that they should be concluded by
the end of 1991. This objective requires completing
negotiations on three elements: the text of the "General
Agreement on Trade in Services", sectoral annexes and
initial commitments.

The time remaining for negotiations can be divided
into two major parts, from now until the end of July, and
from September till the end of 1991. This letter
addresses the first period.

There is a general view among participating
countries that to conclude the negotiations by the end of
1991 the following issues need to be advanced, and
wherever possible resolved, by the end of July 1991:

1.   The scheduling of specific commitments.
Informal consultations are continuing on the basis
of a secretariat paper setting forth options for
different approaches. Settling matters relating to
the scheduling of commitments is essential for an
intensive exchange of offers and requests and the
completion of negotiations on initial commitments.

2.   The application of the MFN provision in the
Agreement. It is important to resolve outstanding
matters relating to MFN and agree on an approach
that meets concerns of individual participants

./.

Mr. A. Dunkel
Chairman of the
Trade Negotiations Committee

0071

without resorting to widespread derogations from
this important principle. Matters relating to both
horizontal arrangements (e.g. bilateral investment
treaties and friendship commerce and navigation
treaties) and techniques for dealing with sectoral
considerations need to be addressed. The
secretariat will prepare a paper on horizontal
agreements once information requested of delegations
is provided.

3.   Labour mobility. The text of a proposed labour
mobility annex has not been agreed. Resolving
labour mobility issues is particularly important for
the process of negotiations on initial commitments.

4.   Guidelines for negotiations on initial
commitments. There are draft texts for substantive
and procedural guidelines. An agreement on these
texts would facilitate the intensification of the
negotiations on initial commitments.

5.   Sectoral annexes. There is a need to address,
prior to 31 July, any special arrangements that need
to be put in place for those sectors for which
participants consider annexes are needed. Such
sectors include telecommunications and financial
services.

6.   Negotiations on initial commitments. While the
discussion on offers is underway, participants have
yet to engage in intensive and structured
negotiations within the GNS. Those negotiations
should begin in July.

At the request of the GNS, the secretariat is making
available notes on dispute settlement, definition of
terms and the evaluation of offers and concessions.
These notes will serve to advance discussions within the
GNS. Also, the final version of the classification list
of services will be made available by the secretariat by
the end of June. In addition, work will proceed on
other issues with a view to completing Parts I to IV of
the Agreement before the end of July.

I would be thankful if you could circulate this
letter to participants.

Yours sincerely,

Felipe Jaramillo   0072
Chairman of the Negotiating
Group on Services

경 제 기 획 원

봉조삼 10502- 나기   503-9149   1991. 6. 24.

수신 수신처참조   통상기구2

제목 UR/서비스협상관련 노동력이동 관계부처 회의결과 통보

　　　노동력이동에 대한 아국의 종전입장을 점검하고 향후 대응방향을 논의한
관계부처회의 결과를 별첨과 같이 송부하니 각 부처(기관)는 해당사항의 추진에
만전을 기해주기 바랍니다.

첨부: 1. 노동력이동에 대한 대응방향 (회의자료) 1부.
　　　2. 노동력이동 관계부처 회의결과 1부.　　　끝.

경 제 기 획 원 장

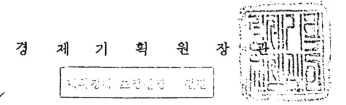

수신처: 외무부장관, 내무부장관, 재무부장관, 법무부장관, 교육부장관,
　　　　문화부장관, 상공부장관, 보건사회부장관, 건설부장관, 교통부장관,
　　　　노동부장관, 체신부장관, 과학기술처장관, 환경처장관, 공보처장관,
　　　　특허청장, 항만청장, 대외경제정책연구원장, 한국개발연구원장,
　　　　대한무역진흥공사장, 김&장법률사무소장

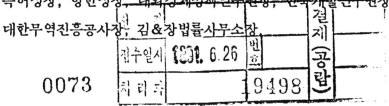

0073

勞動力移動 關係部處會議 結果

I. 會議槪要

- 日　時: '91.6.21(금)　10:00-12:00

- 場　所: 과천청사 3동 225호실 (EPB 제2협력관실)

- 參席者: EPB 제2협력관 (회의주재),
　　　　EPB 통상조정3과장 및 담당사무관,
　　　　인력개발계획과 담당사무관,　建設部 해외협력과장,
　　　　勞動部 고용관리과장,　法務部 입국심사과 담당사무관,
　　　　商工部 산업정책과 담당사무관

- 會議議題

　○ 勞動力移動問題에 대한 協商進展狀況 설명

　○ 아국의 對應現況 및 立場의 再檢討

　○ 향후 對應方向 論議

0074

Ⅱ. 決定事項

> 다음과 같은 事項을 決定하고 各 部處別로 推進하기로 함.

① 勞動力의 移動範圍

- 국내서비스 供給企業이 海外에 진출하기 위해서는 先進國이 主張하는
  Key-personnel (즉 관리자, 중역, 전문가등)만으로는 곤란하며 또한
  國內勞動市場의 需給與件上 開途國이 主張하는 單純勞動人力(Simple
  labour)을 포함시키기도 곤란

  ㅇ 建設, 流通, 運送, 호텔, 病院, 觀光등의 서비스를 해외에 공급하는
    경우를 대비하여 적절한 範圍의 勞動力移動 範圍設定이 필요하며
    또한 아국을 포함한 開途國이 先進國에 비해서 比較優位를 갖고있는
    分野에서 先進國의 主張에 따라 Key-personnel로만 勞動力의 移動
    範圍가 한정되면 UR/서비스協商에 참가하는 國家間에 利益均衡을
    達成하기가 곤란

- 지금까지 熟練勞動人力(Skilled labour)란 용어를 사용해왔으나 同
  用語가 建設分野에만 주로 해당되고 Key-personnel과 單純勞動人力의
  中間領域을 정확하게 지칭하고 있다고 볼수 없으므로 同 用語의
  계속적 使用與否를 再檢討

  ㅇ 앞으로 各 分野別로 필수인력(essential person)의 範圍를 具體的
    으로 검토한후 同 범주의 人力을 代表해서 지칭하는 적절한 用語를
    發掘

0075

② 勞動力移動에 대한 接近方式 (부속서 제정여부)

　- 대부분의 國家가 附屬書를 制定하는 것이 필요하다는 方向으로 接近해
　　가고 있는만큼 我國도 附屬書를 制定하는데 특별히 반대할 必要는 없음.
　　ㅇ 다만 我國에게 不利하지 않는 內容의 附屬書가 制定되도록 努力

　- 필요시 勞動部가 附屬書가 制定되는 것을 前提로 具體的인 附屬書(案)을
　　關係部處와 協議하여 作成

③ 勞動力移動에 대한 MFN일탈문제

　- 현재 我國으로서는 당장현안이 걸려있는 事項이 없기 때문에 강한 MFN
　　原則을 지지하는 我國의 全般的인 立場에 따라 勞動力移動에 대한 MFN
　　일탈에 반대
　　ㅇ 各國의 立場 및 我國의 勞動力輸入 움직임등을 적극적으로 追加檢討

④ 向後 推進方向

　- 會議資料에 포함된 다음과 같은 內容을 關係部處間에 이의없이 確定
　　ㅇ 7月初에 勞動部가 綜合對策資料를 준비하여 UR對策 實務委員會에
　　　상정하고 필요시 對外協力委員會를 開催하여 勞動力移動에 대한
　　　政府의 立場을 論議
　　ㅇ 현재 各部處가 推進中인 分野別 勞動範圍設定(Request案도 포함)
　　　作業을 조속히 마무리
　　ㅇ 현지 協商에 勞動部 및 法務部등 主務部處가 積極參與하여 我國의
　　　理解關係를 反映
　　ㅇ 協商進展狀況에 따라 出入國管理法등 國內關聯 法과 制度를 改善

0076

Ⅱ. 主要論議 事項

(EPB 제2협력관): 勞動力移動問題에 대한 我國立場을 決定하는 節次와
我國立場 自體에 있어서 政府部處間에 다소 混線이 있었는바,
앞으로 協商마무리 단계에서 UR協商 全體次元에서의 關係部處間
의 이견을 調整하고 我國立場을 決定할 必要性 강조

(EPB 담당사무관): 會議資料 報告

(노동부 담당사무관): 別途準備資料報告 (주요내용: 勞動力의 移動範圍는
外國서비스供給企業의 管理者 및 專門家로 한정)

(건설부 해외협력과장): 建設部가 생각하는 熟練勞動人力의 入國許容條件
(필수적인 최소인원이 特定事業期間中에만 滯留하고 사업종료후에
는 철수)을 說明

(상공부 담당사무관): 製造業體 특히 中小企業體(예: 염색업등)의 공동화
를 방지하기 위한 低級單純人力의 輸入도 必要하다는 商工部의
基本立場을 소개

(법무부 담당사무관): 基本的으로 勞動部와 같은 立場이며 各部處가 分野別
로 필수적인 勞動力移動範圍를 設定하면 關聯法規의 개정시 반영할
용의가 있음을 언급하고 향후 協商에 대비하여 필수인력의 범위가
기업의 理事級인지, 部長級인지, 課長級인지를 協商戰略的 次元에서
段階別로 設定하는 것이 必要하다고 지적

0077

(EPB 인력개발계획과 담당사무관): 國內經濟與件上 單純機能人力의 수입은
　　　　곤란하다고 지적

(통상조정3과장): 우선 아국이 勞動力의 輸入國이 될것인지 아니면 輸出國이
　　　　될것인지에 대한 판단이 先行되야 하고 勞動力移動에 대한 自由化約束
　　　　(Commitment)의 性格에 대한 이해가 필요하다고 언급

(노동부 고용관리과장): 附屬書를 制定 自體가 我國에게 커다란 영향을 주는
　　　　것이 아니므로 융봉성을 갖고 대처하되 必要時 勞動部가 我國의
　　　　附屬書案을 關係部處와 協調하여 마련할 용의가 있다고 언급

(EPB 제2협력관): MFN일탈문제는 我國이 利害關係國과 勞動協定을 체결한
　　　　것이 없으며 당장 懸案이 걸려있지 않기 때문에 종전 입장대로 MFN
　　　　일탈에 反對하되 關係部處가 積極的으로 檢討할 것을 제시

(통상조정3과장): 各部處가 分野別로 勞動力移動 許容範圍를 설정할때
　　　　상대국에 要請할 Request(案)까지도 포함해서 檢討할 것을 지적

(EPB 제2협력관): 7월초에 勞動部가 綜合對策資料를 작성하여 UR對策
　　　　實務委員會에서 論議하기로 하고 會議를 마무리

0078

勞動力移動에 대한 對應方向

1991. 6

經 濟 企 劃 院

對外經濟調整室

0079

目　　次

1. 協商進展狀況

2. 我國의 對應現況 및 立場

3. 向後 推進計劃

〈別添〉　1. 開途國 共同提案 및 美國提案의 內容

　　　　　2. 勞動力移動에 대한 附屬書의 主要內容 및
　　　　　　　各國立場

　　　　　3. Initial Offer List에 나타난 各國立場

1. 協商進行狀況

- 서비스協商이 시작된 이래 先.開途國은 계속해서 立場對立

    ㅇ 先進國은 企業의 設立에 필요한 必須 勞動力의 移動을 강조

    ㅇ 開途國은 資本의 移動에 상응하는 모든 範圍의 勞動力
      移動을 主張

- '88.12 開催된 몬트리올 TNC會議에서 서비스供給에 필수적
  (essential)인 勞動力의 國境間 移動을 서비스協定適用
  對象에 포함

    ㅇ 다만 目的의 特定性(Specificity of purpose), 去來의
      不連續性(Discreteness of transaction), 制限된 期間
      (Limited duration)의 관점에서 검토하기로 合意

- '90.6月 以後 勞動力移動에 대한 3회의 作業班(Working party)
  會議를 통하여 4가지 接近方式을 도출

    (1案): 附屬書는 불필요하며 讓許協商을 통하여 各分野別로
          各國의 National Schedule에 기재 (EC,호주,헝가리)

    (2案): 附屬書가 필요하며 同 附屬書는 商業的 駐在와 관련
          되거나 필수적이라고 생각되는 Key-personnel의 移動을
          保障 (美國, 캐나다)

    (3案): 勞動力의 移動이 Framework 제1조(서비스交易의 範圍)
          에 포함되야 하며 또한 附屬書가 필요하고 동 附屬書
          는 市場接近을 약속한 서비스供給에 필요한 모든
          種類의 人力移動을 保障 (개도국)

0081

(4案): 附屬書는 필요하나 各國에게 義務를 부담하는 內容이
될수는 없고 Framework상의 公開主義(제3조), 國內
規制(제6조), 內國民待遇(제16조) 등을 明瞭化하는
內容에 限定

- '90.12 GNS議長은 同 作業結果를 바탕으로 브랏셀 TNC會議에
勞動力移動에 대한 附屬書를 提出

  ○ 主要爭點들이 괄호로 묶여있을 뿐만아니라 附屬書全體가
  괄호로 묶여있는 상태

  ○ 브랏셀 閣僚會議에서 附屬書制定 必要性에 대해서는
  대체적으로 合意 形成

- '91.2 開催된 UR/서비스 韓.美 兩者協議에서 아국은 美側에
대해서 다음과 같은 疑問事項을 問議

  ○ 美側 Offer상의 專門家의 범주에 熟練機能人力(Skilled-
  labor)이 포함되는지 여부
  ○ 入國以前에 該當企業에 1년이상 고용되야 한다는 勞動力
  移動의 事前條件이 建設分野에 적절한지 여부

    〈美側의 答辯要旨〉

  ○ 專門家는 獨占的인 知識(proprietary knowledge) 所有
  與否에 따라 case by case로 판단
    . 다만 國內에서 供給可能한 熟練機能人力은 專門家의
    범주에 포함되지 않음.

  ○ 該當企業에의 1년간 事前雇傭條件은 기업과 고용인 사이의
  關係形成을 위해 필요
    . 이에 대한 我側의 代案을 問議

0082

2. 我國의 對應現況 및 立場

가. 對應現況

- '89.2 勞動力移動에 대한 國內作業班(班長: 勞動部 職業 安定局長)을 設置하고 국내대책을 마련하는 동시에 현지 협상에도 참여

  ○ '90.5월 勞動力移動에 대한 政策協議會 開催

  ○ 제네바에서 開催된 제1차 作業班會議('90.6.25-27)에 研究責任者 참석

- '90.5, 8월 勞動關係部處 會議를 開催하여 我國立場을 論議

  ○ 開途國의 共同提案에 공동서명하는 문제등에 대한 我國 立場을 定立

- '91.1 UR/서비스協商關聯 讓許協商對策 會議에서 各部處 가 所管分野別로 具體的인 移動範圍를 설정할 것을 결정 하고 현재 各部處가 檢討中

  ○ '91.2 各部處의 作業에 도움을 주기위하여 勞動部는 韓國 標準職業分類表中에서 필수인력의 豫示目錄등을 작성하여 배포 (필수인력의 정의: 國內에 商業的 駐在를 한 外國 서비스企業의 管理者 및 專門家)

0083

나. 我國의 立場

① 勞動力의 移動範圍

- UR協商이 시작된 이래 대체로 我國은 先進國과 開途國의 中間立場을 취하여 熟練勞動人力까지 포함시킬 것을 주장
  ○ 특히 建設分野에 대한 分野別 協商時 同 범주의 人力 移動이 必要함을 強調

- 그러나 '90.8경 부터 勞動部등 關係部處는 國內勞動市場의 需給與件變化, 勞動力移動에 따른 社會的인 問題등을 理由로 美國등 先進國과 마찬가지로 Key-personnel만 勞動力의 移動範圍에 포함되야 한다는 견해를 주장
  ○ 이러한 關係部處의 주장에 대하여 UR協商에 參加하는 정부 全體的인 관점에서 아직 立場調整이 결여된 상태

② 勞動力移動에 대한 接近方式 (附屬書의 制定與否)

- 我國은 勞動力移動에 대한 附屬書의 制定이 必要하다는 美國, 開途國의 입장을 묵시적으로 지지하였으나 아직 明確한 立場이 未定인 상태
  ○ 다만 勞動部는 개별적으로 附屬書의 制定이 필요없다는 EC의 立場을 지지

- 또한 附屬書의 性格에 대해서도 명확한 입장이 未定인 狀態
  ○ 즉 同附屬書가 一定한 범주(예: Key-personnel)의 移動을 一律的으로 保障하는 形態가 될 것인지 아니면 Framework 上의 規定(例: 公開主義, 市場接近, 內國民待遇)들의 內容을 明瞭化하는 것이 되야 할 것인지에 대해서 細部的인 檢討缺如

0084

③ 勞動力移動에 대한 MFN일탈문제

- 我國이 特別히 勞動力移動에 대한 國際協定을 締結하고
  있지 않기 때문에 基本的으로 MFN일탈에 반대하는 立場을
  취하고 있으나 아직 細部的인 事項에 대해서는 檢討缺如
  ○ 특히 我國이 中國, 蘇聯등 교포가 살고 있는 國家들과
    勞動力移動에 대한 國際協定을 체결하게 될 경우 이러한
    事項에 대한 MFN일탈을 주장해야 하는지 등에 대하여
    論議가 不足

3. 向後 推進計劃

- 勞動力移動에 대한 我國의 綜合的인 立場을 조속히 확정
  ○ 7월초에 UR對策實務委員會를 開催하여 關係部處間의
    異見을 調整하고 必要時 對外協力委員會 開催

- 현재 勞動部가 推進中인 各分野別 勞動力移動 許容範圍
  設定作業을 조속히 마무리
  ○ 동 작업을 바탕으로 各分野別로 讓許協商 過程에서 我國
    이 Offer 할수 있는 協商案 및 相對國에게 요구할 수
    있는 Request案 등에 대한 技術的인 檢討 遂行

- 現地協商에 積極的 참여하여 我國의 利害關係를 反映
  ○ 主務部處擔當者 및 研究責任者등이 참석하여 主要國家의
    立場 및 協商動向을 깊이있게 파악하고 協商에 對處

- 協商進展狀況에 따라 國內關聯法 및 制度의 改善 推進
  ○ 出入國管理法을 改定하여 入國이 許容되는 人力의 範圍
    를 細分化하고 비자발급 기준을 객관화
  ○ 內國民의 綜合的인 海外進出方案 및 國內進出外國人에
    대한 효율적인 管理方案등 마련

0085

<별첨 1>

開途國 共同提案 및 美國提案의 內容

<開途國의 共同提案(MTN/GNS/W/106)>

o 技術水準 또는 地位에 關係없이 市場接近이 許容된 서비스를 供給하는데 필요한 모든 人力에 適用 (제2조 3항)

o 서비스協定加入國中 經濟的으로 가장 유리한 곳으로 부터 職員採用 可能 (제3조 1항)

o 서비스供給企業의 被雇傭者에 대한 事前承認節次등 特定 條件없이 短期入國許可 附與 (제4조 1,2,3항)

* 멕시코, 인도, 아르헨티나, 콜롬비아, 쿠바, 이집트,
  파키스탄, 페루등 8개국이 共同提案

<美國의 提案(MTN/GNS/Lab/1)>

o 支社, 子會社등을 통하여 서비스가 供給되는 경우 市場接近 約束을 한 分野에 대하여 經營者(managers), 任員(executives), 專門家(specialists)의 移動은 필수적으로 보장 (제1조 3항)

o 勞動力移動分野 附屬書는 일시적인 移動에만 적용되며 그 期間은 3-5년을 超過禁止 (제2조 1항)

0086

勞動力移動에 대한 附屬書의 主要內容 및 各國立場

附屬書의 內容	各國立場	我國立場
第1條(適用範圍) - 自然人의 일시적 이동에 적용	- 이견없음.	
第2條(人力의 種類에 대한 目錄) (1案): 共通 豫示目錄 (illustrative list) 作成 (2案): 共通 豫示目標은 不必要 하며 각체약국들이 相互交換한 人力의 種類를 바탕으로 讓許 協商進行	- 美國, 開途國立場 - EC, 헝가리입장	- (1案) 支持 ○ (1안)이 明瞭하며 향후 勞動力 移動에 대한 多者間規範을 발전시 키는데 유리
第3條(市場接近約束과의 一致) - 勞動力移動에 대한 市場接近 約束은 Framework 第16條 (市場接近)와 一致해야 함.	- 이견없음.	
第4條(勞動力移動에 대한 自由化 約束의 意味) - National Schedule에 記錄된 모든 人力의 서비스供給을 保障	- 이견없음.	

0087

附屬書의 內容	各國立場	我國立場
第5條(市場接近約束의 무효화 금지)		
(1案): 勞動力移動에 대한 市場 接近約束을 입국, 滯留 및 勞動許可등에 관한 國內法 및 規制에 의해서 무효화할 수 없음.	- 開途國	- (1案)支持 ○ 讓許協商過程에서 일단 市場接近約束을 한 사항은 당연히 준수되어야함
(2案): 同條項 削除	- 先進國	○ 다만 이러한 조항은 通信附屬書에도 괄호로 묶여 있는 사항이며 추후 Framework上의 紛爭解決節次規程(제23조)에 비추어 再檢討 必要
第6條(MFN일탈)		
(1案): 勞動力移動에 대한 MFN 일탈허용	- 북구, 아세안	
(2案): 同條項 削除	- 멕시코, 인도, 이집트	- 原則的으로 (2안) 支持 ○ 다만 立場表明을 留保하고 追加的인 檢討必要
第7條(人力市場의 統合)		
(1案): 人力市場의 統合에는 同 附屬書의 適用을 除外	- 북구, 아세안	
(2案): 同條項 削除	- 멕시코, 인도, 이집트	- 原則的으로 (2안) 支持 ○ 다만 立場表明을 留保하고 追加的인 檢討必要

0088

Initial Offer List에 나타난 各國立場

- 我國을 포함하여 많은 國家가 勞動力의 移動에 대하여 Unbound 하거나, 추가적인 檢討事項이라고 언급하거나, 아니면 國內法 및 規制에 종속된다는 無意味한 內容을 Offer

  ○ 韓國, EC, 日本, 스위스, 뉴질랜드, 홍콩, 싱가폴, 터키, 濠洲, 핀랜드, 체코, 오스트리아, 폴란드등

- 美國등 6個國家는 필수인력에 한하여 國境間移動을 許容

  ○ 美國: 市場接近約束을 한 모든분야에 經營者(managers), 重役(executives), 專門家(specialists)를 Offer

  ○ 캐나다: 市場接近約束을 한 모든분야에 서비스판매자 (service sellers), 經營者(managers), 重役 (executives), 專門家(specialists)를 Offer

  ○ 인도네시아: 通信關聯서비스의 경우 最高經營者(top manager)를 허용하되 國內移民關聯法 및 勞動法 과 一致해야 한다고 Offer

  ○ 스웨덴: 管理者(managers), 重役(executives), 專門家 (specialists)의 就業에 대해서는 勞動市場與件 檢査(labor market test)를 免除

  ○ 멕시코: 市場接近約束을 한 모든分野에 理事(members of the Borad of Directors)를 Offer

  ○ 콜롬비아: 管理者(manager), 技術者(technical personnel) legal representatives을 Offer

0089

외 무 부

종   별 :

번   호 : GVW-1187   일   시 : 91 0625 1930

수   신 : 장 관(봉기, 경기원, 재무부, 법무부, 상공부, 건설부, 보사부, 교통부,

발   신 : 주 제네바 대사   체신부, 문화부, 공보처, 과기처, 항만청)

제   목 : UR/GNS 회의(1)

6.24(월) JARAMILLO 의장 주재로 개최된 표제회의 내용을 하기 보고함.

1. 금일 회의 의제중 SCHEDULING OF COMMITMENTS 는 6.25(화) 이후에 HAWES 대사주재의 비공식 협의로 진행할 계획이며 FRAMEWORK 제 1조(정의 및범위)에 대하여만논의하였는바 선.개도국간 종전입장의 반복외에 아무런 진전이 없었음.

2. 선.개도국의 주요 발언내용은 다음과 같음.,

-개도국

0 생산요소(자본, 노동)간 글자 그대로의 균형(영구적 설립이 허용되면 영구적 이민도 허용되어야 한다는 개념)은 실현이 곤란하다 하더라도 경제적 균형을 이룰수있는 방안을찾아야 함.

0 상업적 주재에 제한 조건(한정된 기간,특정목적)이 부과되어야 함.

0 협정상 의무를 부담하는 비정부 규제기관의 범위가 축소되어야 함.

0 특히, 인도는 노동력 이동문제의 해결없이는 다른 분야의 진전이 어렵다고 하였으며 서비스 공급형태의 정의와 SCHEDULING 문제는 별개문제라고 전제하고 SCHEDULING 관련 다음과같이 각 서비스 공급형태별로 의미있는 법규들을 분류하여 동 법규들의 처리에 촛점을 맞추는 접근방법을 제시함.

0 CROSS-BORDER SUPPLY: 통신관계법, BOP조항(본 공급 형태는 인력의 일시적 이동은 포함하지 않는다는 전제)

0 CONSUMPTION ABROAD: 외환규제법

0 자연인의 주재: 이민관계법,노동법, 전문직업자격에 관한 법규, 자율규제단체의 윤리강령등

0 상업적 주재: 투자관계법, 외환규제법

- 선진국

통상국	/차보	2차보	외정실	분석관	청와대	안기부	법무부	보사부
문화부	교통부	체신부	경기원	재무부	상공부	건설부	과기처	해항정
공보처								

PAGE 1   91.06.26   05:50 FN

외신 1과 통제관

0090

O 서비스무역에 필요한 상업적 주재와 투자를 구분하는 것은 일견 타당성이 있으나 투자와 상업적 주재에 관한 법규가 똑같으며 이민관계법도 이민과 인력의 일시적이동에 똑같이 적용된다는 점을 지적함.

O 1조 2항의 서비스 공급형태의 정의는 SCHEDULING목적의 공급형태 구분과는 별개문제이며 1조2항의 정의 규정은 모든 형태의 서비스 무역을 포괄하는 총괄적인 것이 되어야 함(특히 카나다는 두가지 이상의 공급형태가 결합된 형태의 무역이정의 규정에 반영되어야 한다고 함)

O EC 는 1조 3항 A) III) 의 지방정부의 의무에관한 조항이 부적절하며 분쟁해결등 다른 조항에 반영하여야 한다고 한 반면 미국,카나다등은 UR/갓트조문 그룹의 협상결과를 존중하여야 한다고함.

O EC, 미국은 3항 B) 의 '정부 기능 수행과정의 서비스'가 애매한 부분이 많으므로 추가 검토가 필요하다고 함.

3. 표제 회의는 6.25(화) 오후 속개될 예정임.끝

(대사 박수길-국장)

외 무 부

종 별 :

번 호 : GVW-1201   일 시 : 91 0627 1800

수 신 : 장관(통기, 경기원, 재무부, 상공부, 건설부, 보사부, 노동부, 교통부

발 신 : 주 제네바 대사   체신부, 문화부, 과기처, 공보처, 항만청)

제 목 : UR/GNS 회의(2)

6.25(화) 속개된 표제회의는 노동력 이동에 대하여 논의하였는바 주요내용 하기보고함.

1. 노동력 이동 부속서

- 대체적으로 합의가 형성된 사항

0 노동력 이동 부속서 제정과 노동력 이동 자유화추진과는 별개이나 부속서 제정에 대하여는 합의형성

0 개별적인 해외 취업 희망자나 이민대상자는 협정 대상에서 벗어남

0 이민이나 시민권, 영구거주, 취업등에 관한국내법규 및 비자발급 절차, 보건 목적상의규제등 비경제적 이유에 기초한 규제제도는 영향을받지 않음.

0 일단 SCHEDULE 에 인력이동에 관한 시장접근약속을 하고난 후에는 LABOR MARKET TEST, NEED TEST등 추가 규제를 통하여 동 약속을 침해하여서는안됨.

0 노동력 이동 부속서 자체가 인력이동 자유화에관한 의무조항을 포함해서는 안됨.

- 논란이 많은 사항

0 MFN 일탈 여부: ASEAN, 홍콩등이 MFN일탈을 주장하였으나, 호주, 뉴질랜드는모든분야, 모든 종류의 인력에 대한 광범위한MFN 일탈은 곤란하며 세밀한 검토 및 규정이필요하다고 함.

(그외 대다수 국가도 MFN 일탈에 대하여 유보적입장임)

0 서비스 공급인력의 종류에 관한 ILLUSTRATIVELIST 작성 여부(부속서 초안 2항)

. 인도는 광범위한 인력을 포괄하는ILLUSTRATIVE LIST 작성이 시급하다고 함.(노동력이동 자유화 추진 방법 관련 후술)

. 미국, 일본, 캐나다, 호주, 뉴질랜드등은 현실적으로동 LIST 작성은 매우 어렵다고함.

통상국 재무부	차관 상공부	2차보 건설부	경제국 노동부	보사부 과기처	문화부 해항청	교통부 공보처	체신부	경기원

외신 1과 통제관
0092

- 특기사항0 EC 는 한 EC 회원국이 이민 관계법에의한 규제는 분쟁해결 대상이
되지 않는다는조항이 추가되어야 한다고 주장함으로써 회원국간이견이 발생, 토의에
참가하지 않았음.

2. 노동력 이동 자유화 추진방법

- 인도: 모든 형태의 서비스 공급에 필요한 모든종류의 인력 이동이 FRAMEWORK 및
각국의SCHEDULE 인력 이동란에 반영되어야 함.

(상기 사항을 대원칙으로 전제하고 노동력 이동부속서에 ILLUSTRATIVE LIST 를
첨부함으로써시장접근에 관한 양허 협상시 이를 강한 압력수단으로 활용코자 하는
의도)

0 인도는 또한 서비스 공급자가 필요인력을본국뿐만 아니라 가장 경제적인 제
3국에서도조달할 수 있어야 한다고 함.

- 기타 대다수국가: 노동력 이동도 서비스 공급형태의하나인 만큼 협정 제
3부의양허협상 대상이되어야 하며 협정 2부와 같은 일반적 의무사항이되어서는 않됨.

0 미국: MANAGERS, EXECITIVES,SPECIALISTS 는 다자간약속(MULTIATERAL
COMMITMENT) 에 의하여일률적으로 자유화 하고 나머지 범주인력은 양자간양허 협상에
맡김.(동 약속은 각국 SCHEDULE에 등재된 분야에 한하여 적용)

0 캐나다: MANAGERS, EXECUTIVE, SPECIALISTS, SERVICESELLERS 는 모든 서비스
분야에 대하여 다자간약속으로 자유화 하고 나머지 범주의 인력은 양자간양허
협상에맡김.

0 호주,뉴질랜드,오지리: 캐나다 접근방법에 지지의사를 표명하였으나 다만
뉴질랜드는 동 접근방법이 각국 SCHEDULE 에 등재되지 않은분야까지도 적용되는 점에
대하여는 유보적 의사를표명함.

0 기타 헝가리도 원칙적으로 미국,캐나다의접근방법을 환영하는 한편 다른 범주의
인력에관한 양자협상의 중요성을 강조하였음.

3. 관찰 및 건의
가. 협상추이

- 노동력 이동에 관한 일반적 사항을 규정하는부속서를 제정하되 동 부속서가
노동력 이동자유화에 관한 의무조항을 포함해서는안된다는데 합의가 형성됨.

- 따라서 노동력 이동 자유화는 각국 양허협상에의하여 다양하게 결정되는
것이기본 원칙임

PAGE 2

0093

0 미국,캐나다는 KEY-PERSONNEL 에 대해서는각국이 모든 서비스분야에 약속할 수있는사항이므로 다자간 약속(MULTILATERAL COMMITMENT) 에의하여 공통으로 자유화(비자발급, 취업허가등의절차는 계속 부과됨) 하되 나머지 범주의 인력도국가간 양허협상에 의하여 자유화 대상이 된다고밝힘으로써 이에대한 지지가 확산되는 추세임.0인도 역시 부속서를 통하여 광범위한 범주의인력을 일괄 자유화 하고자 하는 것은 아니며 공통ILLUSTRATIVE LIST 를 제정하여 향후 서비스 분야별양허 협상시 이를 압력수단으로 활동하고자 하는입장나. 건의

- 상기 협상 추이를 볼때 KEY-PERSONNEL 이외범주의 인력에 대하여 부속서나 MULTILATERALCOMMITMENT 를 통하여 공통으로 자유화하는 것은불가능함.

0 따라서 아국이 특정분야의 어떤 인력(예:SKILLED PERSONNEL) 에 해외진출기회확대필요성이 있다면 분야별 양허협상을 통하여해결하여야 할것임.

0 그러나 특정분야의 특정범주 인력에 비교우위가있다 하더라도 양허협상과정에서 동 인력을 아국NATION SCHEDULE 에 기재하게 되는 경우 이는국제법상 의무(기속)를지게되는 것을 의미하므로향후(5년내지 10년후) 아국 사정에 변화가 있을경우에도 변경이 불가능함.

- 위와같은 관점에서 하기 사항을 건의하니 입장회시 바람.

0 노동력 이동 자유화 추진방법: KEY-PERSONNEL 에대하여는 다자간 자유화 약속에 의하되 기타 범주인력은 국가간 양허협상에 맡기는 방법 지지

0 분야별 양허협상 대책: 양허협상을 통하여아국도 특정분야에 광범위한 인력이 BINDING되지 않도록 가능한 서비스 협정과 무관하게현재와 같이 인력이동이 계속 또는 확대되는방안 강구.끝

(대사 박수길-국장)

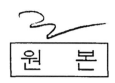

외 무 부

종　별 :

번　호 : GVW-1202　　　　　　　　　일　시 : 91 0627 1800

수　신 : 장관(통기,경기원,재무부,법무부,상공부,건설부,보사부,노동부,교통부

발　신 : 주제네바대사　　　　　　　체신부,문화부,과기처,공보처,항만청)

제　목 : UR/GNS 회의(3)

　　6.26(수)　JARAMILLO　의장　주재로　개최된주요국(30개국)　비공식　협의는
양허협상절차적기준에 대하여 논의하였는바 주요 내용 하기 보고함.

　　1. OFFER 제출 목표 일자

　　- 7.31. 로 합의함.(동 일자는 확정 마감시한이아니기때문에 그후에도 OFFER
제출은 가능함)

　　2. REQUEST 제출 목표일자

　　- 동　일자역시　마감시한이　아니라　목표일자라는데는합의되었으나　구체적
일자는합의하지 못하고의장이 개별접촉하여 6.28(금) 회의시 재논의키로하였음.

　　0 북구,스위스,호주: 9.1 주장

　　0 미국, EC: 9.15 주장

　　0 인도,헝가리,유고등 개도국: 10.1, 10.15, 또는 10.30주장

　　3. 기타

　　- 각국 OFFER 에 대한 다자간 협의, 검토 ,평가

　　0 OFFER 제출을 촉진하기 위하여 미제출 국가도참여 가능함

　　- 양허협상 및 정보 교환

　　0　OFFER 를　제출한　나라만　참여할수　있으나미제출　국가도　특별한　경우(
REQUEST받은경우등)에 참여 가능함

　　- REQUEST 배부

　　0 사무국이 요약하여 OFFER 제출 국가에만 배부함.

　　- 기타 양허협상 방식

　　0 REQUEST/OFFER 방식이 아닌 기타방식(예: 카나다가주장하는 COMMON APPROACH)도
가능함.끝

(외사-국장)

통상국	차관	2차보	경제국	법무부	보사부	문화부	교통부	체신부
경기원	재무부	상공부	건설부	노동부	과기처	해항청	공보처	

PAGE 1　　　　　　　　　　　　　　　　　　　91.06.28　 08:17 DF

외신 1과　통제관

0095

외 무 부

종 별 :

번 호 : GVW-1226

일 시 : 91 0701 1900

수 신 : 장 관(봉기, 경기원, 재무부, 상공부, 건설부, 보사부, 노동부, 교통부, 채신부,

발 신 : 주 제네부 대사   문화부, 과기처, 공보처, 항만청)

제 목 : UR/GNS 회의 (4)

    6.28(금) 오후 속개된 표제회의는 동일 오전 주요 국비공식 협의를 거친 다음사항에 대하여 합의하고 종결하였음.

    1. 양허협상의 실질적 기준

    - 동문제는 FRAMEWORK 제 18조 (양허협상), 제19조 (적용)과 밀접히 연계되어 있는 바 동 조문이 완료되바 문제가 단순해 질것이므로 7월 회의시 논의 완결키로 함.

    2. 양허 협상의 절차적 기준

    - 별첨(FAX 송부)과 같이 합의함

    3. OFFER 평가시 고려요소

    - 사무국 작성 문서 (기파편 송부에 대하여) 호주, 브라질이 다음과 같이 논평함.

    0 호주: 사무국이 주기적으로 각국 OFFER 를종합하여 OFFER 된 분야의 GDP 점유비중등 관련 통계 제공으로 각국의 평가 작업을 돕기바라며 이를 양허협상시 준거기준으로 이용하는 방법도 모색할 필요가 있음.

    0 브라질: OFFER 된 서비스 분야의 현재비중뿐만 아니라 향후 잠재력도 고려 요소가 되어야함.

    4. 양허협상 관련 작업

    - 7.24(수)-7.26(금) 간 각국 OFFER 에 관한 비공식 양자, 복수간 협의를 개최함.

    0 동 협의는 이해관계가 있는 국가간의 양허협상 준비 작업으로서 각국 OFFER 의명료화와 관심사항의 전달, 파악이 될 것으로 추정되는바 상세한 내용은 추후 보고 위계임.

    - 한편 캐나다는 자국의 <u>COMMON APPROACH</u> 를 재차 소개하였는바 EC 및 인도가 처음으로 다음과 같이 논평하였음.

    0 EC: 양허 협상 추진에 시간이 부족한 만큼 동과정을 촉진할 수 있는 유용한

통상국	2차보	보사부	문화부	교통부	채신부	경기원	재무부	상공부
건설부	노동부	과기처	해항청	공보처				

PAGE 1

91.07.02   10:04 WI

외신 1과 통제관

0096

대안이 될수있으며 현재의 규제 수준을 동결하는 것이 또다른 유용한 대안이 될 수 있음.

0 인도: 캐나다 제안은 세가지 서비스 공급형태만 완전 자유화하는 반면 노동력 이동의 자유화 범위는 너무 제한적이며, 시장접근에 관한 조건을 부과할 수 없으므로 점진적 자유화 원칙에 근본적으로 배치됨.

5. 노동력 이동

- 의장은 서비스 공급인력의 종류에 관한 ILLUSTRATIVE LIST 작성 여부 및 동 LIST 의내용, MFN 일탈이 필요한 현존 국제협정에 대한 추가 논의가 필요하다고 전제하고 사무국이 다음회의에 대비하여 비공식 문서를 작성 배부 할것이고 함.

6. SCHEDULING OF COMMITMENTS

- HAWES 대사가 다음과 같이 비공식 협의 경과를 보고함

0 제한 조치를 다음 4가지로 분류 가능함

1) 내.외국인간 차별적인 양적 제한 조치

2) 무차별적인 양적 제한 조치 (서비스 공급자수제한, 서비스의 VOLUME 또는 VALUE 제한)

3) 차별적인 질적 제한 조치

4) 무차별인 질적 제한 조치

0 상기 4가지 형태의 제한 조치중 1) - 3)은 TOP-DOWN(NEGATIVE) 방식으로 기재하는데 대체적 합의가 형성됨. 그러나 회색지대가 있기때문에 추가 검토가 필요함.

0 무차별적인 질적 제한 조치에 대해서는 스케줄 기재대상 조치 유형 목록 작성필요성이 제기됨.

. 이와관련 제 6조 (국내규제) 2항의 기준 (합리적, 개관적, 공평한등)이 추가 보완 되어야 함

0 그러나 스케줄 작성에 관한 명확한 개념부재가 양허협상을 지연시켜서는 안된다는 것이 일반적 인식임.

0 또한 스케줄 작성에 조치의 결정과 관련 시장접근 (제 16조)과 내국민 대우 (제 17조) 규정의 추가 보완이 필요하며 제 6조 2항도 시장접근 약속이 이루어진 분야에 한하여 적용되는 만큼 협정 제3부 (SPECIFIC COMMITMENT) 에 규정하는 것이 보다적당한 것으로 판단됨.

0 일단 스케줄 기재 대상 조치가 결정되면 구체적 작성방법은 기계적 작업이 될것

PAGE 2

이나 많은 나라가 ENTRY 와 OPERATION 을 기준으로 시장접근과 내국민 대우를 구분하는 방식을 지시했음.

7. 스케줄 작성에 관한 세미나

- 동 문제가 기술적으로 복잡하기 때문에 많은 나라들이 요청하여 사무국에서 이에관한 세미나를 개최키로 함

0 구체적 일정은 추후 결정(7.1주 또는 7.8주간에1-2일)

8. 차기 회의 계획

- 7.10(수)-7.19(금): 공식 GNS 회의 (7.11은 갓트이사회 때문에 제외)

0 7.10(수): 금융분야 (MTN,TNC/2/50,52,68,GNS/W/71 을 기초로 금융 부속서에대하여 토의)

0 7.12(금): 통신분야 (통신 부속서 초안을 기초로 토의)

0 7.15(월)- 7.19(금): FRAMEWORK 제 1부- 제4부 (특히 제 1조, 2조, 4조, 6조, 7조, 14조, 16조, 17조, 18조, 19조)

0 특히 의장은 MFN 과 관련, 각국의 우려를 반영하는 가운데 MFN 일탈을 최소화하는 문제의 중요성을 강조하고 동문제의 해결을 위한 대안의 마련이 필요한 바 각국이 맺은 분야별 현존 협정이 실제 상업적으로 운용되고 있는지, 어떠한 상업적 가치를 가지고 있는지를 파악하여 실용적으로 접근할 수 있도록 비밀유지 조건하에 각국이 사무국에 이에 대한 자료를 제출해 줄것을 요청하였음.(수평적 협정도 동일)

- 7.24(수)-7.26(금): 비공식 양자, 복수국간 협의

9. 금번 GNS 회의 관찰 및 향후 협상대책 건의는 별전 보고 계획임.

첨부: 양허협상의 절차적 기준 1부.끝

(GVW(F)-229)

(대사 박수길-국장)

REVISION

Guvc—022P 107011Pro
Guw-1226 현5

Procedural Guidelines for Negotiations
on Initial Commitments

1.   Participants should submit conditional initial offers by
31 July 1991 in which they specify commitments they are
willing to assume in accordance with the provisions of Parts
III and IV of the General Agreement on Trade in Services.

2.   All initial offers shall be circulated to all
participants in the Uruguay Round in order to provide
transparency.

3.   The initial offers will be the subject of multilateral
consultations as well as a periodic review and assessment
process open to all participants.

4.   Negotiations on initial commitments shall proceed on the
basis of the guidelines agreed to by the GNS before 31 July
1991.

5.   Participants who have submitted offers ~~may~~ *are encouraged to* present initial
requests bilaterally by 20 September 1991. Summaries of such
requests shall be made available, through the Secretariat, to
all participants who have made offers.

6.   In order to facilitate negotiations on commitments, each
participant, upon request for specific information by any
other participant who has submitted an offer, shall make
available, clarify and explain regulations affecting trade.

7.   Negotiations will take place among participants which
have submitted initial offers. These negotiations will take
place on the basis of the submitted offers/requests.

8.   Negotiations may also proceed among participants on the
basis of other proposals.

9.   After negotiations on initial commitments are concluded
each participant shall consolidate its schedule of specific
commitments and communicate it to the Secretariat.

0099

/~/

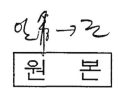

외 무 부

종 별 :

번 호 : GVW-1227   일 시 : 91 0701 1900

수 신 : 장관(봉기, 경기원, 재무부, 법무부, 상공부, 건설부, 보사부, 노동부, 교통부,

발 신 : 주 제네바 대사   체신부, 문화부, 과기처, 공보처, 항만청)

제 목 : UR/GNS 협상

연: GVW-1226

연호 GNS 의장 보고서 (GNS/W/117) 및 6.24주간 GNS 회의에 대한 평가와 향후 협상대책에 관한 당관 건의 사항을 하기 보고함.

1. GNS 의장 보고서 (TNC/W/85 및 GNS/2/117)에 대한 평가

가. 작성 경위

- 농산물 협상 그룹의 OPTION PAPER 작성과 관련, 정치적 쟁점 및 기술적 작업과제가 많다는 점에 유사한 성격을 가지고있고, 미. EC간 농산물과 연계 관계에 있는 서비스 분야도 균형을 이루기 위하여 OPTION PAPER 작성을 시도

- 그러나 OPTION PAPER 작업의 기초 작업 (실제적문제의 탐색, 정리)이 미진한 상태이기 때문에 주요 잇슈와 협상 진행 상황만을 기술한 경과보고서 작성에 그쳤음.

나. 보고서의 구성

- 91년까지 협상 완료를 위하여 하기 휴가전 까지의 우선 협상과제를 예시하고 있는바 다음과 같이 분류할수 있음.

I) 양허 협상 추진 관련 과제

O NATIONAL SCHEDULE 작성방법

O 노동력 이동 (부속서 및 각국의 자유화 약속)

O 양허협상기준(절차적 기준, 실질적 기준)

II) 주요 정치적 쟁점

O MFN 문제 (항공, 해운, 육운, 내수로 운송, 기본봉신, AUDIO VISUAL 분야별 MFN 이탈 여부및 범위, 수평적 협정에 대한 MFN 일탈 여부)

O 노동력 이동(부속서 및 각국의 자유화 약속)

O 분야별 부속서(금융,통신)

통상국	2차보	법무부	보사부	문화부	교통부	체신부	경기원	재무부
상공부	건설부	노동부	과기처	해항정	공보처			

PAGE 1   91.07.02   09:23 WG

외신 1과 통제관

0100

III) 실질양허 협상

다. 평가 및 협상 전망

- 동보고서는 서비스 협상의 주요 과제를 거의 모두 열거하고 있는바 동 문제들이 하기 휴가전까지 해결될 가능성은 극히 적음.

O 특히, 7월 중 본격적인 양허 협상 개시는 미국의 주장에 의하여 반영될 것이나 실현불가능한 사항으로 판단됨.

- 하기 휴가전까지는 양허 협상 추진의 필수 전제조건인 (1) NATIONAL SCHEDULE 작성 방법과, (2) 양허 협상 기준에 대한 합의에만 도달할 가능성이 큼.

O 주요 정치적 쟁점 (MFN, 노동력 이동, 금융.통신 부속서)은 하반기에 양허 협상 과 병행하여 또한 UR 전체 협상 진전 추이에 따라 타결될 것으로 예상됨.

O FRAMEWORK 도 SCHEDULE 작성관련 조항 (제 6조, 16조, 17조, 18조, 19조)이 아닌 다른 조항 (제 10조, 11조, 12조, 14조, 23조, 30조등)은 하기 휴가 이후로 미루어질 전망

- 다른 주요 사항들이 미결상태라 하더라도 SCHEDULING과 양허 협상 기준에 대한 합의만 이루어지면 기술적으로 양허 협상 추진에는 문제가 없으나 인도등 강경개도국들은 노동력 이동의 선결을 조건으로 다른 사항들을 BLOCK 할 가능성이 큼.

2. 6.24 주간 GNS 회의 평가

- 양허 협상 진입 기반 마련을 위하여 SCHEDULING, 노동력 이동에 대한 토의에 집중하였으나 큰진전은 없었음.

O 단, 양허 협상의 절차적 기준에 대하여는 합의도출

O 각국 OFFER 평가에 관한 고려 사항도 사무국 작성문서 배부만으로 거의 일단락된 상태

- 주요 잇슈들은 모두 7월 회의로 넘겨지는 결과초래

O MFN 및 금융, 통신 부속서를 제외한 주요 잇슈들이 모두 SCHEDULING 문제와 맞물려 있기 때문임.

- 7월중 양허협상 진입을 시도한 미국의 노력도 여러가지 여건 미비로 좌절

O 단, GNS 관할하에 양자 복수국간 협의기간을 설정함으로써 하반기 협상에 있어서 시간절약이 가능하게 됨.

3. 협상 대책(건의사항)

- 향후 양허 협상 및 OFFER 개정에 대비한 준비작업에 행정력 집중 요망

PAGE 2

0101

가. 국내 규제 체계의 정확한 파악, 정리

0 SCHEDULING 대상 규제 조치의 범위가 확산되는 추세를 감안하여 내.외국인간차별조치뿐만 아니라 무차별적인 양적 규제, 질적 규제도 파악정리요 (특히 금융분야)

0 또한 법규상의 규제 현황뿐만 아니라 실제운영 상황에 대한 정확한 사실 확인작업긴요

. 인가, 면허, 허가, 등록, 신고등의 절차가 사전에 설정된 객관적 기준에 따라 차별없이 공평하고 합리적으로 운영되고 있는지 여부

. 동 인가등의 과정에 있어서 행정부의 자유재량이 개입할 경우 동 재량 정도 및 자유재량의 준거 기준등

나. 인.허가등 개별적 행정행위와 분쟁해결과의 관계 연구

0 SCHEDULE 에 기재된 분야에 있어서 인.허가등록등의 거부시 국내 구제 절차 (행정 심판 또는 행정소송)에 대한 점검

0 국내 규제 체계에 대한 사실 확인 작업도 인.허가 기준등에 대한 해석상의 분쟁과 수권조항에 기초한 행정부의 재량 행위에 대한 분쟁발생 가능성등 향후 분쟁해결 문제와 연계 검토, 필요시 동 제도를 명확하고 객관적인 방향으로 보완

다. 양허 협상 팀 구성

0 각분야별로 전담자 지정, 하반기 양허 협상에대비 (7.24-26 간 비공식 협의에 참가 여부는 추후결정)

0 동 전담자들은 SCHEDULING 에 관한 일반적 이해와 담당분야의 규제체계 (REGULATORY FRAMEWORK)에 대한 정확한 지식 구비요

첨부: 사무국작성 스케쥴 기재대상 무차별조치예시 목록 1부.끝

(GVW(F)-230)

(대사 박수길-국장)

GVW(TH)- 0230 107011P00

GVW-1227 참부

28.6.91

EXAMPLES OF NON-DISCRIMINATORY MEASURES
WHICH COULD BE SUBJECT TO SCHEDULING

At the meeting of the Group of Negotiations on Services (GNS) commencing on 27 May 1991, the secretariat was requested to prepare an informal note indicating the kinds of non-discriminatory qualitative measures which could be considered for scheduling in those sectors where commitments are undertaken.

This note draws on informal submissions by participants. As some of these submissions include examples of quantitative measures of a non-discriminatory nature as well as examples of non-discriminatory qualitative measures which should not be scheduled, these measures have also been included for completeness.

4-1

B-NDM   0103

- 2 -

Quantitative-type measures

- Legal monopolies, as well as quasi-monopolies that leave only few activities open for other service suppliers

- Measures which limit the number of operators, e.g, through licencing or other form of authorization

- Measures containing quantitative non-objective criteria, i.e, criteria which do not concern the qualifications of the service supplier or the quality of the service per se, e.g, economic needs tests (licences for restaurants, etc.)

- Limits on the number of branches which any one service supplier can have (e.g, banks).

- Limits on the total membership of professional organizations

Limits on the size and number of offices or shops

Qualitative-type measures

- Qualitative non-objective criteria, i.e, criteria which do not concern the qualifications of the service provider or the quality of the service provided per se, such as:
  .. diploma from a domestic educational institution or authorization from a domestic institution required in order to gain the right to practice (e.g. bar examinations from particular universities are required for attorneys);
  .. space limitation systems (e.g. a special approval needed for the establishment of a shop if the floor area is more than X square meters).

- Requirements based on membership/association with specific organization, agreement or arrangement

B-NDM

4-2

0104

- 3 -

Scope of activity limitations, e.g,

.. restrictions on insurance companies from providing not more
   than one type of insurance;

.. prohibition on banks from engaging in insurance activities,
   and vice versa;

.. auditors not permitted to provide tax-related services in
   the same establishment.

Limitations on forms of commercial presence, e.g,

✓ auditors may not be employees of a company, but must become ___ ?
   partners, shareholders, or independent contractors;

.. lawyers may not form associations with each other to provide
   a full range of legal services.

.. requirement that firms (e.g, accountancy) be independent of
   parent company in terms of finance and personnel.

Price controls on services

Restrictions on professionals, e.g, professionals not permitted
to advertise their   services or use   the names of their
international affiliates

Administrative-type limitations, e.g,

.. Formal licencing, accreditation and authorization
   requirements or registration procedures

.. Restriction/limitation/conditions attached to approval
   necessary for marketing of new products (e.g, insurance).

Discretionary power of authorities, e.g, where there are no clear
guidelines for the issuing of licences, permission/approval
systems, etc.

Geographical/regional limitations or requirements e.g,

.. residency requirements

.. requirements to demonstrate particular linguistic abilities

.. limitation of commercial activities to a particular region

B-NDM   0105

4-3

- 4 -

- Requirement that advertising agency be accredited to local newspaper association in order to receive commissions on advertisements placed in local newspapers.

- Subsidy to regionally based/produced services.

- Restriction or any condition imposed on funds leaving the country (e.g, withholding tax, outright bar, prior approval requirement).

- Requirement that engineers, in order to practise, must be registered with a non-government Board of Engineers (registration based on competency standard and years of practice but may vary in restrictiveness between countries that have this requirement).

- Requirement that banks wishing to establish must be a certain threshold size.

- Limitation/restriction/prohibition on purchase of services abroad.

Note: Suggestions have also been made regarding non-discriminatory, qualitative measures which should not be scheduled provided that they do not contain licencing, authorization or registration requirements:

- ethical and other "codes of conduct" and similar regulations that address the on-going operations of a service supplier;
- competition, environmental and consumer protection regulations;
- safety, security, technical and other standards;
- reporting requirements.

B-NDM 0106

4-4

TOTAL P.07

외 무 부

종   별 :

번   호 : GVW-1274   일   시 : 91 0709 1700

수   신 : 장 관(통기, 경기원, 재무부, 상공부, 노동부, 체신부)

발   신 : 주 제네바 대사

제   목 : UR/GNS 의제 송부

　　91.7.10-7.19 간 개최 예정인 UR/GNS 회의 의제를 별첨 송부함.

　　첨부: UR/GNS 회의 의제 1부. (GVW(F)-239)

　　(대사 박수길-국장)

통상국　　2차보　　체신부　　경기원　　재무부　　상공부　　노동부

PAGE 1   91.07.10   08:28 WG

외신 1과 통제관

0107

GVW (h) -0259, 1070P1700
GVW - 12 7X 형시

GATT/AIR/3209   4 JULY 1991

SUBJECT: URUGUAY ROUND: GROUP OF NEGOTIATIONS ON SERVICES

1.   THE GROUP OF NEGOTIATIONS ON SERVICES WILL HOLD ITS NEXT MEETING ON
10-19 JULY 1991, STARTING ON WEDNESDAY, 10 JULY AT 10 A.M. IN THE CENTRE
WILLIAM RAPPARD. THE GROUP MAY CONTINUE ITS MEETING DURING THE WEEK OF
22 JULY IF NECESSARY.

2.   THE FOLLOWING ITEMS ARE ON THE AGENDA:

   2.1 FINANCIAL SERVICES ANNEX:

      -   DISCUSSION OF ANNEX BASED ON MTN.TNC/W/35/REV.1 AND
          SUBMISSIONS MTN.GNS/W/71; MTN.TNC/W/50; MTN.TNC/W/52;
          MTN.TNC/W/68;

   2.2 TELECOMMUNICATION SERVICES ANNEX:

      -   FURTHER WORK ON DRAFT ANNEX (IN MTN.TNC/W/35/REV.1);

   2.3 PARTS I-IV OF THE FRAMEWORK (IN PARTICULAR TO ARTICLES I, II, IV,
        V, VI, VII, XIV, XVI, XVII, XVIII, XIX, XX) AND DISPUTE
        SETTLEMENT;

   2.4 LABOUR MOBILITY: THE SECRETARIAT WILL MAKE AVAILABLE A DRAFT
        ANNEX ON TEMPORARY MOVEMENT OF NATURAL PERSONS PROVIDING
        SERVICES;

   2.5 OTHER BUSINESS.

3.   THE AGENDA ITEM ON FINANCIAL SERVICES WILL BE TAKEN UP ON 10 JULY AT
10 A.M. AND TELECOMMUNICATION SERVICES ON 12 JULY AT 10 A.M. DISCUSSION OF
AGENDA ITEMS 2.3, 2.4 AND 2.5 WILL COMMENCE ON MONDAY, 15 JULY AT 10 A.M.

4.   THE FOLLOWING DOCUMENTS ARE OF RELEVANCE FOR THE DISCUSSION:

   MTN.TNC/W/35/REV.1; MTN.GNS/W/71; MTN.TNC/W/50; MTN.TNC/W/52;
   MTN.TNC/W/68; MTN.GNS/43; AN INFORMAL NOTE BY THE SECRETARIAT ON
   DISPUTE SETTLEMENT WILL ALSO BE MADE AVAILABLE.

5.   GOVERNMENTS PARTICIPATING IN THE MULTILATERAL TRADE NEGOTIATIONS, AND
INTERNATIONAL ORGANIZATIONS WHICH HAVE PREVIOUSLY ATTENDED THE PROCEEDINGS
OF THIS NEGOTIATING GROUP, WISHING TO BE REPRESENTED AT THIS MEETING ARE
REQUESTED TO INFORM ME AS SOON AS POSSIBLE OF THE NAMES OF THEIR
REPRESENTATIVES.

91-0991   A. DUNKEL

                                                                    0108

                              1-1

기 안 용 지

분류기호 문서번호	통기 20644-	(전화: 720 - 2188)	시 행 상 특별취급	
보존기간	영구 . 준영구 10. 5. 3. 1.	장 관		
수 신 처 보존기간				
시행일자	1991. 7. 9.			

보조기관	국 장	전결	협조기관		문 서 통 제
	심의관				
	과 장				
기안책임자	조 현			발 송 인	

경 유 수 신 참 조	건 의	발 신 명 의	

제 목	UR/서비스 협상 정부대표 임명

91.7.12. 제네바에서 개최되는 UR/GNS 통신분야 전문가 회의에

참가할 정부대표를 "정부대표 및 특별사절의 임명과 권한에 관한 법률"에

의거 아래와 같이 임명할 것을 건의하오니 재가하여 주시기 바랍니다.

- 아   래 -

1. 회 의 명 : UR/서비스 협상 통신분야 전문가 회의

- 1 -

0109

2. 회의기간 및 장소 : 91.7.12(금), 제네바
3. 정부대표
ㅇ 체신부 행정사무관   강영철
ㅇ 체신부 통신기좌   박정열
ㅇ 통신개발연구원 연구위원   최병일(자문)
ㅇ 주 제네바 대표부 관계관
4. 출장기간 : 7.10-14
5. 소요예산 : 체신부 소관예산
6. 훈 령
ㅇ 금번 UR/GNS 통신분야 전문가 회의는 지난 90.12월에
확정이 보류된 통신부속서와 각국이 제출한 통신분야
Offer List를 협의하는 중요한 회의이므로, 통신서비스
시장개방 및 통신 서비스 이용 보장 문제가 UR 서비스
다자간 협상을 통하여 해결될 수 있도록 적극적으로
협의에 임하도록 함.

- 2 -　　　　　　　　0110

o 통신부속서 제정에 대해서는 90.6월에 기제출한 아국

　통신부속서의 입장이 반영될 수 있도록 노력하고,

　통신분야 Offer List에 대한 협의는 91.1월에 제출한

　아국 Offer List 범위내에서 능동적으로 대처토록 함.

끝.

체　　　신　　　부

통협34475-4900　　　　　750-2343　　　　　1991. 7. 8.

수신　　외무부장관

제목　　UR/GNS 통신분야 전문가회의 참가

　　　　1. GVW-1134<91.6.19>관련입니다.

　　　　2. 위관련 UR/GNS 통신분야 부속서 제정을 위한 전문가회의가
91.7.12<금> 스위스제네바에서 개최될 예정인 바, 동회의에 대한
통신분야 전문가를 아래와 같이 참석케 하고자 하오니 적극 협조하여
주시기 바랍니다.

　　　　가. 참가자 및 출장기간

소　속	직　위	성　명	출장기간	비　고
체신부	행정사무관	강영철	91.7.10-7.14	통신분야 전문가회의 대표
"	통신기좌	박정열	"	"
통신개발연구원 연구위원		최병일	91.7.10-7.20	통신분야 전문가회의 및 UR 서비스협상 자문위원

붙임 : 1. 훈령<안> 1부.　끝.

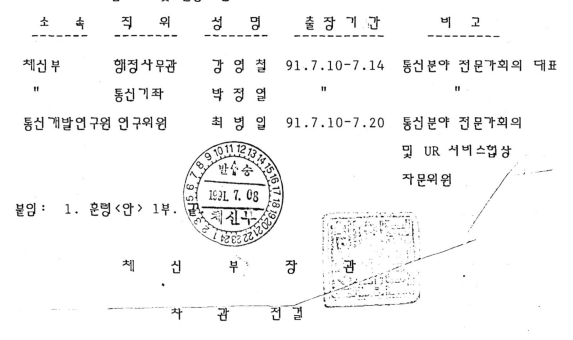

체　　신　　부　　장　　관

차　　관　　전　　결

0112

훈 령 (안)

1. 기본훈령

o 금번 UR/GNS 통신분야 전문가회의는 지난 90.12월에 확정이
   보류된 통신부속서와 각국이 제출한 통신분야 Offer List를
   협의하는 중요한 회의이므로
   - 통신서비스시장개방 및 통신서비스이용보장문제가 UR서비스
     다자간협상을 통하여 해결될 수 있도록 적극적으로 협의에
     임할것

o 통신부속서 제정에 대해서는 90.6월에 제출한 바 있는 아국
   통신부속서의 입장이 반영될 수 있도록 노력하고
   - 통신분야 Offer List에 대한 협의는 91.1월에 제출한 아국
     Offer List 범위내에서 능동적으로 협의함으로써 UR협상의
     원만한 타결에 기여하도록 할 것

2. 세부훈령

o 통신부속서 제정에 있어 공중통신전송서비스의 이용보장문제에
   대해서는
   - 공중통신전송서비스의 이용보장으로 각국이 유보시킨
     서비스가 허용되는 결과가 초래되어서는 안된다는 입장을
     견지할 것

o 원가에 기초한 요금제도도입에 대해서는 요금결정시 각국의
   국내정책이 고려될 수 있어야 한다는 입장을 견지할 것

o 기업내통신의 허용에 대해서는 기업내통신의 허용이 각국의
   공중통신사업자에게 미칠 영향이 충분히 고려되어 결정되어야
   한다는 입장을 견지할 것

o 아국 Offer 내용중 데이타단순전송서비스에는 회선재판매가
   제외된다는 사실을 분명히 할 것

0113

기안용지

분류기호 문서번호	통기 20644-	31832 (전화: 720 - 2188)	시 행 상 특별취급	
보존기간	영구. 준영구 10. 5. 3. 1.	장 관		
수 신 처 보존기간				
시행일자	1991. 7. 9.			

보조 기관	국 장	전 결	협 조 기 관		문 서 통 제 1991. 7. 10
	심의관				
	과 장	대결			
기안책임자		조 현			발 송 인

경유 수신 참조	체신부장관	발 신 명 의		반송 1991. 7. 10 외무부

제 목	UR/서비스 협상 정부대표 임명 통보

1. 91.7.12. 제네바에서 개최되는 UR/GNS 통신분야 전문가

회의에 참가할 정부대표가 "정부대표 및 특별사절의 임명과 권한에 관한

법률"에 의거 아래와 같이 임명 되었으니 통보하여 주시기 바랍니다.

- 아   래 -

가. 회 의 명 : UR/서비스 협상 통신분야 전문가 회의

- 1 -

0114

나. 회의기간 및 장소 : 91.7.12(금), 제네바

다. 정부대표

    ㅇ 체신부 행정사무관   강영철

    ㅇ 체신부 통신기좌   박정열

    ㅇ 통신개발연구원 연구위원   최병일(자문)

라. 출장기간 : 7.10-14

마. 소요경비 : 체신부 소관예산

  2. 출장 결과 보고서는 대표단 귀국후 2주일이내 당부로

송부하여 주시기 바랍니다.   끝.

발 신 전 보

번 호 : WGV-0876　910709 1818　CO　종별 : _____

수 신 : 주　　　제네바　대사. 총영사

발 신 : 장 관 (통 기)

제 목 : GNS 통신분야 전문가 회의

분류번호　보존기간

　　　7.12. 귀지에서 개최되는 UR/GNS 통신분야 전문가 회의에 참가할 정부대표가
아래 임명 되었으니, 귀관 관계관과 함께 참석토록 하기바람.

　　　가 . 본부대표

　　　　ㅇ 체신부 행정사무관　　　　　강영철

　　　　ㅇ 체신부 통신기좌　　　　　　박정열

　　　　ㅇ 통신개발연구원 연구위원　　최병일 (자문)

　　　나 . 출장기간 : 7.10-14

　　　다 . 훈　　　령

　　　　ㅇ 통신서비스 시장개방 및 통신서비스 이용 보장 문제가 UR 협상에서
　　　　　타결될 수 있도록 적극적인 입장으로 협의에 임하도록 함.

　　　　ㅇ 통신부속서 제정에는 90.6월 아국이 기제출한 통신부속서 제안 내용이
　　　　　반영될 수 있도록 노력함.

　　　　ㅇ 통신분야 Offer List 협의에는 아국의 서비스 협상 Offer 범위내에서
　　　　　능동적으로 대처토록 함.　　　　　　　　끝.

　　　　　　　　　　　　　　(통상국장　김 삼 훈)

0116

경 제 기 획 원

봉조삼 10502- 461   503-9149   1991. 7. 9.

수신 수신처참조   외무부 통상기구과

제목 UR/서비스협상관련 분야별 대책회의 개최

　　　1. 6.24-30일간 스위스 제네바에서 개최된 '91년도 제2차 UR/서비스협상
회의에서 7.24-26일간 관심있는 국가간에 양자 또는 복수국간협의(consultation)
를 하기로 결정하는등 향후 양허협상절차면에서 상당한 진전이 있었습니다.
(별첨 1참조)

　　　2. 이에따라 7.24-26일간 스위스 제네바에서 개최될 양자 또는 복수국간
협의에 대처하고 아울러 8-9월중에 있을 우리 Offer List의 보완작업을 위하여
분야별 대책회의를 다음과 같이 개최하니 각 참석대상자는 필요한 자료를 지참
하고 지정된 시각에 회의에 참석해 주시기 바랍니다.

　　　　　　　　　　　　다   음

　　가. 일   시: '91.7.11-16

　　　　ㅇ 7.11   14:00-18:00   운송 및 관광

　　　　ㅇ 7.12   14:00-16:00   금융

　　　　　　　　 16:00-18:00   통신

　　　　ㅇ 7.15   10:30-12:00   건설, 노동력이동

　　　　　　　　 14:00-18:00   사업서비스 (광고, 엔지니어링,
　　　　　　　　　　　　　　　 회계사, 세무사)

　　　　ㅇ 7.16   10:00-12:00   유통

　　　　　　　　 14:00-15:00   시청각서비스

　　　　　　　　 15:00-18:00   우리 Offer List에서 제외시킨
　　　　　　　　　　　　　　　 분야 (보건, 교육, 법무)

　　나. 장   소: EPB 제2협력관실 (과천청사 3동 225호실)

0117

21831

다. 참석범위

    ○ 총괄반(매회의때마다 참석): EPB 제2협력관(회의주재),
       통상조정3과장, 이병화사무관, 김용준사무관, 외무부 통상
       기구과장, KIEP 박태호.김태준박사, 김&장법률사무소
       신희택변호사

    ○ 분과반(해당분야회의에만 참석): EPB 담당자 및 전문가,
       주무부처의 양허협상책임자 및 연구책임자

라. 의   제: 각분야별 규제현황 파악 및 협상대책 (단계별
            협상안 및 대응논리, 상대국에 대한 Request List)
            추진상황점검

마. 회의자료(각 참석자지참): 한국의 Initial Offer List, 각국의
             Offer List, 소관분야의 규제현황 및 협상대책등

첨부: 1. 양허협상일정 및 대응방향 1부.
      2. 한국의 Initial Offer List 1부.   끝.

경 제 기 획 원

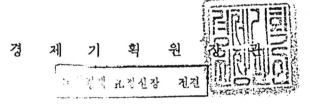

수신처: 외무부장관, 내무부장관, 재무부장관, 법무부장관, 교육부장관,
      문화부장관, 상공부장관, 보건사회부장관, 건설부장관, 교통부장관,
      노동부장관, 체신부장관, 과학기술처장관, 환경처장관, 공보처장관,
      특허청장, 항만청장, 대외경제정책연구원장, 한국개발연구원장,
      대한무역진흥공사장, 김&장법률사무소장.

                                  0118

외 무 부

종 별 :

번 호 : GVW-1273   일 시 : 91 0709 1700

수 신 : 장관(통기) 사본:사본처참조

발 신 : 주 제네바 대사

제 목 : UR / GNS 협상

　　사본처 : 경기원, 재무부, 법무부, 상공부, 건설부, 보사부, 노동부, 교통부, 체신부, 문화부, 과기처, 공보처, 항만청

　　표제 협상 관련 분쟁해결에 관한 갓트 사무국작성문서를 별첨 송부함.

　　첨부: 분쟁해결에 관한 사무국 문서 1부. 끝

　　(GVW(F)-0240)

　　(대사 박수길-국장)

통상국	2차보	내무부	법무부	보사부	문화부	교통부	체신부	경기원
재무부	상공부	건설부	노동부	과기처	해항청			

PAGE 1   91.07.10   08:27 FO

외신 1과 통제관

0119

9.7.91

GVW(기)-240 /070/ /700
GVW-1273 참고

DISPUTE SETTLEMENT AND TRADE IN SERVICES

Points Raised in Discussions

1.   In the meeting of the Group of Negotiations on Services commencing 27
May 1991, a number of issues relating to dispute settlement were discussed.
As requested in the course of that meeting, the secretariat has prepared an
informal note indicating the main issues identified in the discussion,
principal points raised and some questions participants may wish to address
under each of the issues: these cover procedures, local remedies,
individual cases, non-violation cases, the role of experts and retaliation.

2.   The intention of the secretariat in preparing this informal note has
not been to be exhaustive with respect to all the points raised in the
discussion; the note can be modified as considered appropriate by
participants.

PROCEDURES

3.   It is agreed that procedures will need to be adopted for the
settlement of disputes involving trade in services. The present Articles
XXII and XXIII of the draft framework deal only with consultation,
compensation and the suspension of concessions.

Points raised by delegations:

  (i) Traditional GATT procedures alongside improvements agreed in the
       Dispute Settlement Group should provide the basis for dispute
       settlement in GATS.

  (ii) Though GATT procedures should not be transposed to the GATS, the
       sequence followed in GATT could be adopted - i.e. bilateral
       consultations, panels and opinions of Contracting Parties,

P-1   0120

A-MISC3

- 2 -

compensatory mechanism in case panel recommendations were not complied with and retaliation.

(iii) Given the limited experience with multilateral dispute settlement for trade in services, GATT procedures could not be accepted before there was a better appreciation of the specificities of services activities.

(iv) Given the limited experience with trade in services, the settling of disputes should be limited to consultation and conciliation for the time being.

Questions

- Should the provisions of Articles XXII and XXIII of GATT and the result of the Negotiating Group on Dispute Settlement contained in MTN.TNC/W/35/Rev.1 serve as the basis for dispute settlement in the General Agreement on Trade in Services (GATS)?

- Is it necessary to include into the GATS further detailed procedures on dispute settlement, such as those that have been adopted by the CONTRACTING PARTIES under Articles XXII and XXIII of the GATT and, if so, could the GATT decisions on such detailed procedures serve as a basis or should the PARTIES to the GATS adopt different procedures?

- Given the limited experience with multilateral dispute settlement for trade in services, would it be preferable to incorporate the dispute settlement procedures in a decision by the PARTIES, which can be easily modified, rather than incorporating them into the GATS itself, the amendment of which would be substantially more difficult?

9-2

A-MISC3   0121

- 3 -

INDIVIDUAL CASES

4.   Certain factors may determine whether cases involving individual service providers may be brought to the GATS dispute settlement system.

Points raised by delegations:

   (i)   Patterns of practice could be a useful means of determining whether a case could be brought to the GATS.

   (ii) Patterns of practice would not be entirely satisfactory as some Parties may be adversely affected by practices which did not yet reflect an established pattern.

   (iii) Patterns of practice would not suffice for measures which reflected major policies which violate GATS obligations or for isolated/infrequent cases of significant proportions.

Questions

- Should draft Article XXIII contain any reference to the treatment of individual cases?

- If so, should it stipulate the extent to which patterns of practice determined whether a case could be brought to the GATS?

- Should draft Article XXIII specify the types of cases which could be exempted from established patterns of practice?

LOCAL REMEDIES

5.   The use of local remedies primarily relates to the settling of disputes involving natural or juridical persons within individual states - and not between Parties to the GATS.

9-3

A-MISC3

0122

- 4 -

Points raised by delegations:

(i) Should Parties be entitled to bring such cases to the GATS
     dispute settlement system prior to the exhaustion of local
     remedies?

(ii) Though resort to local remedies is desirable as a first step
     towards the settlement of such disputes, a formal requirement to
     do so would unnecessarily restrict governments in bringing cases
     before the GATS disputes settlement system.

Questions

- Would a provision dealing with the exhaustion of local remedies, where
   relevant, be necessary or desirable in the GATS?

- If so, should such a provision be formulated as a best-endeavours
   clause?

- Or, should it be an obligatory clause conditioning resort to the GATS
   dispute settlement system on the exhaustion of local remedies in
   individual cases?

NON-VIOLATION CASES

6. Draft Article XXIII:4 (which is in square brackets) deals with
non-violation cases. As with the GATT dispute settlement system for goods
trade, a distinction could be drawn between violation and non-violation
cases in services.

Points raised by delegations:

(i) Non-violation should be carefully defined and circumscribed in
     order to:

9-4

A-MISC3   0123

- 5 -

- prevent countries from abusing a provision on non-violation cases;

- avoid any confusion with Article VI:2.

(ii) A non-violation provision could apply only to measures introduced after a concession was negotiated or could also apply to measures in place at the time of negotiating the concession.

(iii) A non-violation provision could be important with respect to provisions which will require further elaboration (e.g. areas of subsidies or public/government procurement).

(iv) While in violation cases the obligation falls on the accused Party to remove a measure inconsistent with commitments under the agreement, in non-violation cases the obligation could be limited to compensation.

(v) It is premature to have a provision on non-violation. It could be agreed that this would be addressed in the future.

(vi) There is no need to distinguish between violation and non-violation cases.

Questions

- Should there be a clear and circumscribed definition of non-violation under the framework?

- In what respects should a definition of non-violation be circumscribed (e.g. relationship to other framework articles such as Article VI)?

- Should the scope of a provision on non-violation cover measures introduced after the time a concession was negotiated, measures in place at the time a concession was negotiated or measures which are

0124

9-5   A-MISC3

- 6 -

contrary to the spirit of certain framework articles (e.g. subsidies, government procurement)?

-   Should a distinction be drawn in GATS between remedies that applied to violation cases and those that applied to non-violation cases?

ROLE OF EXPERTS

7.   Panel procedures are not covered in draft Article XXIII though it is recognised that they will need to be agreed.

Points raised by delegations:

(i)   A provision on expert participation could relate to the number of panellists, the scope of expert participation, and the role of experts if they do not participate in panels.

(ii)   The participation of experts should be confined to an advisory role unless Parties to a dispute agreed otherwise.

(iii)   Panellists - whether sectoral experts or not - should bear in mind the need to ensure the integrity of the GATT system as a whole.

(iv)   Whether expert participate as panellists or advisors:

-   a roster of experts should be established;

-   all sectors should be subject to the same procedures regarding expert participation.

Questions

-   What should the role of experts be in settling disputes?

A-MISC3   0125

9-6

- 7 -

- Should expert input be dealt with explicitly in the agreement or in procedures to be agreed in the future?

- If so, should rules and procedures allow for expert participation in panels, advisory bodies alongside panels or both alternatives?

RETALIATION

8. Draft Article XXIII:3 deals with retaliatory measures, through the suspension of the application to any party or parties of such obligations and commitments under the framework which are determined by the parties to be appropriate in the circumstances. Because of the special character of trade in services, some clarification with respect to retaliation is necessary.

Points raised by delegations:

    (i) Further discussion is required with respect to proportionality and "equivalent commercial effect".

    (ii) With respect to the scope of retaliation:

- countries should, to the extent possible, constrain retaliation to the sector concerned;

- the provisions should not be overly rigid with respect to retaliation across services sectors;

- an additional decision might be envisaged by the parties as to whether retaliation could go beyond certain sectors in certain cases (including into goods sectors);

- retaliation should not be extended between services and goods;

9-7

0126

A-MISC3

- 8 -

    - given the structure of trade, it may not be feasible in practice to limit the sectoral scope of retaliation;

    - a hierarchy should be established commencing with retaliation in the same sector, retaliation across services sectors, to retaliation between services and goods;

    - independent dispute settlement systems for services and goods should prevent countries from retaliating beyond services sectors.

(iii) Retaliation against acquired rights of natural or juridical persons:

    - may necessitate a provision stipulating that retaliation should not cause "injuries" to acquired rights;

    - may be limited to the prohibition of the entry of, or limitation of rights granted to, new juridical or natural persons.

(iv) With respect to the relationship of GATS dispute settlement provisions to those of other agreements:

    - GATS dispute settlement and retaliation provisions should take precedence over the relevant parts of other existing/subsequent agreements;

    - GATS dispute settlement and retaliation provisions should not take precedence over the relevant parts of other existing/subsequent agreements;

    - it is premature to assume that dispute settlement and other provisions of the framework could take precedence over other existing or subsequent agreements.

A-MISC3

0127

9-8

- 9 -

Questions

- Which of the following elements dealing with retaliatory measures
  could be elaborated upon in draft Article XXIII:3: clear definition
  of proportionality and equivalent commercial effect; arbitration in
  cases when the Party concerned objects to the level of suspension
  proposed; the amount of trade covered by recourse to suspension of
  concessions; the temporary nature of recourse to suspension of
  concessions?

- What should be the scope of application of retaliation under the
  framework?

- With respect to acquired rights of natural and juridical persons, is a
  multilaterally agreed definition of the term "acquired rights"
  considered necessary?

9-9

A-MISC3

0128

외 무 부

종 별 :

번 호 : GVW-1288   일 시 : 91 0711 1930

수 신 : 장 관(통기,경기원,재무부,상공부)

발 신 : 주 제네바대사

제 목 : UR/GNS 회의(1)

    7.10(수) 개최된 표제회의는 JARAMILLO GNS의장과 MR.FRANK SWEDLOVE(캐나다 재무부)공동주재로 금융분야 부속서에 대하여 논의하였는바 주요 내용 하기 보고함.

    1. 회의개요

    - 금융분야를 GNS 에서 공식 논의한다는 의미에서 스위스(TNC/W/50), 말련(TNC/W/52), 콜롬비아(TNC/2/68) 가 각각 제안 설명을 하였음

    - 실질문제에 대한 토의는 TWO TRACK APPROACH 와 PRUDENTIAL REGULATION 에 집중되었으나 별다른 진전은 없었으며 다만 9월회의 이전까지의 작업 계획에 대하여 합의하였음.

    2. 주요 회의 내용

    가. TWO TRACK APPROACH

    - TNC/W/50 공동제안 4개국이 종래 논란이 많았던 다음사항을 명시한 수정제안 (TNC/W/50/ADD.1) 을 제출하였음

    O 각국이 자유화 추진 방식을 자유로이 선택할 수 있음

    O 상기 자유화 선택과 자유화 약속 수준과는 별개 문제임.

    O MFN 등 협정상의 어떤권리, 의무도 자유화방식 선택에 따라 변동되지 않음

    - 선진 4개국이 동 제안을 제출함에 따라 SEACEN등 개도국으로 부터 종전의 반대논리 전개는 없었으며 호주, 오지리가 지지의사를 표명하였음.

    O 다만, 인도 및 이집트는 FRAMEWORK 에 따르더라도 높은 수준의 자유화 추진이가능한 바 굳이 TWO TRACKAPPROACH 를 택하는 이유가 불분명하다고 함

    O 스웨덴은 동 부속서에 의할 경우 각국의 COMMITMENT 내용이 명확해지며 향후분쟁발생시 PANEL 의 해석 작업이 용이해져 분쟁해결이 쉽게되는 잇점이 있다고 함

통상국   2차보   경기원   재무부   상공부

- 아국은 TNC/W/50 의 제 3부가 협정 제3부에 있는 사항뿐만 아니라 여러 다른 요소(독점, 정부조달, NEW SERVICE, 무차별 조치등)를 포함하고 있는 바, LOW TRACK 을 택하는 나라가 동 사항에 대해서도 아무런 의무 부담이 없는지 아니면 SCHEDULING에 관해서만 POSITIVE APPROACH채택이 허용되는지 질의한 바

O 스웨덴은 동 사항들에 대한 의무는 없으나 이에 대한 COMMITMENT 여부는 각국에 달려 있다고함

나. PRUDENTIAL REGULATION- 미국, 스위스등은 TNC/W/52 에 대하여 금융정책 당국에 백지수표를 위임하는 결과가 된다고 지적한 반면

O 싱가폴은 TNC/2/50 에 따른 경우 금융당국이 예외적인 경우에만 동 조항을 원용할 수 있을뿐만 아니라 관련 조치가 자의적이지 않고 정당한 것 이라는 입증을 하여야 하는 바 동 입증이 매우 어려우며 동 조치들을 통지하여야 하는 부담이 있다고 함.

- 아국은 규제완화 과정에서 과당경쟁이 초래되어 많은 금융기관들이 도산하고 경제침체에 심각한 영향을 미치게 되는 실례를 들어 강력한 PRUDENTIAL REGULATION 조항이 마련되어야 한다고 하였음.,

다. 제도적 규정

1) 서비스 분야간 보복

- 말련이 서비스 분야간 보복금지 입장을 표명한데 대하여 캐나다는 같은 분야내에 보복이 불가능 할 경우에는 어떻게 할것인지 의문을 제기함

O EC 는 금융분야는 매우 민감한 분이이기때문에 타분야로 부터의 SPILLOWER 위험을 감안하여 신중하게 다루어야 한다고 함

2) 금융서비스 기구

- 대부분의 나라가 동 기구의 필요성을 인정하였으며 이씨, 캐나다, 항가리, 인도등은 FRAMEWORK 과의 일관성 유지, 신뢰성 제고를 위하여 금융분야 전문가에 의지할필요성등 두가지 요소가 함께 고려되어야 한다고 함.(동 기구의 기능에 대하여는 논의진전 미비)

O 다만 유고는 GATS 에 이사회가 설치될 것임을 들어 등 기구의 명칭과 기능에 대하여 의문을 표시하였으며 통신도 복잡한 분야임을 들어 FRAMEWORK 하에서 수평적으로 다루어져야 한다고 하였음

O 헝가리는 TNC/W/52 의 2항, 3항이 너무 엄격하다고 지적하고 주요 문제의 처리는 이사회 소관이므로 보다 신축적으로 규정하여야 한다고 함.

PAGE 2

0130

3. 향후 작업계획

- JARAMILLO 의장이 제시한 다음사항에 대하여 합의함

0 GNS 의장이 FRANK SWEDLOVE 조력하에 GNS담당자 및 금융전문가들과 비공식 협의를 개최함

0 9월 첫째 GNS 회의의제에 금융부속서가 포함 될 것이며 상기 비공식 협의 결과를 제시함

0 금일의 토론에 기초하여 해결되어야 할 과제들을 모은 INFORMAL NOTE 를 작성하도록 노력함.

첨부: TNC/W/50/ADD.1 1 부(GVW(F)-0244). 끝

(대사 박수길-국장)

GVW(h)-0244 /0711 1P30

"GUW-1288 첨부"

MULTILATERAL TRADE

NEGOTIATIONS

THE URUGUAY ROUND

RESTRICTED

MTN.TNC/W/50/Add.1
9 July 1991

Special Distribution

Trade Negotiations Committee

Original: English

COMMUNICATION FROM CANADA, JAPAN, SWEDEN AND SWITZERLAND

Addendum

At the Ministerial Meeting in Brussels in December 1990, the delegations of Canada, Japan, Sweden and Switzerland presented a proposal for a Financial Services Annex to the draft General Agreement on Trade in Services (GATS). The proposal was distributed as MTN.TNC/W/50.

An important element of the proposed Annex was the introduction of a common approach for making commitments with respect to financial services. Under the heading "PART III: SPECIFIC COMMITMENTS - I. Application" the text enables a Party to make its commitments simply be inscribing in its schedule the term "financial services sector". Where a Party makes such an inscription, the provisions of Part III of the Annex shall apply unless otherwise specified in that Party's schedule. These provisions of the Annex were, however, not intended to prevent any Party from undertaking commitments with respect to financial services pursuant to Article XIX of the Framework.

Since the presentation of the proposed Annex, some delegations have raised questions and expressed concern with regard to the precise functioning of this so-called two-track approach. Specifically there has been concern that financial service providers of Parties that undertake commitments pursuant to Article XIX of the Framework would not be given full m.f.n. or national treatment.

It was never the intent of our delegations that the choice of a Party with respect to how it undertakes its commitments should affect the rights and obligations of that Party under the Agreement. In order to clarify this issue we propose that the attached text be inserted to replace the language in paragraphs 1 and 2 under the heading "PART III: SPECIFIC COMMITMENTS - I. Application" of MTN.TNC/W/50.

./.

GATT SECRETARIAT

UR-91-0073

0132

2-1

經濟企劃院 對外經濟調整室

427-760
京畿道 果川市 中央洞 1番地
政府 第2廳舍
Tel (02) 503-9130
Fax (02) 503-9138

Facsimile 送信表紙

日字 : 199*1. 7. 15*

受信 : 외무부 통상2과 김기환

經由 :

發信 : E.P.B 통상조정3과

題目 :

發送枚數 : *9* (表紙包含)

※ 내용중 명확하지 않은 부분이 있거나 누락된 부분이 있을 경우에는 연락하여 주시기
바랍니다.

0133

3. 서비스 市場開放 協商

— 美國은 쇠고기, 담배, 農產物등 商品市場開放 要求外에도 서비스
  分野에까지 그 開放要求幅을 擴大

  ○ 金融, 保險, 廣告, 通信, 海運, 航空, 映畵등에서 雙務協商이 進行

(1) 保 險

— 通商法 301條 關聯 韓·美間 協商은 '79年 美國의 生命保險
  會社인 AHA (The American Home Assurance Co.)가 韓國保險
  會社와 同等 競爭할 수 있는 機會 剝奪을 理由로 301條
  調查申請을 提起한 것이 最初

  ○ 同 調查申請은 財務部가 '77.4月에 AHA에게 海上保險業,
    火災保險 pool 參與 許容約束을 履行하지 않으므로써 提起

  ○ 同 調查始作後 韓國政府가 '81.5까지 AHA에 海上保險取扱許可,
    火災保險 pool 을 大部分 廢止할 것을 約束함으로써 調查 終了

— 그러나 '85.9 레이건大統領은 AHA에 대한 專業許可 約束不履行과
  對美 差別을 理由로 韓國의 保險市場에 대해 第301條 調査를
  命令하여 同 月 USTR이 調査를 開始하였고

  ○ 그결과 '86年 通商協定에서 保險에 관한 覺書가 交換되어
    美國 生命保險會社 進出許容, 火災保險 pool 에 美國會社 參與
    許容을 約束

― '86. 通商協定締結以後에도 保險關聯覺書 合意事項履行 問題와
　　追加開放 要求가 持續

　　○ 그 結果 '87.9 第2次 保險協商에서 '88.1부터 支店·合作·
　　　子會社등 進出形態에 關係없이 美保險會社의 韓國 進出을
　　　許容하고 '88.1까지 合作基準등을 마련 美政府와 協議키로
　　　合意

　　○ '88.3. 第3次 保險協商에서 國內 15大 財閥은 合作對象에서
　　　除外시킴을 確認하고 다만 16～30大 財閥은 50%未滿 持分
　　　으로 國內市場 參與를 許容키로 合意

― 이에 대하여 美國은 國內進出 美生命保險會社의 國內營業上
　　制限撤廢 및 保險仲介業 許容등 追加開放을 要求함으로써 以後
　　懸案으로 尚存

(2) 廣 告

― '87.12 廣告代行業에 대한 投資比率 50% 未滿의 制限的 合作
　　投資를 許容하고

　　○ '88.10. 韓·美 經濟協議會에서 '90.1. 合作投資 持分撤廢,
　　　'91.1. 支社 및 子會社設立을 許容하는 것을 內容으로 하는
　　　追加開放日程에 合意

―33―

0135

(3) 映畵

ー 美國 映畵 輸出協會(MPEAA)가 映畵業에서의 外國人 活動禁止,
스크린 쿼타制(外畵上映日數制限)에 의한 外畵輸入編數의 實質的
制限등 韓國의 外畵輸入制限에 대해 '85.9. USTR에 301條
提訴

   O '85.11. 兩國間 協議에서 '87.1부터 外國映畵社 國內 支社
設置許容과 輸入쿼타 制限없이 MPEAA 會員社 映畵필름
輸入을 許容키로 合意

   O '88.9.15. 同 MPEAA 는 韓國 檢閱節次가 數量制限的임을
理由로 USTR에 301條 請願을 提出하고 '85年 合意事項
履行을 促求하는 한편 韓國의 直配 反對示威의 是正을 要求

ー 이에 따라 '88.12.30 檢閱申請節次·編數 制限 緩和, 輸入外畵
複寫벌수 段階撤廢등에서 讓步함으로써 合意

(4) 海運

ー '86.11月 韓·美 海運協議時(每年開催) 美國은 韓國內 貨物
運送(Trucking) 事業의 許容을 要求한 이래 港灣使用料
差別撤廢 및 鐵道直契約 許容등을 계속적으로 要請

   O 그간 港灣使用料 差別의 撤廢('90.4), 부두에서 콘테이너
野積場까지의 貨物運送許容方針 表明('91.1)

-34-

0136

— 한편 美關聯 海事委員會(FMC)는 '87年 美船社의 要請에
따라 우리.나라의 海運 및 陸運 分野에 있어서의 不公正專例
調査를 開始

   ○ '91.4.17 貨物運送事業參與制限, 鐵道使用時 直契約制限을
   理由로 不公正 慣行國으로 判定함에 따라 美 FMC는
   '91.6.7. 美商船法에 依據 對韓 制裁案을 發表하였고 이어
   開催된 '91.7. 韓·美 海運協議에서 貨物運送의 段階開放과
   鐵道運送直契約을 일부 許容함으로써 懸案問題는 일단 解消된
   것으로 判斷

(5) 航 空

— '57.4月 韓·美航空協定을 締結한 以後 數次例의 會談을 開催
하여 '71年, '79年 2次例 協定內容을 改正하였으나 韓·美間
不平等 狀況은 계속 維持됨.

   ○ 美國은 韓國內 諸地點에 대한 運輸權과 餘他 地點에 대한
   以遠權(韓國經由 蘇聯, 中國등 運航權)을 確保

   ○ 韓國은 美國內 3個地點(뉴욕, L.A., 호놀룰루)에 한하여
   運輸權 保有

— 한편 美國은 '86.10. 以後 美航空社의 컴퓨터 豫約制度(CRS)의
韓國內 營業許容과 貨物艙을 提供問題를 계속 提起

-35-

0137

一 우리는 韓·美間 不平等을 解消하기 위하여 '79年 以後 數次例
會談을 開催하였으나 지금까지 妥協을 이루지 못하였던 것이나
'91.6.13 會談에서 그간 美國이 要求해왔던 貨物廳舍新築 및
CRS開放을 條件으로 韓國이 要求해왔던 追加運輸權 및 以遠權
確保問題에 대하여 一括合意

O 美國은 韓國內 自體 CRS 設置可能 및 專用貨物廳舍 確保

O 韓國은 美國內 追加 10個地點(都合 13個地點)에 대한
運輸權 및 3個地點에 대한 以遠權 確保

(6) 通 信

一 情報化 社會의 到來와 함께 通信分野는 美國의 主要戰略産業으로
浮上하였고 高度技術을 要하는 資本集約産業으로서 높은 收益率
및 高賃金을 保障하는 産業

O 그러나 各國은 通信의 特性上 國家別 規制를 持續하고 있어
美 輸出이 크게 制約되는 反面 輸入은 크게 늘어 深刻한
逆調 狀態

O 이에 따라 美國은 主要國과 通信市場開放을 위한 協商을 展開

一 美國은 '88美 綜合通商法에 通信關聯 優先協商對象國(PFC)
指定 條項을 揷入함으로써 各國과의 協商을 이에 따라 推進

O 美側은 韓國에 대해 附加價値 通信事業(VAN)開放 및 通信
機器 標準化 問題, 形式承認品目擴大, 國産化政策 撤廢등 要求

— 韓國은 '89 年 以前에도 形式承認品目擴大, 公共機關 컴퓨터
　　購買時 國産化要求廢止('88.1) 등 一部 對美 通信分野 讓許를
　　해 왔으나

　○ '89.2 協商에서 通信市場開放範圍 및 時期에 대한 異見으로
　　協商이 決裂되었으며, 이에따라 '89.2.21 EC와 함께 通信分野
　　優先協商 對象國으로 指定됨

— 以後 '89.9 부터 '90.2 까지 5차례 걸친 通信會談이 開催
　　되었던 바, '90.2.14. 5次 最終會談에서 일부 意見調整後
　　諒解錄에 假署名하였고, 美側은 協商期限을 '91.2 月까지 延長
　　하였음.

　○ 通信서비스開放範圍 및 時期는 原則的으로 UR / 多者間協商에서
　　論議하되 優先的으로 情報檢察 (DB), 情報處理 (DP)서비스의
　　自由化 實施 (國內 : '90.7, 國際 : '91.7)

　○ '90.7 까지 通信裝備標準 및 認證節次를 改善하여 明瞭한
　　標準制定 및 承認節次 마련

　○ 通信裝備調達市場은 '91.1 까지 GATT 의 政府調達協定에 加入
　　하여 開放하도록 努力하되, 調達協定加入이 實現되지 않을 경우
　　一般通信裝備는 '92 年까지, 通信網裝備는 '93 年까지 GATT
　　調達節次에 準用하는 國內節次를 마련

—37—

— '91.2月 優先協商對象國 指定時限을 앞두고 開催된 協商에서
  美國은 우리의 通信市場開放計劃과 '90.2 合意內容의 誠實한
  履行을 肯定的으로 評價하여 다시 優先協商對象國 指定을 1年
  延長하기로 決定

— 앞으로의 通信市場開放問題는 UR/서비스協商을 中心으로 論議될
  것이나 美國과의 合意事項中 開放을 約束한 分野는 兩者協商을
  통해 계속 協議될 것으로 展望

  O '91.7까지 VAN市場의 開放約束을 韓·美 兩者間 國際 VAN
    協定을 締結하여 履行('91.6.17)하였고, 通信裝備調達市場開放,
    VAN事業에 대한 外國人投資 緩和問題는 追後協議豫定

(7) 金 融

— 金融分野에 대한 市場開放要求는 美國을 中心으로 지난 '80年代
  中盤부터 本格化되기 시작함.

  O 처음에는 部分的 市場接近(market access)要求
    (例) 外銀支店 設置, 保險市場 參與要求등

  O 다음段階에는 內國民待遇(national treatment)로 發展
    (例) 돈市場 參與, 複數支店 許容要求등

  O 最近에는 互視政策變數의 運用 및 構造調整次元에서의 金融自律化
    까지 擴散되는 양상을 나타냄
    (例) 外換自由化, 金利自由化 幅 擴大등

— 이러한 움직임을 反映하여

　ㅇ '84年 및 '86年에 美財務部가 議會에 提出한 內國民待遇報告書
　　에서는 우리나라에 대해 外銀支店 增設制限 또는 不動産取得制限등
　　營業上의 一部 制限만을 지적하였으나

　　・ '90.12 提出한 內國民待遇 報告書에서는 韓國이 利子率規制,
　　　信用割當, 外換規制등을 통해 金融市場을 强力히 統制한다는
　　　理由로 日本, 臺灣과 함께 美金融機關에 대한 內國民待遇를
　　　가장 심하게 拒否하고 있는 國家로 評價

　ㅇ '90.2에 開催되기 시작한 韓・美金融政策會談(FPT)에서 美財務部는
　　單純히 美金融機關의 營業範圍擴大 또는 內國民待遇要求가 아니라
　　우리金融市場, 外換市場 및 資本市場 自由化 또는 이의 日程提示를
　　要求

　ㅇ '91年 들어서는 美財務部外에 商務部, 國務部, USTR등 汎部處的으로
　　金融市場開放問題 集中 要求

— 韓・美通商關係에 있어서 이러한 金融・外換・資本市場開放壓力
　强化의 意味는 個別懸案이 점차 解決되어 감에 따라 經濟政策의
　協議등 構造調整問題가 提起되는 것을 意味하는 것으로 볼수
　있으며 이에 대한 對應態勢 準備가 시급함을 暗示해 준다 할
　것임.

-39-

외 무 부

종 별 :

번 호 : GVW-1317 일 시 : 91 0716 1700

수 신 : 장관(통기),경기원,재무부,법무부,상공부,건설부,보사부,노동부,교통부

발 신 : 주제네바 대사   체신부,문화부,과기처,공보처,항만청)

제 목 : UR/ 서비스 양자협의

7.24-26 간 개최될 표제 양자 협의 관련 현재까지 계획된 아국 관련,
협의 일정을 하기보고함.

1. 협의일정(대상 분야)

- 7.24(수) 15:00: 캐나다 (모든 분야)

17:00: 호주(금융,통신을 제외한 모든 분야)

7.25(목) 09:30-11:00: EC (금융을 제외한 모든분야)

11:00-13:00: 뉴질랜드(시청각, 에지니어링, 건축,회계, 해운, 관광, 통신,
외국인 부자 및노동력 이동)

15:00-17:00: 일본(모든 분야)

2. 협의 성격

- 주로 양국 OFFER 의 명료화 작업이 될것이나 일부 국가의 경우 개괄적인 관심
사항 전달도 포함될 것임.

3. 상대국 참석자

- 캐나다: 본부(대외무역성 및 산업성) 서비스담당자 및 제네바 대표부 담당자 4-5
인

- 호주, 뉴질랜드: 본부 및 제네바 대표부 GNS담당자 각 1인

- EC : 통신, 전문직업, 운송, 유통분야 전문가참석 예정

- 일본: 제네바 대표부에 근무하는 서비스 분야별 담당자 참석 예정

4. 기타: - 상기 협의시 아국이 토의를 원하는 분야가 있을 경우 통보 바람.

- 아국대표단은 EC 및 일본의 분야별 전문가가 참석하는 점을 감안, 소규모 분야별
전문가가 참석하는 것이 좋을 것으로 판단됨.

- 상기 관련 현재 당지 출장중인 최병일 연구위원의 출장 연장 조치를 검토 회시

통상국	법무부	보사부	문화부	교통부	체신부	경기원	재무부	상공부
건설부	노동부	과기처	해항청	공보처				

PAGE 1

바람.

- 아국의 협의 요청할 국가가 있는 경우 동국가명 및 관심분야 통보 바람.

- 여타 국가와의 협의는 요청이 접수 되는대로 추보예정임. 끝

(대사 박수길-국장)

PAGE 2

외 무 부

종 별 :

번 호 : GVW-1312　　　　　　　　　　　　　일　시 : 91 0716 0900

수 신 : 장 관(통기, 경기원, 상공부, 체신부)

발 신 : 주 제네바 대사

제 목 : UR/GNS 회의(2)

　7.12(금) 속개된 표제회의는 GNS 의장과 MR.ROBERT TRITT (캐나다 통신부 통상정책과장)공동주재로 통신 부속서에 대하여 논의하였는바 주요 내용 하기 보고함.

　1. 회의개요

　- 표제 공식회의는 오전에 종료되었는바 각국의 기존입장 반복에 불과하였고 오후에 개최된 주요국 비공식 협의에서 미국은 부속서 초안 11,12,16,17항에 대하여 종래의 자국제안 (GNS/W/97)에 가까운 수정안을 구두로 제시하였으나 서면제안의 미비로 토의가 진행되지 못하여 향후 협상진전의 기반도 마련하지 못한채 9월 GNS회의시 재논의키로 하였음.

　2. 공식 회의 주요내용

　가. 부속서의 적용범위

　- 미국은 어떤 무역협정이든 정부의 조치를 적용대상으로 하는 것이지 민간기업을 구속할 수 없는 것이라고 하여 AT AND T 를 부속서 적용으로부터 배제하려는 입장을 재표명함.

　- 이씨 및 스웨덴은 사기업의 행위가 공중통신망의 접근 및 사용에 영향을 미치는

　만큼 상대국의 혜택을 고려하여야 한다는 점, 미국은 잘발달된 경제촉진 체계를가지고 있기때문에 공중 통신망의 접근 및 사용보장에 별문제가 없을 것이라고 반박함.

　0 미국은 자국의 경쟁촉진법 체계가 잘 발달된점은 인정하나 동 법규의 시행을 강제하는 것은 전체 GATT 규율체계 및 무역체제, 국내법률 체계에 혼란을 초래할 것이며 각국의 경쟁촉진법 체계가 다르고 국제표준도 없기때문에 이의 시행을 강제하는것은 불가능하다고함.

　나. 기업내 통신

통상국　　2차보　　　체신부　　　경기원　　　상공부

외신 1과 통제관
0144

- EC 의 일반적 논평 이외에 발언국 없음

다. 정보에의 접근

- 싱가폴 및 말련은 14항 말미의 법규변경시 (사전) 통지 및 협의 규정에 대하여FRAMEWORK 6 조 (국내규제)상의 각국의 입법권보장 부분을 들어 유보 의사를 표명한바

0 미국은 모든 법규 변경을 대상으로 하는 것이아니라 시장접근 약속의 무효화,침해되는 경우에만 해당하는 것이라고 반박함.

라. 공중통신망(PTTS) 에의 접근 및 사용

- 인도, 이집트는 제 13항 (가격제정)을 삭제하자고 하였으며 유고는 동 조항이삭제되어야 하나 타협안으로서 BEST ENDEAVOUR 조항은 수용 가능하다고함

0 미국, 이씨, 스웨덴등은 부당하게 높은 가격으로 시장접근 약속이 침해되는 경우에 대비하여 동조항이 규정되어야 한다고 함.

- 한편 미국은 11,12,16,17항이 부적절하며 통신부속서 제정 가치를 의심스럽게한다고 하였는바 동일 오후 비공식 협의에서 보다 구체적으로 논의되었음.

3. 주요국 비공식 협의

- 미국은 타국의 경우 국내사업자도 공중통신망 접근 및 사용에 제한이 많기 때문에 11항의 내국민 대우 규정만 가지고는 불충분하다고 전제하고 다음안을 구두로 제시 함.

0 11항 말미의 MFN, 국내규제,내국민 대우 조항언급 부분 삭제

0 12항에 과거 미국제안상의 여러가지 전용회선 상호접촉, 기기접속 의무 규정 (GNS/W/97 의 3.6.2-3.6.6 및 3.7) 추가

0 제 16항 A) 의 BYPASS 문구 삭제 및 기타문귀 수정

0 제 17항의 재구성 및 일부 표현 수정

- 인도는 본내 내국민 대우는 FRAMEWORK 상에 의무가 아니라 목표로 되어있으나공중통신망 접근에 있어서는 내국민 대우를 의무로 수용해주었는바 내국민 대우 수준을 넘어서는 의무는 어떤것도 받아들일수 없다고 하였으며

0 EC 역시 미국 제안은 초 내국민 대우규정으로서 COMMON ADDITIONAL COMITMENT를 추구하는바 수용곤란 하다고 함.

- 한편, 모든나라가 동제안이 매우 복잡한 문제이므로 서면 제안이 있어야만 토의가 가능하다고 하였으나 미국은 국내검토 작업이 아직 끝나지않아 서면으로

PAGE 2

0145

제안할수 없다고 하여 9월 회의이전까지 서면으로 배부하고 9월 GNS 회의에서 재논의키로하고 회의를 종결하였음. 끝

　　(대사 박수길-국장)

외 무 부

종 별 :

번 호 : GVW-1316   일 시 : 91 0716 1700

수 신 : 장관(통기, 경기원, 재무부, 법무부, 상공부, 건설부)

발 신 : 주 제네바대사

제 목 : UR/GNS 회의(3)

배부처:보사부,노동부,교통부,체신부,문화부,공보처,과기처,항만청

7.15(월) JARAMILLO 의장 주재로 속개된표제회의 내용을 하기 보고함.

1. 금주 회의 진행 계획

- 7.15 오전(공식 GNS): 분쟁해결, 노동력 이동부속서(공식회의 이후 비공식 협의를 거쳐 사무국이부속서 초안 개정 예정)

오후(비공식 GNS): 제 2조(MFN)

- 7.16 오전(비공식 협의): SCHEDULING 및 제 6조,7조, 14조, 16조, 17조, 19조,20조 (HAWES 대사 주재)

오후(비공식 GNS): 제 1조 및 노동력 이동

- 7.17 오전 (비공식 GNS): INITIAL COMMITMENT 에관한 실질적 기준(제 4조, 18조, 19 조 관련)

오후 (비공식 GNS): 제 5조

- 7.19 오전(비공식 협의): HAWES 대사 주재로필요시 개최

오후: 공사 GNS 회의

2. 주요 회의 내용

가. 분쟁해결

- 사무국 작성문서(기송부)에 대하여 EC 는 자세하지 못하다고 실망을 표하는 한편 7월회의에서 분쟁해결을 우선적으로 다루는데 의문을 제기한바, 각국이 개별적으로 사무국에 의견을 제시하고 9월 GNS 에서 논의하기로 결정함.

나. 노동력 이동

- 6월 GNS 회의시 토의에 불참하였던 EC 로부터 노동력 이동 부속서 초안에 대한다음과 같은 논평이 있었음.

통상국	2차보	법무부	보사부	문화부	교통부	체신부	경기원	재무부
상공부	건설부	노동부	과기처	해항청	공보처			

PAGE 1   91.07.17   08:20 DN
외신 1과 통제관

0147

O 제 1항: 서비스 공급관련 자연인이 개별 서비스공급자와 서비스 공급기업의 종업원등 두종류가 있음을 감안하여 서비스 공급자의 정의 규정이 마련되어야 함.

특히 서비스 공급기업에 고용된 비체약국 국적의인력, 인력시장에의 접근 문제등도 다루어져야 함.

시장접근 약속을 무효화 하지 않는 이상 국경에서 시행되는 모든 국내 법규가 침해되어서는 안되며, 제 5항도 FRUSTRATE 라는 용어보다는 NULLIFY또는 IMPAIR 라는용어가 보다 적절함.

O 제 2항: ILLUSTRATIVE LIST 를 작성할 가치가 별로없음.

O 제 6항: 서비스 무역에 한정되지 않는 광범위한 인력 이동에 관한 협정이 있음을 인식하여야 하나 다른 체약국에 대한 시장접근 약속을 보호할수 있는 세이프 가드가 있어야 함.

O 부속서 초안에 누락된 사항: 근로조건(최저임금법)등에 관한 국내 법규 적용문제,분쟁해결 절차

- 또한 EC 는 캐나다가 제시한 고급인력에 대한 공통 자유화 약속 접근 방식에 대한 지지의사를 표명하였는바,

O 인도는 어떤 COMMON APPROACH 도 참가국간 이익 분균형을 심화시키므로 수용할수없다고 하였으며

O 헝가리는 동 접근 방식이 특히 상업적 주재와관련된 고급인력만 취급하는 것은불충분하며,국경간 서비스 공급 관련 인력과 다른 범주의인력 이동도 해결되어야 한다고 함.(이집트, 멕시코동조)

O 또한 싱가폴 및 말련 역시 COMMON APPROACH 에 유보의사를 표명함.

다. MFN

- 의장은 개인자격으로 별첨(FAX 송부)과같이 MFN 문제에 관하여 논평함.

- 대부분의 나라가 MFN 일탈은 최소한에 그쳐야하며, 현존 협정에 한하여일탈을허용하되 PHASE-OUT 시한을 설정하여야 한다는 의사를 표명함.

O 캐나다는 UN LINER CODE 가 현존 협정인바 동협정하에서 맺어지는 양자 협정들은 새로운 협정이 될것이므로 현존 협정의 의미가 보다 명확해져야 한다고 함.

- 미국은 각국의 시장접근 약속 수준을 알기전에 MFN 문제를 결정하는 것은 공평치 못하다고 전제하고 양허 협상을 통하여 각국의 시장접근약속 수준도 알고 MFN 일탈 거론 분야에 대한 정보도 확충한 이후에 최종 결정하는 것이 실용적 접근 방법이 될수

PAGE 2

0148

있다고 함.

0 브라질은 어느나라의 약속 수준이 만족할 만한것인지 여부는 주관적인 것이며 MFN 문제가 먼저하결 되어야 양허 협상에 진입할수 있다고반박함.

 - 한편, 종래의 분야별 부속서에 의하여 공통으로 특정 ACTIVITIES 에 대한 MFN일탈을 규정하는 다자간 접근 방법에 덧붙여 개별 국가별유보 방법 및 WAIVER 방식이 제기되었으며, 동시에 동 방법은 각국의 이익 균형을 도모할수 있도록 주의 깊은 규정이 필요하다는 점이 지적됨.

0 또한 많은 나라로 부터 MFN 일탈을 원하는 나라가 구체적 목록을 제출할 의무가 있으며, 사무국이 이를 취합하여야 한다는 지적이 있었음.끝

첨부: MFN 에 관한 의장 논평 1부. 끝

(GVW(F)-250)

(대사 박수길-국장)

@

· 15.7.91

GVW(?)-0250 10716 1700
GVW-1316 첨부,

MOST-FAVOURED-NATION CLAUSE

Statement of the problem

It is important to note that Article II of the draft
Agreement states that the m.f.n. clause applies to measures
affecting trade in services. It follows that it is not the
bilateral, plurilateral agreements or discretionary domestic
legislation per se, which may not be in conformity with the
m.f.n. obligation, but rather measures affecting trade in
services which may be taken pursuant to such arrangements or
legislation. Mandatory legislation, however, constitutes a
measure.

Measures which may not be in conformity with the m.f.n.
obligation may be taken in accordance with:

- horizontal agreements or arrangements that apply
  across services sectors and include Bilateral
  Investment, Friendship, Commerce and Navigation,
  taxation, juridical assistance and visa exemption
  agreements;

- sectoral agreements or arrangements which, by their
  nature, are limited to a specific sector. Examples
  are found in the transport (air, maritime, inland)
  and audiovisual sectors. As for horizontal
  agreements, these too are of a bilateral or
  plurilateral nature and provide preferential terms
  and conditions for signatories.

3 -/

0150

F-MFN

- 2 -

· What these agreements have in common is that if the benefits derived from the measures adopted in accordance with the agreement are not extended to all signatories of the General Agreement on Trade in Services (GATS) following its date of entry into force, the parties concerned would be in violation of the m.f.n. obligation. It should be borne in mind, however, that these agreements do not preclude the extension of the benefit accruing to signatories to third parties.

In addition, there are instances where parties may seek to invoke measures in accordance with domestic legislation, the application of which is inconsistent with the m.f.n. obligation. Such measures include retaliatory action on a unilateral basis.

With respect to existing arrangements, most participants have expressed the view that it would be impossible to conform to the m.f.n. provision for all activities in all sectors at the time of entry into force of the agreement. There are various reasons for this:

- Most countries have indicated that they could apply the m.f.n. provision for the majority of activities in the sectors where agreements exist, providing they have a period of time in which to phase out the non-conforming measures.

- There are some activities, however, where for a large number of participants, irrespective of the time available, there is no desire to apply the m.f.n. obligation.

3 - 2   F-MFN   0151

- 3 -

- There are also instances where non-conforming measures may not be in place at the time of entry into force of the agreement but domestic legislation would permit such measures to be invoked in the future.

- In other cases, some participants consider that m.f.n. may be applied if a satisfactory level of concessions is reached with third parties.

It follows that the legal solutions to the problems faced by individual parties wishing to maintain or introduce a non-conforming measure may well be based on a number of considerations relating to the measures themselves. For example:

- whether all or only some parties are seeking exemptions;

- the motivation for the exemption;

- whether the measure is a pre-existing measure with continuing effect after the entry into force of the GATS;

- the extent of the sector affected by the exception - that is the scope of the activities covered by the exemption.

0152

3-3

외 무 부

종 별 :

번 호 : GVW-1320 일 시 : 91 0716 1830

수 신 : 장관(통기), 경기원, 재무부, 법무부, 상공부, 건설부, 보사부

발 신 : 주 제네바 대사 , 노동부, 교통부, 체신부, 문화부, 공보처, 과기처, 항만청

제 목 : UR/GNS 회의(4)

7.16(화) 속개된 표제회의 내용을 하기 보고함.

1. 전체 GSN 비공식

- JARAMILLO 의장 주재의 상기 회의에서는 6월GSN 회의 및 7.15. GNS 회의시 각국발언내용을 반영 사무국이 재작성한 노동력 이동에관한 부속서 초안(별도 FAX 송부)을 배부하고 동초안에 누락된 사항에 대한 각국의 논평을요청함.

0 캐나다와 호주는 캐나다 작성 초안상의 '노사분규문제 불개입'원칙이 빠졌다고지적하였으며 그외특기할 만한 사항은 없었음.

- 의장은 동 초안에 대해 의견이 있는 국가는서면 논평을 제시해 줄것을 요청하는 한편금주말에 다시 협의 하겠다고 하고 곧 회의를종결하였음.

2. SCHEDULING 에 관한 비공식 협의

- 한편 동일 오전 HAWES 대사 주재로 SCHEDULING에 관한 비공식 협의가 개최되었는바

,0 차별적인 양적규제, 질적 규제 및 무차별적인양적 규제는 TOP-DOWN 방식으로기재하되무차별적인 질적 규제는 특정요건(객관적기준에 기초할것, 필요이상의 부담을 초래하지않을 것, 그 자체가 서비스 공급에 대한 제한이되지 않을것)에 합치하지않는 경우에만SCHEDULE 에 기재하는 방식으로 합의가 형성되고있음.,- 또한 이와관련 제 6조(국내규제), 제16조(시장접근), 제 17조(내국민 대우)에 대한 조문작성이 진행중인바, 최종안이 나오는대로 상세보고 예정임.

첨부: 노동력 이동 부속서 수정안 1부.(GVW(F)-0251).끝

(대사 박수길-국장)

통상국	차관	1차보	2차보	구주국	청와대	안기부	법무부	보사부
문화부	교통부	체신부	경기원	재무부	상공부	건설부	노동부	과기처
해항정	공보처							

PAGE 1

91.07.17 20:24 DZ

외신 1과 통제관

0153

DRAFT
16.7.91

GVW.(주)-0251   10716 1830
"GVW-1320 첨부,

Incorporation of result of the
Chairman's consultations[1]

[ANNEX ON THE TEMPORARY MOVEMENT OF
NATURAL PERSONS PROVIDING SERVICES]

1.   The provisions of the Agreement relate to temporary movement of natural
persons performing particular services in respect of which access commitments
have been undertaken. They do not apply to individual job seekers, and do
not concern, and should not affect, national laws and regulations **or
international agreements and arrangements** regarding citizenship or
immigration related to residence or employment on a permanent basis.

[2. An illustrative list of natural persons performing particular services
covering broad categories of sectors and skill levels is attached to this
Annex.]

[2. Negotiations shall proceed on the basis of lists of categories of
persons exchanged by the Parties without prejudice to whether access in
respect of any such categories of persons is subsequently bound.]

[3. **In the application of Article III of the Agreement, Parties shall ensure
that relevant information on the procedure and regulations concerning the
granting of entry for temporary stay is made publicly available.**]

4.   Market access commitments specifying the categories of natural persons
for the provision of a particular service on a **temporary basis** shall be
negotiated in accordance with Articles XVI, XVII and XVIII of the Agreement,
drawing on the [illustrative] list(s) as a reference point.

_____

[1]Changes from the draft annex contained in MTN.TNC/W/35/Rev.1 are .
indicated in bold.

0154

3-1   LAB2-LAB

- 2 -

5.   Once such a market access commitment is inscribed in the schedules, all categories of natural persons covered by the commitment shall be allowed to provide the service.

[6.   The benefits from any specific commitment covering labour mobility shall not be frustrated through the application of national laws or regulations relating to the entry, stay and work on a temporary basis of natural persons.]

[6.   Parties shall apply their laws and regulations to entry, stay and work on a temporary basis of natural persons, in such a manner as not to nullify or impair the benefits accruing to any Party under any such specific commitment.]

[7.   Nothing in the Agreement or its annexes shall prevent a Party from adopting and enforcing such measures relating to the temporary movement of natural persons providing services as it considers necessary to protect the integrity of, and the orderly movement of natural persons across, its international borders.]

[8.   Parties may require that [measures relating to all working conditions] [relevant domestic regulations] (e.g. minimum wage requirements, social security regulations, health and safety standards, etc.), applicable in the country, province or state where the service is provided, are respected by natural persons providing services under the Agreement.]

[9.   Notwithstanding Article II of the Agreement, Parties may undertake bilateral or plurilateral arrangements providing for preferential movement of natural persons with other countries, and may impose conditions and limitations on such movement. In applying such arrangements or in imposing such conditions and limitations, Parties shall endeavour to act in the least restrictive manner possible with respect to foreign providers of services.]

[9.   Any agreements or arrangements providing for preferential conditions for the temporary movement of natural persons from the other countries party to,

0155

LAB2-LAB

2-2

- 3 -

or benefiting from, such agreements or arrangements shall not be considered
to be in conflict with the provisions of Article II of the Agreement.
Parties shall ensure however that such agreements or arrangements shall not
nullify or impair specific commitments regarding the movement of natural
persons from other parties.]

[10. It is understood that nothing in the Agreement shall be construed to
prevent agreements or arrangements the effect of which is the substantial
integration of labour markets.]

[11. A Party may not invoke the provisions of Article XXIII with respect to
the denial or the revocation of an authorization for temporary entry of a
natural person subject to a specific commitment unless:

   (a) the rules being applied as a pattern of practice for the denial or
       revocation do not conform to the commitment undertaken; and

   (b) available local remedies have been exhausted.

외 무 부

종   별 :

번   호 : GVW-1358　　　　　　　　　　　　일   시 : 91 0719 1200

수   신 : 장관(봉기,경기원,재무부,법무부,상공부,건설부,보사부,

발   신 : 주 제네바 대사　　노동부,교통부,체신부,문화부,과기처,공보처,항만청)

제   목 : UR/GNS 회의(5)

7.18(목) 속개된 표제회의(전체 비공식) 내용을하기 보고함.

1. MFN

- 갓트 사무국(법률국)에서 작성 배부한 **MFN 일탈에 관한 법률적 검토문서(별도FAX송부)**에 대한 각국의 논평 및 기술적 사항에 대한 법률국장의 답변이 있었음.)

　가. 각국의 논평

- 대부분의 나라가 4항 B) 의 방법(각국별일방적 MFN 유보)는 규율 체계를 문란하게 하는 위험한 것이라고 지적하였으며, 4항 A) 의 방법(GATS 또는 부속서에 규정하는 방법)을 지지함.

- EC 등 많은 나라가 MFN 일탈을 원하는나라가 구체적 정보를 제출하여야 하며,동 자료를 바탕으로 9월중에 집중적인 협상이 진행되어야 한다고 하였으나 동 방법이 실제 관리가능한지(스위스), 동 방법이 얼마나 확실성을 증대시킬 수 있는지(카나다) 하는 의문도 제기되었음.

0 한편 미국은 9월중에 관련 정보를 제공할 용의도 있음을 시사함.

- 기타 많은 나라가 MFN 일탈을 최소한에 그쳐야하며, 한시적임과 동시에 계속 재검토 되어야한다고 지적함.

- 미국은 권리,의무의 균형면에서 MFN 일탈 및 적용에 대한 당사국 및 상대국의댓가 문제를 거론하였으나 인도는 MFN 을 적용하더라도 대부분의 나라가 선진국 시장에 진입하는 것은 사실상 불가능하브로 무임승차 문제는 허구에 불과하다고 함.

　나. 기술적 사항에 대한 법률국 답변

- 각국의 MFN 일탈 대상 제출은 당해국에 관한 것만 제출하여야지 타국도 일탈대

통상국	2차보	경제국	법무부	보사부	문화부	교통부	체신부	경기원
재무부	상공부	건설부	노동부	과기처	해항정	공보처	우주국.	정아애

PAGE 1　　　　　　　　　　　　　　　　　　　　　　　91.07.19　　22:43 DF

외신 1과 통제관

0157

상으로 할것을 전제로 제출하는데 대한 이의(호주)에 대하여갓트 관례상 일반적으로 이용 가능한 사항도특정국가가 제시할수 있다고 함.

  - MFN 일탈 조치의 점진적 제거에 관한메카니즘이 누락되었다는 EC 의 지적에 대해법률국은 어떤 조치든 대개 일정기간후 일시에사라지는 것이 상례라고 함.

  - MFN 일탈 대상 조치의 구체적 정의는 각국국내 법규에 맡기는 것이 보다 실용적일 것이라는 북구의 지적에 대하여 이는 법률적으로는 가능하나 당사국에 너무 많은 재량을 주게되어 규율 체계가 혼란스러워 진다고함.

  - 새로운 서비스의 MFN 일탈 필요시 처리방법(오지리)에 대하여는 동 서비스 출현이전의 규정가지고는 불가능하며, 웨이버나 조문 개정으로 대처하여야 할것이라고함.

  2. 양허 협상에 관한 실질적 기준

  - 한편 7.17(수) 오전의 GNS 비공식 회의에서는양허 협상의 실질적 기준에 대하여 논의하였으나다음과 같은 선.개도국간 입장 대립으로 추후의장이 어떤 제안을 하고재논의 키로 하였음.

  0 미국은 시장접근 약속시 개도국에 대한 신축성 부여는 허용가능하나 제4조(개도국 무역 비중증대), 제 8조(양허협상) 2항이 면책 조항이 될 우려가있다고 하면서 양허 협상의 실질적 기준 자체가 필요 없을지도 모른다고 발언함.

  0 EC 는 브랏셀 이전의 양허 협상 절차적 기준안에 협상력을 강화하는 어떤 조치도 취하지 않겠다는 정치적 약속이 포함되어 있음을 지적하고 동 동결정신이 양허협상의 실질적기준에 반영되어야 한다고 함.(일본, 스위스,스웨덴 동조)

  0 인도, 멕시코, 이집트 등은 제 4조 및 18조에 대한합의가 완료되기 전에는 양허 협상의 실질적기준에 대한 합의가 곤란하다고 하였으며,대부분의 개도국이 동결 약속에 반대입장을 견지하였음.

  0 아국은 18조 3항 C 의 자발적 자유화 조치에 대한 고려가 양허 협상의 실질적기준안에는 반영되어 있지 않아 UR 개시이후 취해진 자발적 자유화 조치에 대한 고려가 불충분하다고 지적함.

  첨부: MFN 에 관한 사무국 작성 문서 1부 끝

  (GVW(F)-265)

  (대사 박수길-국장)

GVW(재)-0265   10718 /200

"GVW-1358첨부"

EXEMPTIONS FROM THE
MOST-FAVOURED-NATION TREATMENT (MFN) CLAUSE OF THE
GENERAL AGREEMENT ON TRADE IN SERVICES (GATS)

1. **Which governmental actions are covered by the MFN clause and therefore require exemption from it ?**

The MFN clause of Article II of the GATS applies to measures affecting the supply of services through the modes of delivery specified in Article I of the GATS. An exemption from the MFN clause must be formulated as a permission to take a specified measure on specified conditions notwithstanding that clause. Measures within the meaning of the MFN clause can be administrative actions affecting the supply of a service or legislation which mandatorily requires the executive authorities to take such actions. The maintenance of discretionary legislation merely permitting the executive authorities to act inconsistently with the MFN clause, but not requiring it to do so, would normally not constitute a measure affecting trade in services.

Bilateral or plurilateral agreements relating to trade in services are also normally not measures within the meaning of Article II; it is their implementation through legislative or administrative actions, not their mere existence, which affects trade in services. Moreover, most agreements relating to trade in services, while guaranteeing certain benefits to the treaty partner, do not prevent the extension of these benefits to third parties. It is thus normally not the implementation of these agreements that is inconsistent with the MFN clause, but the non-extension of the benefits granted under it to third parties.

The formulation used in the note to Article II of the draft GATS in MTN.TNC/W/35/Rev.1 (page 334), that is

"The provisions of this Article do not apply to international agreements on taxation, investment protection or juridical and/or administrative assistance".

0153

- 2 -

exempts for these reasons from the MFN clause something that is not covered by it. Also the formulation used in paragraph 2 of Article II of this draft, namely

"The provisions of paragraph 1 of this Article shall temporarily not apply to those activities in specific sectors covered by other international agreements as are identified and set out in the annexes to this Agreement"

does not clearly define the exempted measures in terms of the obligations under the MFN clause, which does not relate to "activities covered by agreements".

2. **What categories of exemptions from the MFN clause can be distinguished?**

The measures that could be exempted from the MFN clause can be distinguished as follows:

(a) measures taken in any service sector and measures taken in specified sectors;

(b) measures taken by any Party and measures taken by a specified Party;

(c) measures applied on the date of acceptance of the GATS (grandfathering) and measures taken subsequent to the date of acceptance of the GATS;

(d) measures taken up to a specified date (time-bound exemption) and measures taken at any time (permanent exemption).

The choice among the above categories of exemptions will depend on the reasons for which the exemption is sought. For instance, if a country needs some time to adjust sector-specific domestic legislation to the requirements of the MFN clause, it might request for itself a time-bound exemption for a measure in force on the day of acceptance of the GATS.

0160

- 4 -

4.   What legal techniques could be used to implement MFN exemptions?

There are essentially three legal techniques available for implementing the MFN exemptions:

(a)   the exemption could be included in the text of the GATS, either in the body of the Agreement or in an Annex forming an integral part of it;

(b)   Parties could be allowed to make unilateral reservations upon their acceptance of the Agreement;

(c)   the PARTIES could, after the entry into force of the Agreement, grant waivers to particular Parties.

The first of the above options has a number of advantages over the other two. The parties would know at the time of acceptance of the Agreement precisely what their rights and obligations are. To permit unilateral reservations at the time of the acceptance of the Agreement entails the risk of unravelling the results of the negotiations. Since waivers can be granted only _after_ the entry into force of the Agreement, this legal technique would be available only for requests for exemptions after the entry into force of the Agreement.

Exemptions from the MFN clause could also be included in the protocol by which a government accedes to the GATS in accordance with Article XXXVIII:2. However, this legal technique would be available only for the parties that accede to the GATS after its entry into force.

0161

기 안 용 지

분류기호 문서번호	통기 20644-	기 안 용 지 (전화 : 720 - 2188)	시 행 상 특별취급	
보존기간	영구 . 준영구 10. 5. 3. 1.	차 관	장 관	
수 신 처 보존기간		전결		
시행일자	1991. 7.19.			
보조 기관	국 장	협 조 기 관	제2차관보 :	문 서 통 제
	심의관			
	과 장			
기안책임자	조 현			발 송 인
경 유 수 신 참 조	건 의	발신명의		
제 목	UR/서비스 협상 정부대표 임명			

91.7.24(수)-26(금)간 제네바에서 개최되는 UR/서비스 협상에

참가할 정부대표단을 "정부대표 및 특별사절의 임명과 권한에 관한

법률"에 의거 아래와 같이 임명할 것을 건의하오니 재가하여 주시기

바랍니다.

- 아   래 -

1. 회 의 명 : UR/서비스 협상 (주요국간 양자협의)   0162

2. 회의기간 및 장소 : 91.7.24(수)-26(금), 제네바
3. 정부대표
○ 본부대표
- 경제기획원 대조실 제2협력관　　　　이윤재
- 경제기획원 통상조정3과장　　　　　하동만
- 경제기획원 통상조정3과 사무관　　신호현
- 경제기획원 통상조정3과 사무관　　김용준
○ 자　문
- 대외경제정책연구원 연구위원　　　박태호
- 통신개발 연구원 연구위원　　최병일(제네바 출장중)
4. 출장기간 : 91.7.22(월)-28(일) (6박7일)
5. 소요경비 : 경제기획원 및 KIEP 소관예산
6. 훈령
○ 양자협의는 아국의 Offer list에 대한 질문 사항을
명료화하는 선에서 회의를 진행하며 본격적인 양자협상은

0163

9월이후로 유보함.

ㅇ 상대국 Offer list에 대해서도 적극 질문하여 향후

Request list 제출에 필요한 정보를 입수함

별 첨 : 양자협의 일정.   끝.

0164

서비스 양자협의 일정

일 시	상 대 국	장 소	참 석 자
7.24			
11:00-13:00	북 구	GATT ROOM 1055	스웨덴, 핀란드, 노르웨이의 서비스 협상 담당자
15:00-16:00	카 나 다	GATT사무차장방	David Lee(본부), Francois Nadeau(제네바), 대외무역성 및 산업성의 서비스 담당자 각 1인등 4-5명
17:00	호 주	GATT ROOM A	Peter Gray(본부), Michael Wood(제네바)등
7.25			
09:30-11:00	E C	GATT ROOM 64	통신, 전문직업, 운송, 유통 분야의 전문가 참석 예정
11:00-13:00	뉴질랜드	GATT ROOM X	Malcoln McGoun(본부), Jo Tyndall(제네바)
15:00-17:00	일 본	미정(GATT)	제네바 대표부 소속 각부처 주재관 참석 예정

0165

경 제 기 획 원

봉조삼 10502- 484   503-9149   1991. 7. 19.

수신 외무부장관

참조 봉상국장

제목 UR/서비스 양자협의 참석

　　1. 스위스 제네바에서 개최되는 UR/서비스 양자협의(7.24-26)에 참석할
본부대표단(자문역포함)을 다음과 같이 송부하니 협조해 주기 바랍니다.

다   음

　　가. 출장자

소 속	직 위	성 명
경제기획원 대외경제조정실	제 2협력관	이 윤 재
"	봉상조정3과장	하 동 만
"	봉상조정2과 사무관	신 호 현
"	봉상조정3과 사무관	김 용 준
대외경제정책연구원 (자문역)	연 구 위 원	박 태 호

　　나. 출장기간: '91.7.22-28 (6박 7일)
　　다. 경비부담: 당원 및 KIEP

첨부: 1. 출장일정 1부.
　　　2. 협상대책자료 1부(별도송부). 끝.

경 제 기 획 원 장

0166

출 장 일 정

'91. 7. 22(월)	12:40	서울 발 (KE 901)
	19:10	파리 착
	20:45	파리 발 (SR 729)
	21:45	제네바 착
7. 24(수)		
~		UR/서비스 양자협의
7. 26(금)		
7. 27(토)	10:50	제네바 발 (SR 1855)
	12:15	프랑크푸르트 착
	14:20	프랑크푸르트 발 (KE 916)
7. 28(일)	09:50	서울 착

0167

"질서앞에 혼란없고 절약앞에 가난없다"

체   신   부

통협 34475-5203   750-2341   91. 7. 20.

수신 수신처 참조

제목 UR/GNS Offer List협의 참가 협조요청

　　1. 통협 34475-4900(91. 7. 8)관련.

　　2. UR서비스 협상을 가속화하기 위하여 91.7.24-7.26일간 개최될 Offer List양차 및 다자간 협의에 효율적으로 대처하기 위하여 아래의 통신분야 전문가를 정부 대표단 자문위원으로 참석케 하고자 하오니 적극 협조하여 주시기 바랍니다.

　　　　가. 참가자 및 출장기간

소 속	직 위	성 명	출 장 기 간	비 고
통신개발연구원	연구위원	최명일	91.7.22-7.28	UR/GNS Offer List 협의참가

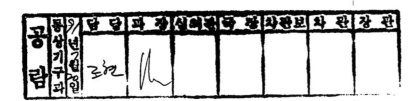

체   신   부   장

통신정책국장 전결

수신처 : 외무부장관·통신개발연구원장·

0168

		34229	기 안 용 지			
분류기호 문서번호	통기 20644-		(전화 : 720 - 2188)		시 행 상 특별취급	
보존기간	영구. 준영구 10. 5. 3. 1.		장 관			
수 신 처 보존기간						
시행일자	1991. 7. 20.					
보조 기관	국 장	전 결	협 조 기 관		문 서 통 제	
	심의관	홍정성				
	과 장	대결				
기안책임자		조 현			발 송 인	
경수참	유신조	경제기획원장관	발신명의			
제 목	UR/서비스 협상 정부대표 임명 통보					

1. 91.7.24(수)-26(금)간 제네바에서 개최되는 UR/서비스 협상에

참가할 정부대표단이 "정부대표 및 특별사절의 임명과 권한에 관한

법률"에 의거 아래와 같이 임명 되었음을 통보합니다.

- 아   래 -

가. 회 의 명 : UR/서비스 협상(주요국간 양자협의)

- 1 -

0169

나. 회의기간 및 장소 : 91.7.24(수)-26(금), 제네바
다. 정부대표
ㅇ 본부대표
- 경제기획원 대조실 제2협력관   이윤재
- 경제기획원 통상조정3과장   하동만
- 경제기획원 통상조정3과 사무관   신호현
- 경제기획원 통상조정3과 사무관   김용준
ㅇ 자 문
- 대외경제정책연구원 연구위원   박태호
- 통신개발 연구원 연구위원   최병일(제네바 출장중)
라. 출장기간 : 91.7.22(월)-28(일) (6박7일)
마. 소요경비 : 경제기획원 및 KIEP 소관예산
2. 출장 결과 보고서는 대표단 귀국후 2주일이내 당부로
송부하여 주시기 바랍니다.   끝.

- 2 -
0170

발 신 전 보

분류번호	보존기간

번   호 : WGV-0918   910720 1045 FN 종별 : 암호통신

수   신 : 주 제네바   대사. 총영사

발   신 : 장 관 (통 기)

제   목 : UR/GNS 협상

      대 : GVW-1317

1. 귀지에서 7.24-26간 개최되는 UR/GNS 협상 주요국간 양자협의에 참가할 본부대표가
   아래 임명 되었으니 귀관 관계관과 함께 참석토록 조치바람.

   ○ 본부대표

      - 경제기획원 대조실 제2협력관   이윤재
      - 경제기획원 통상조정3과장   하동만
      - 경제기획원 통상조정3과 사무관   신호현
      - 경제기획원 통상조정3과 사무관   김용준

   ○ 자   문

      - 대외경제정책연구원 연구위원   박태호
      - 통신개발 연구원 연구위원   최병일 (출장기간을 28일까지로 연장)

2. 금번 양자협의에서는 아국의 Offer list에 대한 질문사항을 명료화하는 선에서
   회의를 진행하고 본격적인 양자협상은 9월이후로 유보 바라며, 본부대표가 지참
   예정인 자료를 기초로 상대국 Offer list 제출에 필요한 정보를 입수바람.

                                        끝.   (통상국장 김용규)

기 안	1
통 제	M

| 앙고재 | 91년7월9일 | 통기과 | 기안자성명 조현 | 과장 M | 심의관 전결 | 국장 | 차관 | 장관 山 | 외신과통제 |

0171

UR/서비스 協商實務委資料

725 - 1737

특상가나의 근원 서기관

┌─────────────────────────────┐
│　　　UR / 서비스 협상 관련　　│
│   │
│ 勞動力 移動分野 對應方案   │
└─────────────────────────────┘

1991. 7. 20

勞　　動　　部

1. UR/서비스會議(6.24 - 28) 協商動向 및 展望

가 . 勞動力 移動에 대한 論議 事項

◦ 勞動力 移動自由化 推進方法

- 大多數國家

. 미 국 :KEY-PERSONNEL (MANAGERS, EXECUTIVES, SPECIALISTS)은 多者間
約束으로 自由化하고 其他 人力은 讓許協商으로 決定

. 캐나다 : MANAGERS, EXECUTIVE, SPECIALISTS, SERVICESELLERS는
自由化,其他 讓許協商 (호주,뉴질랜드,모지리 지지표명)

- 印 度 : 모든 形態의 서비스에 필요한 인력을 FRAMEWORK 및 각국의
SCHEDULE 에 反影

◦ 勞動力 移動附屬書 制定에 대하여 合議形成

- 個別的인 海外就業希望者,移民對象者는 對象에서 除外

- 就業 등에 관한 國內法規 등 非經濟的 이유에 基礎한 規制는 可能

나 . 向後 展望

◦ KEY - PERSONNEL은 多者間 約束에 의해 自由化하고 나머지 範疇人力은
讓許協商에 의해 自由化하자는 趨勢임 (미국,캐나다)

* KEY - PERSONNEL 以外 範疇人力에 대해 附屬書나 多者間 約束을 통하여
共通으로 自由化하는 것은 不可能

◦ 次期會議時 NATIONAL SCHEDULE 作成方法과 讓許協商基準에 대한 合議 可能

0173

2. 我國의 勞動市場 與件

ㅇ UR서비스協商에서의 勞動力移動과 관련, 우리나라 勞動力의 輸出可能性 보다는 輸入 可能性이 더욱 높음.

- 우리나라의 賃金등 勤勞條件이 상대적으로 優位에 있음.

< 主要國 月平均 賃金 水準 比較 >

(단위 : 미달러, %)

구분	한 국	일 본	대 만	홍 콩	멕시코	브라질
임금	805 (100.0)	2,501 (310.7)	802 (99.6)	556 (69.1)	262 (32.5)	202 (25.1)

자료 : 대한 무역진흥공사

- 就業關聯 外國人 入國의 漸增 및 國內勤勞者 海外進出의 減少 趨勢

  · 就業關聯 外國人 入國者 漸增(雇傭, 敎育, 興行目的入國者)

$$\frac{4,403}{'85} \rightarrow \frac{9,334}{'90} \quad (112\% \uparrow)$$

  · 國內勤勞者 海外進出 激減

$$\frac{120,245}{'85} \rightarrow \frac{55,774}{'90} \quad (46\% \downarrow)$$

- 勞動力 進出의 주종이었던 建設分野의 海外進出이 激減하고 있으며, 國內에서도 人力供給이 不足한 狀態임.

- 勞動力 國際間 移動은 주로 高級專門人力과 單純人力部門에서 강하게 이루어지는데 우리나라의 경우 高級專門人力에 있어서 先進國에 비해 比較劣位에 있고, 單純人力에 있어서도 개도국에 비해 比較 劣位에 있음

0174

o   外國勞動力 流入의 경우, 經濟 및 社會一般에 廣範圍한 否定的 效果를
    若起할 可能性이 높음.

肯定的인面	否定的인面
o 短期的으로 勞動集約的 産業인 建設 등 …部業種의 單純人力 不足解消	o 國內勤勞者 失業問題 深化
o 海外進出에 必要한 先進技術, 知識 習得 및 人的資本 確保 容易	o 住宅, 醫療등 諸般社會 問題 若起
	o 經濟構造調整 및 企業의 生産性提高 沮害
o 國際間 理解增進 및 交流에 寄與	o 外國勤勞者의 低級한일에 從事할 경우 內國人의 勤勞觀 變化로 國家 將來 惡影響 招來

3. 對應 方案

가. 我國의 基本立場 整理

KEY - PERSONNEL 은 多者間 約束에 의하여 自由化하고

其他 範疇人力은 讓許協商에 의해 業種別로 勞動力 移動許容範圍 決定

니. 段階別 對應方案

o 勞動力移動附屬書(案) 對應

- 各國立場 把握 後 再檢討

- 勞動力移動에 대한 附屬書의 主要内容 및 各國 立場 : 별첨<1>참조

o 各 部處에서는 '91.2.22 旣 通報한 必須人力 移動許容範圍 豫示目錄을 參考하여 業種別로 範圍設定

- 豫示目錄以外의 職種 追加時는 法務部및 勞動部와 協議하여 決定

- UR 서비스協商關聯 人力移動許容範圍 設定 參考 資料 : 별첨<2>참조

0175

o 讓許協商 進行狀況 수시 把握하여 CASE -BY-CASE 별로 신속히 對處

< 별첨 1 >

勞動力移動에 대한 附屬書의 主要內容 및 各國 入場

附屬書의 內容	各國入場	勞動部 意見
제1조 (適用範圍) - 자연인의 일시적 이동에 적용	이견 없음	이견없음
제2조 (人力의 種類에 대한 目錄)		
(1안) 공통예시목록작성	- 개도국	
(2안) 공통예시목록은 불필요하며 각 체약국들이 상호교환한 인력의 종류를 바탕으로 양허협상 진행	- 미국, EC, 헝가리	각국간의 共通的인 基準 作成는 現實的으로 困難
제3조 (市場接近約束과의 一致) - 노동이동에 대한 시장접근 약속은 FRAMEWORK 제16조 (시장접근)와 일치 해야함	이견없음	이견없음
제4조 (勞動移動에 대한 自由化約束의 意味) - National Schedule 에 기록된 모든 인력의 서비스공급을 보장	이견없음	이견없음
제5조 (市場接近約束의 無效化 禁止)		
(1안) 노동력이동에 대한 시장접근약속 후 입국, 체류및노동허가등에 관한 국내 법및규제에의해서 무효화할수없음	- 개도국	FRAMEWORKT 상의 분쟁해결 절차 규정 (제23조)에 따라 재검토
(2안) 동조항 삭제	- 선진국	
제6조 (MFN 逸脫)	거주요건	별다른 문제점 없음 —?
(1안) 노동력이동에 대한 일탈허용	- 북구, 아세안	반대 입장.
(2안) 동조항 삭제	- 멕시코, 인도, 이집트	
제7조 (人力市場의 統合)		입장유보, 재검토 필요 —?
(1안) 인력시장의 통합에는 동부숙사 적용을 제외	- 북구, 아세안	삭제, (FTA.
(제2안) 동조항 삭제	- 멕시코, 인도, 이집트	

0176

< 별첨 2 >

UR서비스협상관련 인력이동허용범위 설정 참고 자료

Ⅰ. 배 경

ο UR/서비스협상의 양허협상에 대비, 국내에 상업적 주재를 하는 외국서비스
기업의 서비스공급에 필수적인 인력의 이동허용범위를 서비스업종별로
설정함에 참고토록 하기위하여 작성됨.

Ⅱ. 기본방향

ο 우리나라는 인력이동에 관하여, 국내노동시상의 여건과 전망, 노동력이동에
따른 사회적 측면에 대한 고려등으로 서비스업종별로 필수인력에 한해
제한적인 이동만을 허용해야 한다는 입장에 있음.

ο 서비스업종별 주무부처에서 제Ⅲ항의 필수(ESSNTIAL)인력 예시목록을 참고,
   당해 서비스업종에 필수적(KEY)인 인력의 허용범위를 설정.

   - 예시목록 이외의 직종추가는 업무무 및   설정.

   - 회계사등 전문가의 경우는 해당업종의   주무부처의
     신중한 검토 요망.

Ⅲ. 필수인력의 일반적 정의 및 예시목록

ο 일반적 정의

   국내에 상업적 주재를 한 외국서비스기업의 종사자로서 다음에서 정의하는
   관리자 또는 전문가에 해당하는 협정 체약국의 국민.

   - 관리자 : 주로 조직 및 그 하부조직의 목표와 활동을 계획·조직·지휘·
             감독 하는자로서 조직의 주요한 의사 결정을 하거나
             이에 참여하고, 다른 전문직·관리직 종사자들의 업무를 결정
             하고 이들을 지휘·감독하는 자.
             이에는 전문직이 아닌 종사자에 대한 일선관리자가 제외되고
             서비스의 생산에 필요한 업무를 주로 수행하는 자도 제외 됨.

   - 전문가 : 조직의 서비스·연구설비·기술·관리등에 관하여 고도의
             전문적·독점적 지식과 경험을 가진 자.

0177

관리 번호	91/506

외 무 부

종 별 :

번 호 : GVW-1374

일 시 : 91 0722 1730

수 신 : 장관(봉기, 경기원)

발 신 : 주 제네바 대사

제 목 : UR/서비스 협상(MFN)

대: WGV-0912

표제 협상 관련, 향후 서비스 협정 발효이후 아국과 북한과의 관계 증진시 봉일 추진의 준비작업으로서 서비스 분야에 특정 거래가 발생할 경우 MFN 문제가발생 가능한바 관련 문제점 및 대처 방안등 당관 검토 사항을 하기 보고함.

1. MFN 관련 발생가능 문제점

- 향후 북한과의 봉일 논의가 진전되어 서비스 분야의 교류가 증진될 경우 다음 사례에 대하여 MFN 적용이 문제될 가능성이 있음.

0 봉신 분야: 남. 북한간 기본 봉신망 연결을 위한 합작법인 설립등

0 해운 분야: GABOTAGE 허용 (원산에서 부산, 목표, 인처간등) 등

0 항공분야: SOFT RIGHTS 관련 각종 우대 협정

0 금융분야: 금융기관 본.지점 설치 자유화 등

0 AUDIO VISUAL 분야: 남. 북한 합작 방송국 설립등

2. MFN 적용 배제 방안

- 상기 사항에 대하여 법률적 차원에서 검토 가능한 MFN 배제 방안은 다음과 같음.

0 WAIVER 획득: 향후 1 항의 사례가 구체화 될 경우 체약국(부표수의 2/3 이상 및 체약국의 과반수)의 동의를 얻어 MFN 적용 의무 면제를 받을수 있으나 이에 대한 확실한 보장이 없을 뿐만 아니라 협정 발효이전에는 WAIVER 획득이 불가능함.

0 가입의정서(PROTOCOL OF ACCESSION)에 반영: 서비스 협정 발효이후에 아국이 동 협정에 가입 할 경우에는 아국의 가입 의정서에 남. 북한 봉일관련 활동에 대한 MFN 적용 배제 조건을 반영할수 있으나 아국이 동 협정의 원서명국이 될경우에는 불가능함. (원 서명국에게는 PROTOCOL OF APPLICATION 이 공봉 적용되므로 아국에만 특유한 사항 반영 불가. 다만, 논리적으로는 유보 또는 특별 선언등 형식으로

통상국 경기원	장관 농수부	차관	1차보	2차보	외정실	분석관	청와대	안기부

91.07.23   06:07

외신 2과 통제관 CH

0178

아국입장을 명시할수 있으나 타국으로 부터 상당한 이의 제기 예상)

0 FRAMEWORK 에 반영: 서비스 협정 제 2 조(MFN)에 대한 FOOTNOTE 는 제 14 조 (예외)에 반영(제 2 조에 대한 FOOTNOTE 방식의 경우 현재는 남. 북한 서비스교역 사례가 없으므로 미래의 불확실한 사항을 대상으로 한다는 문제점이 있음)

- 이외에 GNS 에서 공식적으로 문제를 제기하지 않고 향후 구체적 사례 발생시 남. 북한 교역을 국내 거래로 간주하는 종전 입장에 기초하여 당사국간 협의로 해결하는 방안도 선택 가능

3. 남. 북한 교역(쌀거래 포함)을 국내 거래로 간주하는 방침과의 관계 검토

- 상기 대안을 검토할때 법률적으로는 서비스 협정 자체에 MFN 예외를 반영하는 것이 바람직한 것으로 판단되나 남. 북 거래문제와 관련 다음과 같은 문제점이 있음.

0 남. 북한 직교역 문제에 대하여 아국은 "국내거래"로 간주하는 접근 방법을 취하면서 서비스 문제에 있어서는 국가간 서비스 거래임을 전제하고 이에 대한 MFN 예외를 주장함으로써 일관성을 상실하게 될 우려가 있음.

4. 종합검토 및 건의

- 따라서 GNS 에서 동 문제를 제기하여 반영될 경우 향후 관련 사항에 대한예외를 사전에 확보한다는 잇점이 있으나 여타 상품 교역과의 일관성 문제, 남.북한 직교역에 대한 여타 GATT 체약국의 주의 촉발 가능성도 수반될수 있는바 이에 대한 입장 검토 회시 바람.

0 GNS 에서 동 문제를 공식 제기하기로 결정할 경우에는 MFN 에 대한 논의가 본격화 될 9 월 GNS 회의에 이에 대한 서면 제안(1 PAGE 정도)또는 STATEMENT발표가 바람직한 것으로 판단됨.

- 또한 향후 발생 가능한 여러 사태에 대비하기 위하여 " 남. 북 교류 협력에 관한 법률"에 서비스 분야의 명시적 포함등 관련 조치의 검토도 필요한 것으로 판단됨. 끝

(대사 박수길-차관)

예고 91.12.31. 까지

외 무 부

원 본

종   별 :

번   호 : GVW-1375   일   시 : 91 0722 1730

수   신 : 장 관(통기, 경기원, 재무부, 법무부, 상공부, 건설부, 보사부, 노동부, 교통부,

발   신 : 주 제네바 대사   체신부, 문화부, 과기처, 공보처, 항만청)

제   목 : UR/GNS 회의(6)

7.19(금) 속개된 표제회의 내용을 하기 보고함.

1. 각국 OFFER 제안 설명

- 새로이 OFFER 를 제출한 유고 (GNS/W/121), 말련 (GNS/W/122), 베네주엘라 (GNS/W/123), 중국 (GNS/W/124), 알젠틴 (GNS/W/125) 로 부터 OFFER 제안 설명이 있었음. (현재까지 총29개국 제출)

2. SCHEDULING OF COMMITMENTS

- HAWES 대사가 그간의 협상 경과를 정리한 문서 (제 16조, 제 17조)를 배부하고다음과 같이 설명함. (동 사항은 최종 합의된 것이 아니기 때문에 추후 송부예정)

0 양적 규제는 차별조치든 무차별 조치든 16조 3항에 따라 TOP-DOWN 방식으로 시장 접근란에 기재함.

0 질적 규제중 차별 조치는 명목상의 차별조치든 사실상의 차별조치든 TOP-DOWN방식으로 17조에 따라 내국민 대우란에 기재됨.

0 질적 규제중 무차별 조치에 대하여는 아직 분명한 이해 및 가인드 라인이 없는 상태임.

- 다음주 (7.22주)에 SCHEDULING 에 관하여 계속협의를 개최할 예정임.

3. 노동력 이동

- JARAMILLO 의장은 사무국에서 재 작성한 노동력 이동 부속서 초안 (추후 송부예정)을 배부하고 다음주에 계속 협의하겠다고 함.

4. 양자협상의 실질적 기준

- JARAMILLO 의장은 동 사항은 제 4조, 18조, 19조와 함께 검토되어야 하나 이견 해소에 문제가 있다고 전제하고 다음주에 계속 협의 하겠다고함.

통상국	2차보	법무부	보사부	문화부	교통부	체신부	경기원	재무부
상공부	건설부	노동부	과기처	해항청	공보처			

PAGE 1   91.07.23   16:19 WI

외신 1과 통제관

0180

5. MFN

- JARAMILLO 의장은 자신이 제시한 MFN 관련 두가지 INFORMAL NOTE 의 성경을 재요약한 다음각국이 9월20일까지 MFN 예외를 원하는 사항에 대한 분명한 목록을 사무국에 제출해줄것 (보안 유지조건)을 요청함.

6. 다음주 회의 계획

- SCHEDULING OF COMMITMENT, 노동력 이동 부속서, 양허협상의 실질적 기준에 대하여 비공식 협의를 계속한 다음 7.25(목) 오후 GNS 공식 회의를 개최하여 논의를 종결할 예정임.

7. 9월회의 계획

- 9.17(화) 금융부속서

- 9.19(목): 봉신부속서

- 9.23.주간: 기타 협상의제.끝

(대사 박수길-국장)

외 무 부

종   별 :

번   호 : GVW-1417   일   시 : 91 0726 1500

수   신 : 장관(통기, 경기원, 재무부, 법무부, 상공부, 건설부, 보사부, 노동부, 교통부,

발   신 : 주 제네바 대사   체신부, 문화부, 과기처, 공보처, 항만청)

제   목 : UR 서비스 양자 협의

　　7.24(수)-25(목)간 개최된 일본, 북구, 캐나다, 호주, EC, 뉴질랜드와의 표제
협의 내용을 하기보고함.

　　1. 아국 OFFER 에 미반영 분야중 상대국이 관심을 표명한 분야

　　- 북구: 복합 운송

　　- 캐나다: CONSULTING ENGINEERING, GEOPHYSICAL CONSULTING, ENVIRONMENT
(WASTE MANAGENENT), FISHING MINING. FORESTRY

　　- EC: LEGAL SERVICES, REAL-ESTSTE, PRESS AND PUBLISHING, SURVEYING, URBAN
PLANNING, MEDICAL, MARKET RESEARCH (OPINIONPOLLING), BUILDING CLEANING, PUBLIC
RELATIONS, 귀중품운송 보안

　　- 뉴질랜드: AGRICULTURAL CONSULTANCY (기타 아국 OFFER 중 CONSULTING,
AUDIOVISUAL, ENGINEERING, ARCHITECTURE, 통신에 관심이 있다고 함)

　　2. 아국 OFFER 중 주요 관심사항

　　- 일본을 제외한 모든 나라가 엔지니어, 회계사등 외국 전문직업인의 자격
인정문제에 대하여 지대한 관심을 표명하였으며, 엔지니어링 서비스분야중
CROSS-BORDER SUPPLY 가 UNBOUND 된데 대하여 많은 질문을 제기함.

　　- 유통분야에 있어서 설립이 허용되는 도소매업의 범위와 설치 가능한 영업장 수(
캐나다)

　　- 시청각 서비스에 있어서 시장접근 및 내국민대우는 OFFER 내용에 불구하고 MFN이
적용될것이라고 지적하고 외국에서 제작된 광고물의 수입 추천에 객관적 기준이있는지
여부(일본)

　　- 금융 분야에 합작 부자, 자회사 등 외국인 부자허용 여부(북구)

　　- 특히 EC 는 집행위와 함께 참석한 회원국 (독일, 프랑스)이 다음과 같이 강한

통상국	2차보	법무부	보사부	문화부	교통부	체신부	경기원	재무부
상공부	건설부	노동부	과기처	해항청	공보처			

불만을 제기함.

0 한국 회사는 독일에서 자유롭게 영업하는 반면 한국의 규제제도는 지극히 엄격하여 자국회사가 많은 어려움을 겪고 있으며, 특히 'PATTERN OF PRACTICE' 가 없어 규제의 예측 가능성이 없음.KEY

- PERSONNEL 의 입국 및활동에도 많은제약이 있으며, 전 문직업인의 자격 인정이 이루어지지 않아 어려움이 많음.(독일)

0 금융분야 OFFER 주석에 ' 전통적 내국민 대우규정'과 자율 규제 단체에 대한 언급이 있는바 효과적 시장접근이 이루어져야 하며, FRAMEWORK 제1조상 정부 기능을 수행하는 민간 단체도 협정상의 의무가 적용되어야 함.

또한 실제적 문제점으로서 외국 금융기관나 (특히 보험회사)의 설립이 매우 어려움(프랑스)

- 또한 EC 집행위는 아국 OFFER 의 개정계획에 대하여 많은 관심을 표명함.

0 SECTORAL COVERAGE 확대

0 TRANSPARENCY 증대

0 자유화 약속의 증대0 OFFER 수정안의 구체적 제출일자 등

3. 노동력 이동

- 모든 상대국이 노동력 이동에 대하여 아국이 어떤접근 방법을 고려하고 있는지문의한바,

0 아국은 미국, 캐나다의 COMMON APPROACH 를 긍정적으로 검토하고 있으나 KEY PERSONNEL 에 대하여 MULTILATERAL COMMITMENT 를 하더라도 기타 범주의 인력에 대해서는 분야별로 국가간 양허 협상이 이루어져야 한다는 점을 강조함.

(캐나다의 접근 방법중 COMMITMENT 를 모든 서비스분야에 적용하는 문제, SERVICE SELLER 의 포함, 서비스 공급 기업내의 1년 이상 사전 고용조건, SPECIALIST 의 범위 및 정의등에 대하여는 유보의사 표명)

- 상대국들 역시 일본 (보다 보수적 입장)을 제외하고는 모두 미국, 캐나다의 접근 방법을 지지하고 있다고 밝혔으나

0 캐나다의 접근 방법과 관련 SERVICE SELLER 는 포함하는 입장이었으나 COMMITMENT 를 모든 서비스분야에 적용하는 것은 유보적 입장이었음.

0 다만, 호주는 KEY-PERSONNEL 을 대상으로 하더라도 SPECIALISTS 는 캐나다 보다 더 좁은 범위로 상정하고 있으며, COMMITMENT 도 다자간 방식은 국내 사정상

PAGE 2

0183

어려우며, 개별 방식이 될것이라고 함.

　　4. 양국 OFFER 에 대한 질의 답변

　　- 상세 내용 금 파편 송부 계획임.

　　- 일본, 북구, 호주 등으로 부터 서면 질의가 있을 예정인바, 입수 즉시 송부하겠음. 끝

　　(대사 박수길-국장)

PAGE 3

외 무 부

종 별 :

번 호 : GVW-1418

일 시 : 91 0726 1500

수 신 : 장관(통기, 경기원, 재무부, 법무부, 상공부, 건설부, 보사부, 노동부, 교통부,

발 신 : 주 제네바 대사 　　　　　　체신부, 문화부, 과기처, 공보처, 항만청)

제 목 : UR/GNS 회의(7)

7.25(목) 개최된 표제회의 결과를 하기 보고함.

1. SCHEDULING OF COMMITMENTS

- HAWES 대사가 주요국 비공식 협의를 거쳐 재작성된 시장 접근 (제 16조)과 내국민 대우 (제17조)에 관한 조문 초안 (별도 FAX 송부)을 배부하고 다음과 같이 설명함.

0 동 초안은 계속 보완이 필요한 상태이며, 어느국가도 기속하는 것이 아님.

0 의 장의 논평 (COMMENTARY) 부분은 7.19 자문서의 논평과 함께 읽어야 함

0 제 16조 3항은 각국의 OFFER, 실제 교역상의 사례등에서 추출된 시장접근에 대한 제안들을 포괄하기 위한 것이나 문안이 완전하지는 않으며 어떤 조치가 포함되는지 불분명한 부분이 있음.

0 16조 4항 역시 문제가 많은 부분이나 많은나라들이 제 17조가 효율적으로 규정되어 외국인이 불리한 사례가 잘 다루어진다면 16조 4항은 별로중요하지 않다는 의견 임.

0 제 17조의 실질적 문제는 오직 2항 B 의 존치여부임.

0 SCHEDULING 에 관한 작업이 아직 미결 상태이나 현재 초안을 기초로 각국이 OFFER 를 개정할수있을 것임.

- 홍콩은 17조 주석의 분쟁해결시 패널에 통계자료를 제출할수 있다는 부분에 대하여 본래 어느나라든 관련 자료를 제출하는 것은 자유이므로 동 주석이 불 필요하다고 하는 한편

0 16조 3항 C 의 상업적 주재 형태의 제한에 대하여 국내 규제목적상 내,외국인 공히 지사는 허용하면서 자회사는 금지하거나 또는 그 반대의 경우 관련 시장 접근 조치로 볼 것인지 의문을 제기함.

통상국 상공부	2차보 건설부	법무부 노동부	보사부 과기처	문화부 해항청	교통부 공보처	체신부	경기원	재무부

PAGE 1

91.07.27　　08:44 WG

외신 1과 통제관

0185

2. 노동력 이동

- GNS 의장이 새로운 부속서 초안 (별도 FAX송부)을 배부하였으며, 논평국가 없었음 (동초안은 합의된 것이 아니며 하기 휴가이후 계속 논의 대상임)

3. MFN

- 의장은 MFN 일탈 방법으로서 GRANDFATHERING, 단자간 공통적 예외 허용등의 방법이 있음을 언급하고 무역에 미치는 영향을 최소화 하는 가운데 법률적 관점에서 이를 처리할 공통 구조를 마련하기 위하여 MFN 일탈을 원하는 분야가있는 국가는 다음 사항에 대한 자료를 9.20까지 사무국에 제출 할 것을 요청함.

  0 MFN 예외를 원하는 서비스 분야 (예: AUDIOVISUAL, 운송)
  0 MFN 예외를 원하는 ACTIVITIES (예:PRODUCTION)
  0 MFN 예외을 원하는 MEASURES (예: 영화공동 생산 협정)
  0 국가간 협정에 따라 발생하는 MFN위배조치의 범위를 당해국 국내 법규에 따라 규정하도록 할 것인지 여부
  0 MFN 예외대상을 현존 조치에 한할 것인지 미래의 조치까지 포함할 것인지
  0 현존 조치의 유효기간등

4. 양허 협상의 실질적 기준

- 의장은 상기 사항에 대한 합의가 없음을 밝히고 다만 제 18조 (양허 협상)의 개정초안 (합의된 것은 아님)을 배부함.

  0 의장은 7.30 TNC 이전 까지 계속 협의하여 동 TNC 에 보다 긍정적인 보고를 할수 있도록 노력하겠다고 함.

5. 향후 협상일정

가. 차기 회의

- 9.17: 해운
- 9.19: 통신부속서
- 9.20: 금융 부속서
- 9.23 주간

0 양허 협상의 실질적 기준 (4조, 18조 포함:최우선적으로 다룸)
0 SCHEDULING (6 조, 7조, 14조, 16조, 17조, 18조, 19조,20조)
0 MFN
0 기타 조문(5조, 12조, 23조, 34조 등)

PAGE 2

0186

0 노동력 이동 부속서 (1조 포함)

0 INITIAL COMMITMENT 에 관한 추가 작업

나. 9월 이후 회의 일정 : 10.21-11.1

- 11.8 - 11.26

- 12.9 주간

다. 기타

- 북구는 해운 분야 관련 다음 사항에 대하여 공통으로 자유화 하는 APPROACH 에 관한 제안을 다음주에 제출 예정이며 9.17 회의에서 논의되기를 바란다고 하는 한편 서비스 분야 분류표중 해운분야의 세분화를 사무국에 요청함.

0 동결 및 일정 기간내의 제한 조치 철폐 약속 ✓

0 CABOTAGE 의 포함

0 기타 해운 서비스의 BINDING COMMITMENT

0 서비스의 사용 및 접근에 관한 공통 약속

- 북구 제안에 대하여 EC, 폴란드, 일본, 캐나다, 유고등이 지지의사를 표명한 반면, 인도, 이집트, 말련등이 반대입장을 견지함.

- 또한 캐나다는 10월 회의에서 원산지 규정에대한 논의가 있어야 한다고 전제하고 사무국에 배경문서 작성을 요청하여 동 문서 작성에 합의함.

- 코스타리카, 우루과이, 페루 등이 OFFER 를 제출함으로써 총 32개국이 OFFER를 제출하게됨.

0 구체적 OFFER 를 제출한 국가 (28개국): 스위스, 미국, 일본, EC, 호주, 뉴질랜드, 홍콩, 캐나다, 스웨덴, 아국, 노르웨이, 핀란드, 싱가폴, 인도네시아, 터키, 멕시코, 오지리, 콜롬비아, 아이슬랜드, 칠레, 브라질, 유고, 말레이지아, 중국, 알젠틴, 폴란드, 우루과이, 페루

0 일부 분야에 대한 동결 약속만 제시한국가 (4개국): 첵코, 루마니아, 베네주엘라, 코스타리카

- 한편 7.30 TNC 회의와 관련 의장은 개인자격으로 GNS 협상 진행 상태에 대하여 보고하겠다고 함.

첨부: 1. 시장접근 및 내국민 대우 조문 초안 1부

2. 노동력 이동 부속서 초안 1부

3. 제 18조 조문 초안 1부. 끝

PAGE 3

0187

(GVW(F)-277)
(대사 박수길-국장)

0188

*Gvwch)-02 77 1072615*0*

Gvw-14l8 전부

25.7.91

COMMENTARY

Status of Work on Market Access
and National Treatment:
Implications for Scheduling

1.   While the attached texts on Market Access (Articles XVI) and National
Treatment (Article XVII) are still under discussion, consultations to date
indicate that participants broadly agree that if a country places
limitations on market access and national treatment in sectors or
sub-sectors where commitments are being undertaken, the following types of
measures will have to be scheduled in a top-down manner:

- quantitative restrictions of both a discriminatory and
  non-discriminatory kind which are specified in Article XVI:3, and

- discriminatory measures of a formal and also a de facto kind
  which are covered by Article XVII, paras. 1 and 2.

2.   What is less clear is how to treat qualitative measures of a
non-discriminatory character, in particular, those relating to
qualifications, standards and licensing requirements which in the current
draft are specified in Article XVI:4. Further commentary is set out below
in paragraphs 5 and 6.

Article XVI

3.   Article XVI:3 has been developed as a means of identifying those
quantitative restrictions, whether discriminatory or non-discriminatory,
which constitute limitations on market access. While the language may need
further refinement, the aim has been to try and capture all of the
examples, brought to light in discussions thus far of instances where

12—1

K-HAW   0189

- 2 -

quantitative measures of one kind or another would constitute limitations
on access.

4.   The reference to "limitations on the form of commercial presence"
contained in Article XVI:3 sub-paragraph (c) will require further
consideration. In essence, however, it is an initial attempt to address
those situations in which requirements concerning joint venture operations
or limitations on the form of foreign participation (e.g. specification of
maximum percentage limits on foreign shareholding) would also constitute
market access limitations.

5.   As regards the qualitative, non-discriminatory measures relating to
technical standards, licensing and professional qualifications
requirements, it seems accepted that a top-down scheduling of these
measures could not take place in the absence of clear definitions of the
criteria in Article XVI:4. Nonetheless, discussions suggest that
participants would wish that any approach which is developed to handle such
measures should be consistent with certain principles and objectives:

    -    that such measures should not be allowed to frustrate commitments
         on market access and national treatment;

    -    that they should be administered in a reasonable, objective and
         impartial manner;

    -    that participants should not be prevented from negotiating
         commitments in respect of such measures;

    -    that in any sector or sub-sector where market access commitments
         are undertaken, relevant regulatory information concerning
         measures under Article XVI:4 should be identified for the
         purposes of transparency.

6.   Against this background, the following operational considerations seem
to be relevant:

K-HAW 0190

12—2

- 3 -

- the non-frustration provision in paragraph 5 could be moved to Article VI, some participants consider that it should be a general obligation;

- options regarding the negotiation of commitments on these measures seem to be:

   (a) to leave paragraph 4 of Article XVI where it is and adjust the language to reflect a bottom-up scheduling approach; or

   (b) to provide for the negotiation of such commitments under Article XVIII;

- the specification of relevant regulatory information for transparency purposes could be done through an additional column in the schedule of a non-binding character, or through developing a separate mechanism. In this regard, it will be important to strike a balance between the need to provide adequate information and the need to avoid repetitive listings of large tracts of regulatory information;

- the content of Article XVI:6 relating to the development of disciplines in the areas of qualification requirements, technical standards and licensing based on the criteria referred to in paragraph 3 could be moved to Article VI. In any event, further consideration will have to be given to Article VI itself.

Article XVII

7. In respect of this Article, it would appear that the main substantive issue refers to the need to maintain paragraph 2(b). The debate continues to focus on the different views set out in the commentary attached to the text dated 19 July 1991.

12—3

K-HAW 0191

25.7.91

Article XVI

MARKET ACCESS

1.   With respect to market access through the modes of supply identified in Article I, each Party shall accord services and service providers of other Parties treatment no less favourable than that provided for under the terms, limitations and conditions agreed and specified in its schedule.

2.   In sectors or sub-sectors where a Party undertakes market access commitments with respect to more than one mode of supply, service providers of other Parties shall be free to choose their preferred mode.

3.   In sectors or sub-sectors where market access commitments are undertaken, and unless otherwise specified in its schedule, a Party shall not maintain any of the following measures either on the basis of a regional sub-division or on the basis of its entire territory:

   (a)   limitations on the number of service providers whether in the form of numerical quotas, monopolies, exclusive service providers or the requirement of an economic needs test;

   (b)   limitations on the total value of services transactions or assets in the form of numerical quotas or the requirement of an economic needs test;

   (c)   limitations on the form of commercial presence;

   (d)   limitations on the total number of service operations or on the total quantity of service output expressed in terms of designated numerical units in the form of quotas or the requirement of an economic needs test*;

----

   *Limitations on the hours of operation or sales floor area need not be scheduled.

F-HAW 0192

- 2 -

(e) limitations on the total number of natural persons necessary for and directly related to the supply of a services in the form of numerical quotas or the requirement of an economic needs test.

4. In sectors or sub-sectors where market access commitments are undertaken, and unless otherwise specified in a Party's schedule, all measures relating to qualification requirements, technical standards and licensing requirements should:

   (a) be based on objective criteria;

   (b) not be more burdensome than necessary;

   (c) not in themselves constitute restrictions on the supply of services.

5. In services or sub-sectors where specific commitments are undertaken, a Party shall administer all measures in a reasonable, objective and an impartial manner.

6. The PARTIES shall, through appropriate bodies that they may establish, develop the necessary disciplines to ensure that qualification requirements, technical standards and licensing requirements shall conform with (a), (b) and (c) of paragraph 4.

F-HAW 0193

25.7.91

Article XVII

NATIONAL TREATMENT

1.   Where a sector or sub-sector is inscribed in its schedule, and subject to any conditions and qualifications as are set out therein, each Party shall accord to services and service providers of other Parties, in respect of all measures affecting the supply of services, treatment no less favourable than that it accords to its own like services and service providers.*

2.   When a measure of a Party accords formally identical treatment to the services or service providers of other Parties it shall nevertheless be considered to be less favourable within the meaning of paragraph 1 if:

    (a) the measure modifies the conditions of competition
         significantly in favour of its own like services or service
         providers;**   and

    (b) a less trade distortive measure is reasonably available [to
         achieve the policy objective].

Interpretative notes:

*   Regarding paragraph 1, a Party may accord no less favourable treatment to the services and service providers of other Parties through the application of the same measures as are applied to its own services and service providers, or through different measures as long as they provide equivalent treatment.

[Note: This paragraph could provide useful bridging text between existing paragraphs 1 and 2 above.]

/2-6   I-HAW   0194

- 2 -

** The application of paragraph 2 (a):

- shall not be based on economic performance in the relevant market, including market share achieved;

- shall not prevent a Party from submitting statistics and other relevant factual data for the consideration of a panel;

- shall not be construed to require a Party to eliminate competitive disadvantages that result from the foreign character or origin of the relevant services or service providers.

25.7.91

<u>ANNEX ON MOVEMENT OF NATURAL PERSONS
PROVIDING SERVICES UNDER THE AGREEMENT</u>

1.   The Agreement applies to the entry and temporary stay of natural persons
who are service providers of a Party, or who are employed by a service
provider of a Party, in respect of the delivery of a service for which
specific commitments relating to such entry and temporary stay have been
undertaken.

2.   The Agreement shall not apply to natural persons seeking access to the
employment market of a Party, nor shall it apply to measures regarding
citizenship, residence or employment on a permanent basis. Furthermore,
nothing in the Agreement shall prevent a Party from applying measures
regarding entry [and stay] [, stay and work] on a temporary basis
[, including those] necessary to protect the integrity of, and to ensure the
orderly movement of natural persons across, its borders.

[3. An illustrative list of natural persons performing particular services
covering broad categories of sectors and skill levels is attached to this
Annex.]

[4. In the application of Article III of the Agreement, Parties shall ensure
that relevant information on the procedure and regulations concerning the
granting of entry for temporary stay [, labour laws and professional
qualifications, including those imposed by non-governmental entities,] is
made publicly available.]

5.   In accordance with Parts III and IV of the Agreement Parties may
negotiate specific commitments applying to the temporary movement of natural
persons providing specified services [drawing on the illustrative list as a
reference point].

6.   Natural persons covered by a specific commitment shall be allowed to
provide the service in accordance with the terms of that commitment. Parties

12—8

0196
LAB4-LAB

- 2 -

shall apply their laws and regulations to entry, stay and work on a temporary basis of natural persons, in a manner as not to nullify or impair the benefits accruing to any Party under the terms of any such specific commitment.

[7. A Party may require that measures relating to all working conditions and relevant domestic regulations, applicable at the national or sub-national level to the provision of a service in its territory, [whether based on laws or collective agreements,] are respected by natural persons providing services under the Agreement.]

[8. Nothing in the Agreement or its annexes shall be construed as permitting the temporary movement of natural persons performing particular services in respect of which access commitments have been undertaken where the intent or effect of such movement is to interfere with or otherwise affect the outcome of any labour/management dispute or negotiation.]

It is recognised that the concerns reflected in the following paragraphs should be considered further in the discussions of Articles II, V and XIV of the framework.

[9. Notwithstanding Article II of the Agreement, Parties may undertake bilateral or plurilateral arrangements providing for preferential movement of natural persons with other countries, and may impose conditions and limitations on such movement. In applying such arrangements or in imposing such conditions and limitations, Parties shall endeavour to act in the least restrictive manner possible with respect to foreign providers of services.]

[9. Any agreements or arrangements providing for preferential conditions for the temporary movement of natural persons from the other countries party to, or benefiting from, such agreements or arrangements shall not be considered to be in conflict with the provisions of Article II of the Agreement. Parties shall ensure however that such agreements or arrangements shall not nullify or impair specific commitments regarding the movement of natural persons from other parties.]

0197

LAB4-LAB

- 3 -

[10. It is understood that nothing in the Agreement shall be construed to prevent agreements or arrangements the effect of which is the substantial integration of labour markets.]

It is recognised that the concerns reflected in the following paragraph should be considered further in the discussion of Article XXIII of the framework.

[11. A Party may not invoke the provisions of Article XXIII with respect to the denial or the revocation of an authorization for temporary entry of a natural person subject to a specific commitment unless:

(a)   the rules being applied as a pattern of practice for the denial or revocation do not conform to the commitment undertaken;   and

(b)   available local remedies have been exhausted.]

Note:

-   The following text which has been proposed for paragraph 1 may require further consideration (proposed changes are indicated in bold type):

"1.   The Agreement applies to the entry and temporary stay of natural persons who are service providers of a Party, or **natural persons of a Party** employed by a service provider of a Party, in respect of the delivery of a service for which specific commitments relating to such entry and temporary stay have been undertaken."

12 — 10

LAB4-LAB

0198

25.7.91

Article XVIII

Negotiation of Commitments

1.   In pursuance of the objectives of this Agreement, Parties shall enter into successive rounds of negotiations, beginning not later than ... from the date of entry into force of this Agreement and periodically thereafter, with a view to achieving a progressively higher level of liberalization. Such negotiations shall be directed to the reduction or elimination of the adverse effects on trade in services of measures as a means of providing effective market access. This process shall take place with a view to promoting the interests of all participants on a mutually advantageous basis and to securing an overall balance of rights and obligations. [A least developed Party shall benefit from the extension of all concessions exchanged under this Agreement.]

2.   The process of liberalization shall take place with due respect for national policy objectives and the level of development of individual Parties, both overall and in individual sectors. There shall be appropriate flexibility for individual developing countries for opening fewer sectors, liberalizing fewer types of transactions, progressively extending market access in line with their development situation and, when making access to their markets available to foreign service providers, attaching to it conditions aimed at achieving the objectives referred to in Article IV.

3.   For each round, negotiating guidelines and procedures shall be established. [As part of this process][For the purposes of establishing such guidelines], the PARTIES shall carry out an assessment of international trade in services in overall terms and on a sectoral basis with reference to the objectives of the Agreement, including those set out in Article IV:1. Negotiating guidelines shall establish modalities for the treatment of liberalization undertaken autonomously by Parties since previous negotiations, as well as for the [special] treatment of the least-developed [and developing] countries under the provisions of Article IV[:3].

4.   The process of progressive liberalization shall be advanced in each such round through bilateral, plurilateral or multilateral negotiations directed towards increasing the general level of bindings assumed by Parties with respect to the specific commitments under Part III of this Agreement. Such negotiations shall take place among Parties on the following:

(a)   new market access commitments with respect to unbound sectors, sub-sectors or modes of delivery through binding levels of market access;

(b)   new national treatment commitments with respect to unbound sectors, sub-sectors or modes of delivery;

(c)   total or partial elimination of any limitations and/or conditions on market access in bound sectors, sub-sectors or modes of delivery;

12 — 11

XVIII-ART   0199

- 2 -

(d) total or partial elimination of any conditions and/or qualifications on national treatment in bound sectors, sub-sectors or modes of delivery;

[(e) upon request, additional commitments to provide market access through the modification or elimination of measures which restrict the range of activities or otherwise deny service providers of other Parties competitive opportunities on the market of the Party concerned equal to those of its own providers.]

[(e) upon request, additional commitments regarding measures not falling within the scope of Articles XVI:3 or XVII.]

0200

12-12

XVIII-ART

TOTAL P.07

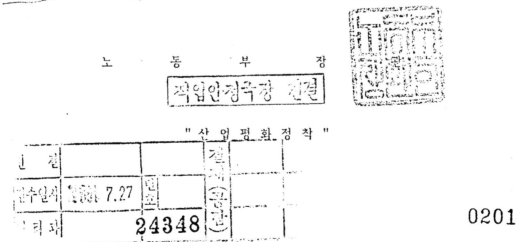

"노 사 관 계 안 정 "

노   동   부

해고 32481-/0 ∂/2   503-9750   1991. 7. 26.

수신 외무부장관

참조 통상국장

제목 UR 서비스협상 관련 노동력이동 범위통보

1. GVW-1201(91.6.27) 및 고관 32402-14532(90.10.18)의 관련입니다.

2. 노동력이동 자유화 추진방법에 대한 주 제네바대표부의 건의사항에 대하여 다음과 같이 당부입장을 통보하오니 동 대표부에 훈령 시달하여 주시기 바랍니다.

가. 노동력이동 (특히 외국근로자 수입) 문제는 이미 통보한바와 같이 사회,문화적으로 부정적 측면이 심각하고 국내노동력도 총량적으로는 부족한 상태가 아니므로 내국인으로 대체 불가능한 전문인력 등 특수분야를 제외하고는 반대하는 것이 정부의 기본입장임.

나. 따라서 노동력이동 허용범위는 Key-Personnel (Managers, Executives, Specialists)에 한하여 다자간 약속으로 자유화하고 기타 범주인력은 양허협상에 의해 업종별로 노동력이동 허용범위를 결정하도록 추진하여야 할것임. 끝.

노   동   부   장

"산 업 평 화 정 착 "

7.27   24348

0201

"노사관계안정"

노 동 부

해고 32480-10916   503-9750   1991. 7. 27.

수신 수신처참조

제목 UR/서비스협상관련 노동력 이동분야 책임자 교체통보

1. 통조삼 10502-208(91.3.25)의 관련입니다.

2. 우리부 사무분장 조정에 따라 UR/서비스 협상에 대비한 노동력
이동분야 양허협상 책임자가 다음과 같이 변경되었음을 알려드립니다.

구 분	변 경 전	변 경 후
담당부서 책임자	직업안정국 고용관리과	직업안정국 해외고용과
	과 장 김 영 갑	과 장 신 재 면
(전화 번호)		503-9750-1, 500-5579,80

* 자문관은 변동없음.   끝.

노 동 부 장

수신처 : 경제기획원장관,외무부장관,법무부장관

"산 입 정 화 정 착"

24566

0202

외 무 부

종 별 :

번 호 : GVW-1439   일 시 : 91 0729 1800

수 신 : 장관(통기, 경기원, 재무부, 법무부, 상공부, 건설부, 보사부,

발 신 : 주 제네바 대사   노동부, 교통부, 체신부, 문화부, 과기처, 공보처, 항만청)

제 목 : UR/ 아국 서비스 OFFER 관련 질의서 송부

　　7.24-25 간 개최된 양자 협의 관련 일본 및 스웨덴이 당관에 송부하여온 표제 관련
질의서를 별첨과 같이 송부하니 검토후 아국 입장회시 바람.

　　첨부: 1. 일본 질의서 1부.

　　　　 2. 스웨덴 질의서 1부. 끝

　　(GVW(F)-281)

　　(대사 박수길-국장)

통상국	2차보	법무부	보사부	문화부	교통부	체신부	경기원	재무부
상공부	건설부	노동부	과기처	해항청	공보처			

PAGE 1   91.07.30   07:50 DF

외신 1과 통제관

0203

GVW(기)-0281 1092p1800
Gw-143f 참조

GNS (Bilateral clarification on voluntary offers)

Questions for Korea

I. General

1. Commercial presence

(1) Concerning restrictions on foreign direct
investments which will remain after 1992, what
are the exact items and how do they match up with
the "Exceptions" under the current version of
Article XIV ?

(2) Are restrictions on "monopolistic or predatory
practices" under the Foreign Capital Inducement
Act necessary if injunctions and remedies are
available under anti-monopoly and other laws
regulating unfair trade practices?
Will the terms and conditions differ between the
two legal régimes (i.e. foreign capital and
antimonopoly et al)?

(3) Foreign Exchange Control
What are "certain services by domestic residents
requiring payment of foreign exchange" whose
contracts require approval? What is the reason
for this? Does the Republic of Korea still maintain
foreign exchange controls for balance of payment
reasons?

8 — 1

0204

- 2 -

II. Specific sectors

1. Audio-Visual Services

(1) What is the practical significance of binding oneself to "No conditions or qualifications on national treatment on cross-border supply if market access is unbound on this mode of delivery ?

(2) What is the legal status of "... guidelines for Foreign Investment" ?

(3) Is the note on foreign motion pictures, etc. part of the offer or just a statement of fact?

(4) Concerning your statement that there will be no limit to the number of foreign motion pictures after 1993, will this be applied in a non-discriminatory manner, i.e. with no derogations from the MFN clause?

2. Business Services

(1) Concerning advertising

(i) what are the criteria for the "letter of recommendation"?

(ii) What is the purpose of a 1% national shareholding requirement?

(iii) What is the legal status of the Newspaper Advertising Council of the Korea Newspaper Publishers Association and its "Rules"?

0205

- 3 -

(2) Concerning engineering services, are there approval processes and criteria for registration under the Engineering Services Promotion Law? If so, what are they?

(3) Concerning computer-related services, how are the "limitations, conditions and qualifications" applied? We would appreciate similar information on other sectors where there are no limitations, conditions or qualifications on market access or national treatment, if time allows.

(4) Is it possible to make an offer on leasing ?

3. Telecommunications services

(1) Does Computer communication services include media conversion services (for example, conversion from data to facsimile)?

(2) In which service is packet switched service without protocol conversion included ?

(3) What is the meaning of "less than 50% foreign equity"? Does it only mean direct investment or does it include both direct and indirect (through subsidiaries) investment ?

0206

8—3

- 4 -

4.   Construction Services

Why is the market access commitment "unbound"
for cross-border supply in the sub-sectors of
"engineering service", "engineering design",
"project management", "general construction" and
"special construction" services, while in
"architectural services" it is inscribed as
"registration required". ?

5.   Transportation services, Bus, Taxi and Railway,
in particular;

(1)   What kind of requirements should applicants meet
in order to get a license with regard to these
modes of transport (eg. an economic needs test,
safety standard, financial requirement, etc.)?

(2)   Does Korea envisage putting these (sub) sectors
on its initial offer list in the future? If not,
please give us the reason for it.

6.   Distribution Service

(1)   Why are "books and newspapers, brokers-chain market,
general foreign trade, foreign trade brokers"
excluded for the offer on "wholesale"?

8 ~4

0207

- 5 -

(2) Why are "antiques and art, cosmetics, books, oil
     service stations, gas service stations, coal
     briquettes, fuel oil, bottled gas" excluded from
     your offer on "retail"?

(3) Could you provide more details on regulations
     for retail stores whose "floor area ... is not
     less than 700m^2 ... subject to approval under
     individual law"?

(4) Could you provide more information on regulation
     for "import distribution of motion pictures"?

7. Engineering Service
    Why is "engineering" unbound for cross-border
    delivery ?

8. Financial Service
    Is it possible to make an offer on sales credit?

0208

Swedish Mission   July 24, 1991
Geneva

GATT/UR CONSULTATIONS ON TRADE IN SERVICES:

QUESTIONS ON TELECOMMUNICATIONS SERVICES FROM THE NORDIC
COUNTRIES

Satellite communications

1. Is two-way satellite communications permitted?

    a. If so, is cross-border communications permitted?

    b. Or only communications within the national
    territory?

    c. Are there any licencing/authorization
    requirements or other conditions that have to be
    fulfilled?

2. Is one-way satellite communication permitted?

    a. If so, is reception permitted?

    b. Or sending?

    c. Is cross-border traffic permitted?

    d. Or only traffic within the national territory?

    e. Are there any licencing/authorization
    requirements or other conditions that have to be
    fulfilled?

Private leased lines

1. Is it permitted to lease lines for private use?

    a. For communications within the national territory?

    b. For cross-border communications?

    c. For communications between which type of users?

    d. For communications between which type of
    companies?

8-6   0209

e. Do the companies have to be related/affiliated?
If so, how do you define the affiliation required?

f. Are there any licencing or authorization
requirements or other conditions that have to be
fulfilled to qualify for (a)-(e)?

2. If leased lines are permitted:

a. Is it permitted to connect a leased line with
the public switched network?

b. On what conditions (if any)?

c. For which type of users or companies?

d. Which entity in your country decides/determines
the conditions?

e. For what purposes can leased lines be obtained?

f. Which entity in your country decides/determines
what purposes are permitted?

g. Is that entity a monopoly holder?

h. Are the conditions transparent?

i. Are they publicly available?

j. Are they transparent or do they vary on a
case-by-case basis?

k. Does your country permit "shared use"? If so,
can two un-related companies share a leased line?

3. Are "closed user groups" permitted in your country?

a. If so, is there a maximum limit for how many
users may share the same leased line?

b. Is it permitted for a closed user group to
perform its own switching?

4. Can leased lines be used for the supply of data base
services?

a. Into your country? To specific clients? To the
public generally?

b. Are there conditions that have to be fulfilled?

0210

8-7

Definition of "value added"/"enhanced" services

1. Does your country have a definition of "value added"/"enhanced" services?

    a. If so, how is that definition expressed? In monetary terms, as value-added calculations, technical specifications, other-form?

    b. Where (how) does your country draw the line between "value added"/"enhanced" services and other services? Other telecommunications services? Other services outside the telecommunications sector?

Telecommunications services/equipment?

1. Is equipment that is permitted to connect to the public switched network in your country considered as part of the network or is it considered to constitute a service? (Example: a telefax machine connected to the network - is it considered to be a service?)

2. What equipment can be connected to the public switched network?

3. What equipment cannot be connected to the public switched network?

4. Where (how) does your country draw the line between the network and a service? Network with or without any connected equipment?

Private networks

1. Can any user (any company) establish a private network?

    a. If so, within the company area/building?

    b. Outside the company area/building?

    c. Cross-border?

2. Is such a network "operator" permitted to perform its own switching?

0211

8 ← 8

공 란

공   란

공   란

공 란

공   란

공　　　　　란

공 란

경 제 기 획 원

통조삼 10502- ⁵⁹│   503-9149   1991. 8. 23.

수신 외무부장관 (통상국장)

제목 주제네바대표부 경제협력관의 일시귀국 협조요청

　주제네바대표부 이종화 경제협력관을 다음과 같이 일시귀국시키고자
하니 협조하여 주시기 바랍니다.

다   음

가. 기간: '91.8.29-9.5 (7박 8일)

나. 사유

－ UR/서비스협상과 관련하여 아국은 '91.1월 GATT사무국에 제출한
　Offer List의 수정작업을 하고 있는바 동 수정작업에 직접 참여

－ 9월중순부터 본격화될 분야별 UR협상의 동향 및 향후 전망과
　주요국협상전략등에 대하여 동 기간중 개최예정인 UR대책 실무
　위원회에 참석 직접 설명토록하여 협상대책의 수립.추진에 협조

끝.

경 제 기 획 원 장

28279   0219

경 제 기 획 원

봉조삼 10502- 528   503-9149   1991. 8. 5.

수신 수신처참조

재목 UR대책 실무위원회 결과봉보

'91.8.2일 개최된 UR대책 실무위원회의에서 결정된 사항을 별첨과 같이 봉보하니 각부처(기관)는 서비스협상대책 추진에 만전을 기해 주시기 바라며 협상대책 작성에 필요한 자료를 기일엄수 제출해 주시기 바랍니다.

별첨: 1. UR/서비스협상 동향과 대응방안, 노동력이동에 대한 협상대책
          (회의자료) 각1부. 〈기송부〉.

       2. UR대책 실무위원회(서비스분야) 회의결과 1부.

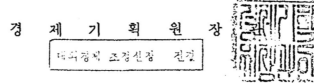

경 제 기 획 원 장

수신처: 외무부장관, 내무부장관, 재무부장관, 법무부장관, 교육부장관,
        문화부장관, 상공부장관, 건설부장관, 보사부장관, 노동부장관,
        교통부장관, 체신부장관, 과학기술처장관, 환경처장관, 공보처장관,
        특허청장, 항만청장, 대외경제정책연구원장, 한국개발연구원장,
        대한무역진흥공사장, 김&장법률사무소장.

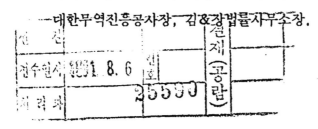

0220

UR對策實務委員會(서비스分野) 會議結果

Ⅰ. 會議槪要

- 日　　時: ʼ91.8.2,　15:00-16:00

- 場　　所: 과천 정부종합청사 1동 721호 (EPB 소회의실)

- 參席者: 經濟企劃院　對外經濟調整室長(회의주재)

　　　　　　　"　　　　第二協力官

　　　　　　　"　　　　通商調整3課長

　　　　外　務　部　通商局長

　　　　法　務　部　滯留審査課長

　　　　財　務　部　國際金融局長

　　　　商　工　部　國際協力擔當官

　　　　建　設　部　海外建設課長

　　　　保　社　部　國際協力課長

　　　　文　化　部　映畫振興課長

　　　　勞　動　部　雇傭管理課長

　　　　交　通　部　國際協力課長

　　　　遞　信　部　通信協力課長

　　　　科學技術處　技術用役課長

- 會議議題

　○ UR/서비스協商 動向 및 對應方案 (경제기획원 보고)

　○ 勞動力移動分野 協商對策 (노동부 보고)

0221

Ⅱ. 議決事項

1. 서비스協商 對策마련을 위한 作業推進日程을 다음과 같이 결정 추진토록 함.

作業推進課題	所管部處	日 程
① 우리 讓許表의 修正.補完作業		
- 所管業種別 各種規制制度를 EPB에 提出	각부처	~8.16
- 讓許表作成 方式에 대한 實務者 會議開催	E P B	8.20
- 各業種別 讓許表 修正試案作成	각부처	8.16~8.31
- 各業種別 讓許表에 대한 綜合檢討	E P B	9. 5~9.13
② 讓許協商對策 推進		
- 各業種別 讓許表에 대한 說明資料 補完 內容을 EPB에 提出	각부처	~9.15
- 國家別.業種別 Request List를 EPB 에 提出 (GATT에 제출시한: 9.20)	각부처	~9. 5
③ MFN逸脫에 대한 我國立場整理		
- MFN逸脫要請事項을 EPB에 提出	각부처	~8.31
- UR對策 서비스實務小委員會 開催	E P B	~9. 5

0222

作業推進課題	所管部處	日 程
④ Framework 및 分野別 附屬書協商 　對策推進		
- 各業種別 勞動力移動 許容範圍을 　勞動部, 法務部 및 EPB에 提出	각부처	~9.15
- 讓許表作成方式에 대한 我國立場 　整理	E P B	~9.15
- 分野別 附屬書協商에 참여 　○ 海運(91.7), 通信(9.19), 　　金融(9.20)	각부처	~12월

2. 勞動力移動에 대한 基本立場의 定立

- 基本人力(manager, executive, specialist등)은 多者間 約束에
  의해서 自由化하고 其他 範圍의 人力은 讓許協商에 의해서
  업종별로 移動許容範圍를 결정

- 다만 建設서비스輸出에 필요한 熟練技能人力을 다른 서비스
  분야에 영향을 주지 않고 多者間 約束을 하는 것이 가능한지
  에 대해서 建設部, 勞動部등 關係部處間에 別途檢討

0223

외 무 부

종 별 :

번 호 : GVW-1504

일 시 : 91 0809 1800

수 신 : 장관(봉기,경기원,재무부,법무부,상공부,건설부,보사부,노동부,교통부,

발 신 : 주 제네바 대사   체신부,문화부,과기처,공보처,항만청)

제 목 : UR/ 서비스 아국 OFFER 관련 질의서 송부

연: GVW-1417

연호 7.24-25간 개최된 UR/ 서비스 양자협의관련 호주가 당관에 보내온 표제 질의서를 별첨송부하니 서면 답변 작성, 기발간된 관련 자료제공, 차기 협의시 구두답변등 사안별로 적의준비바람.

첨부: 호주 질의서 1부(GVW(F)-0293). 끝

(대사 박수길-국장)

통상국	2차보	법무부	보사부	문화부	교통부	체신부	경기원	재무부
상공부	건설부	노동부	과기처	해항청	공보처			

PAGE 1

91.08.10   09:01 WG

외신 1과 통제관

0224

Australian Permanent Mission to the
General Agreement on Tariffs and Trade

6 August 1991

GUW(규)-0213   10809 1800
" GUW-1504 첨부,

Mr Chol Soo Han
Assistant Attache (Economic Affairs)
Permanent Mission of the Republic of Korea to
 the International Organizations in Geneva
Case postale 566
Route de Pre-Bois 20
1215 GENEVE 15

Dear Mr Han

As foreshadowed at our bilateral meeting on 24 July, please find attached a
list of questions regarding the services offer submitted by the Republic of
Korea (MTN.TNC/W/61) on which my authorities would welcome
clarification. I wish to emphasise that the questions are aimed at seeking to
clarify technical aspects of the Korean offer and do not reflect Australian
interest in negotiating an exchange of concessions in any particular sector
or subsector.

As mentioned during our meeting, we recognize that preparation of written
responses to some of the questions may involve a considerable amount of
work and may therefore be more conducive to discussion at our next
meeting.

I would appreciate your contacting me when your authorities have had an
opportunity to consider how they would wish to handle our requests for
clarification.

Yours sincerely

(Michael Mugliston)
Counsellor

0225

12-1

Questions: Korean Offer

II Commercial Presence (P.3)

Could ROK provide an explanation of the "procedural
requirements" contained in the Foreign Capital Inducement Act
and the Foreign Exchange Control Act? What government
authorities are responsible for the administration of these
pieces of legislation?

Could ROK provide a copy of the Negative List for foreign
investment?

Could ROK explain under what conditions and "additional
requirements" direct foreign investment will be allowed in
sectors on the Negative List?

Could the ROK explain what are the "different limitations
and/or conditions" for the establishment of a branch office
from those of a joint venture-company or subsidiary?

Could the ROK provide details of the conditions which must be
satisfied under the Foreign Exchange Control Act and the
Foreign Capital Inducement Act for the approval of mergers and
acquisitions of Korean companies by foreigners through the
acquisition of issued and outstanding stocks?

Could the ROK explain what it considers "foreign direct
investments which are likely to lead to monopolistic or
predatory practices in the domestic market"? Can the ROK give
examples? What "restrictions" has the ROK applied in such
cases?

Could ROK please provide details of the restrictions on the
"registration of foreigner and foreign legal entity"?

2. Acquisition and Usage of Land (P.4)

Could the ROK provide details of what restrictions exist under
the Alien Land Acquisition Law on the acquisition of land by
foreigners or "domestic companies which are deemed
foreigners"?

Could ROK provide us with a list of the domestic companies
which are "deemed foreign"?

Under what conditions are Korean companies "deemed foreign"
for the purposes of land acquisition?

Which ROK government authorities are responsible for the
administration of the Alien Land Acquisition Law?

Under what conditions are the branch offices of foreign
service providers permitted to hold lease right over land?

0226

12-2

3. Foreign Exchange Control (P.4)

Could ROK please provide details of the kinds of contracts for services by domestic residents involving payment of foreign exchange which require government approval? Which government authority is responsible? What legislation/regulation is used to assess applications?

Could the ROK please provide details of the criteria set out in the "Guidelines for Foreign Investment"? Is ROK prepared to negotiate on these Guidelines?

4. Movement of Personnel (P.4)

Could ROK provide us with an illustrative list of the categories of service providers which might be allowed to enter ROK subject to the procedural requirements of the Immigration Control Law?

Could ROK provide us with details of the provisions in the Immigration Control Law which affect foreign service providers?

On what aspects of the Immigration Control Law is ROK prepared to negotiate? What aspects of the movement of personnel is ROK "further examining"? On what aspects of movement of personnel is ROK willing to make a more "specific commitment" in each sector?

0227

/2 -3

III. Sectoral Commitment (P.5)

2. Business Services (P.5)

Advertising (P.5)

Could the ROK please provide details of the criteria used to
approve the importation and use of foreign made advertising
material? Could the ROK provide us with details of the
relevant legislation/regulation, particularly Article 10 of
the Motion Picture Act and Article 8 of the Disk Law? Is the
ROK prepared to negotiate on these conditions?

We understand that under Article 10 of the Motion Picture Act
and Article 8 of the Disk Law, foreign advertising agencies
require a letter of recommendation from the minister
responsible for advertising. Which minister is responsible?
What criterion are used to govern the issue of such letters?

Could the ROK please confirm that as of January 1991 branch
offices or subsidiaries were permitted to establish in the
ROK? What conditions on establishment have been applied?

What are the conditions for accreditation to the Korea
Broadcasting Advertising Corporation (KOBAC)? Are there
different conditions of accreditation for foreigners than for
ROK citizens?

What rules of the Korea Newspaper Publisher's Association are
relevant to the establishment of foreign advertising
companies?

Engineering Services (P.5)

Could the ROK please provide details on what limitations and
conditions currently apply in the engineering sector?

Could the ROK please provide details of the conditions for the
registration of foreign engineering service providers
contained in Article 3 of the Engineering Services Promotion
Law? Do these conditions discriminate against foreign service
providers? Is the ROK prepared to negotiate on these
conditions?

Engineering Design (P.6)

Could the ROK provide a definition of the engineering design
sub-sector?

Could the ROK please provide details of the conditions for the
registration of foreign engineering design service providers
contained in Article 3 of the Engineering Services Promotion
Law? Do these conditions discriminate against foreign service
providers? Is the ROK prepared to negotiate on these
conditions?

Project Management (P.6)

0228

/2-4

Could the ROK please provide details of the conditions for the
registration of foreign project management service providers
contained in Article 3 of the Engineering Services Promotion
Law? Is the ROK prepared to negotiate on these conditions?

Certified Public Accountant (CPA) Services (P.7)

Could the ROK please provide us with details of the
qualifications and conditions applying for registration as a
CPA under Articles 2,4, and 5 of the Certified Public
Accountant Act)? What are the licensing requirements?

Could the ROK please provide more details of the licensing
requirements for a foreign CPA to provide audit services to a
company more than 50% owned by corporations or citizens of the
CPA'S country? What are the reciprocity requirements?

We understand that non Korean nationals are not permitted to
sit for local tests to qualify as CPA? Can the ROK confirm
this? Are tests given in English?

Does the ROK intend to expand its offer to allow qualified
foreign practicing accountants the same conditions of practice
as Korean national accountants?

Could the ROK provide specific information on the limitations
on market access for commercial presence which currently exist
in the market?

Certified Tax Accountant (CTA) Services (P.9)

Could the ROK please provide us with details of the
qualifications and conditions applying for registration as a
CTA? What are the licensing requirements?

Could the ROK please define what precise areas of tax
accounting practice require certification? Are there any areas
of tax accounting practice which do not require certification?

What foreign accountancy qualifications are recognised by the
ROK government? Does the ROK recognise foreign accountancy
qualifications held by Koreans for the purpose of practicing
tax accounting in the ROK? Does the ROK recognise foreign
accountancy qualifications held by foreigners for the purpose
of practicing tax accounting in the ROK? What are the
reciprocity requirements?

What is the average pass rate for foreigners taking the
taxation certification examination? How many foreign
accountants have certification to practice as tax accountants
in the ROK?

What are the conditions on establishment, particularly in
relation to office property?

We understand that non Korean nationals are not permitted to
sit for local tests to qualify as CTA? Can the ROK confirm
this? Are tests given in English?

0229

12 - 5

Does the ROK intend to expand its offer to allow qualified foreign practicing accountants the same conditions of practice as Korean national accountants?

Could the ROK provide specific information on the limitations on market access for commercial presence which currently exist in the market?

3. Telecommunications (P.10)

Why has Korea not included its proposed liberalisation of mobile communication in its offer?

We understand that Korea intends to enter into IVAN agreements with Japan, US, UK et.al. What status will these agreements have in the context this offer?

Will these condition be extended to all countries or do they simply confirm existing levels of market access to the Korean market?

On-line Database and Remote Computing Services (P.10)

Could the ROK provide definitions for "Computer-Related Services" and "Software Development" in order to indicate the coverage of their offer?

Could the ROK please provide us with more details of the conditions applying to domestic On-line Database and Remote Computing services under Article 9 of the Foreign Capital Inducement Act, and Article 73-2 of the Public Telecommunications Business Law? What are the registration requirements? Is the ROK prepared to negotiate on these conditions?

Data Transmission Services (P.10)

Could the ROK please provide details of the registration requirements for foreign data transmission service providers, particularly Article 9 of the Foreign Capital Inducement Act, and Article 73-2 of the Public Telecommunications Business Law? Is the ROK prepared to negotiate on these requirements?

0230

12 — 6

4. Construction (P.12)

Could the ROK provide details on what limitations and
conditions on market access currently apply in the
construction sector?

What are the current foreign equity restrictions?

General Construction (civil works, building) (P.12)

Could the ROK please provide us with details of the licensing
requirements for general construction service providers,
particularly those conditions contained in Article 6 of the
Construction Business Act? Are these requirements administered
in a non-discriminatory manner? Does the treatment of foreign
and ROK construction companies differ?

Special Construction (special construction, specialist
construction, electrical works, communication works, anti-fire
equipment installation) (P.12)

Could the ROK please provide us with details of the licensing
requirements for special construction service providers,
particularly those conditions contained in Article 6 of
Construction Business Act, Article 5 of the Communication
Construction Business Act, Article 42-2 Anti-fire Act?

 Architectural Services (P.12)

Could the ROK please provide us with details of the
registration requirements contained in Article 23 of the
Architect Act?

Could the ROK please provide us with details of the licensing
requirements contained in Article 7 and 23 of the Architect
Act?

5. Distribution Services (P.11)

Retail (P.11)

Could the ROK please provide us with details of the
limitations and conditions on market access applying to
businesses establishing a single shop with a floor area larger
than 700 m2?

6. Financial Services (P.13)

Banking (P.13)

Could the ROK please provide us with details of the Guidelines
for the establishment of representative offices, and branches
for banking service providers? Is the ROK prepared to
negotiate on the Guidelines?

Could the ROK please provide us with more details of the
Conditions and Qualifications on National Treatment for
banking service providers? What restrictions exist for banking

0231

12-ᄉ

business other than the acceptance of deposits, loans, and
exchange business? What criteria are used by the Monetary
Board for the approval of capital increases? What conditions
govern ATM establishment? Are these criterion and conditions
negotiable?

We understand that foreign banks do not have access to the main
interbank market and have no lender of last resort facility
with the Central Bank. Can the ROK confirm this? Is the ROK
government prepared to negotiate on this restriction?

We understand that foreign banks are required to capitalise
each branch separately and that capital for each branch is
limited to 3.75 - 6.25 Million Australian dollars plus
retained earnings and surplus. Can the ROK confirm this? Can
the ROK confirm that these limitations do not apply to
domestic banks? Is the ROK prepared to negotiate on these
limitations, if they exist?

We understand that prior to the establishment of a subsidiary
or branch, a parent bank applying for a license must be one of
the top 500 banks in the world, ranked by total assets. Can
the ROK government confirm this? Is the ROK government
prepared to negotiate on this restriction?

We understand that foreign banks are restricted in where they
may place surplus funds, and are asked to direct funds to
industries designated by the ROK government? Can the ROK
government confirm this? Is the ROK government prepared to
negotiate on these restrictions?

We understand that restrictions by the Central Bank on the
ability of banks to raise local currency deposits and to make
swap currency transactions severely limit trade-related
finance. Can the ROK government confirm this? Is the ROK
government prepared to negotiate on these restrictions?

Services Auxiliary to Banking (P.13)

What restrictions exist for auxiliary banking services other
than the sale of commercial bills and trade bills, mutual
instalment deposits and guarantees? Are these restrictions
negotiable?

Trust Business (P.13)

Could the ROK please provide us with details of the Guidelines
for the establishment of branches for trust businesses? Are
these Guidelines negotiable?

Could the ROK please provide us with details of the conditions
and requirements for trust businesses contained in the Trust
Business Law? Are these conditions and requirements
negotiable?

0232

12-8

Securities Business (P.13)

Could the ROK please provide us with more details of the conditions and requirements for the approval of representative offices, branches and joint ventures?

Is the ROK prepared to negotiate on the restriction of securities businesses to brokerage, dealing and underwriting? What are the minimum capital requirements ? What are the conditions for membership of the Stock Exchange?

We understand that foreign securities firms are only permitted a maximum holding of 10% in ROK securities firms? Can the ROK government confirm this? Is the ROK government prepared to negotiate on this restriction?

We understand that there have been complaints about the lack of transparency characterising the ROK's liberalisation plans for the securities market? Can the ROK confirm this? can the ROK provide us with more details of the liberalisation plan?

Insurance (P.14)

Could the ROK specify current conditions on the application of national treatment in this sector?

What are the guidelines applying to the establishment of a commercial presence in either direct insurance or reinsurance?

We understand that approval for new insurance policies and rates must be sought from the Ministry of Finance and that approval makes the new product available to all insurance companies. Can the ROK confirm that these restrictions exist? Is the ROK government prepared to negotiate on these restrictions?

Direct Insurance (P.15)

Is the ROK prepared to negotiate on the limitation of direct insurance to marine cargo?

What are the licensing requirement for direct insurance? What conditions apply? What is the relevant legislation? Is the ROK prepared to negotiate on the limitation of branch or equity participation to 20% in non-life insurance business?

Reinsurance and Retrocession (P.15)

Could the ROK please provide us with more details of the obligation of priority reinsurance cessions to domestic insurers?

Is the ROK prepared to negotiate on the limitation of branch or equity participation to 20% in non-life insurance business?

Insurance Auxiliary Services (consulting, actuarial, claim handling, risk management) (P.16)

0233

/2 - P

Could the ROK please provide us with more details of the registration requirements administered by the Insurance Supervisory Board? Could the ROK please provide us with an explanation of the Guidelines used by the Ministry of Finance for the approval of Insurance Auxiliary Licence applications?

We understand that "standstill" on qualifications on national treatment for commercial presence will mean continued discrimination in favour of the US. Could the ROK explain why this discrimination remains, when there are other forms of insurance exports to the ROK which do not suffer discriminatory treatment?

7. Transportation (P.15)

A. Air Transportation (P.17)

Ground Handling (P.17)

Could the ROK please provide us with more details of the criteria for the approval of Joint Ventures with less than 50% foreign equity from January 1997? What conditions exist currently?

Selling and Marketing of Air Transport Services (P.18)

Could the ROK please provide us with more details of the criteria for the approval of Joint Ventures with less than 50% foreign equity from January 1997? What conditions exist currently?

Computer Reservation Systems (P.18)

Australia notes that its initial offer proposed binding this sector free of specific limitations and restrictions on market access or national treatment. Is the ROK prepared to offer the same binding?

Is the ROK prepared to negotiate to increase the foreign equity limit on domestic computer reservations systems from 50%? What are the registration requirements contained in Article 9 of the Foreign Capital Inducement Act and Article 73-2 of the Public Telecommunications Business Law? What "further considerations" apply to international services?

Aircraft Repair and Maintenance (P.18)

Australia notes that its initial offer proposed binding this sector free of specific limitations and restrictions on market access or national treatment. Is the ROK prepared to offer the same binding?

Could the ROK please provide us with more details of the criteria for the approval of Joint Ventures with less than 50% foreign equity from January 1997? What conditions exist currently?

0234

12-10

B. Maritime Transportation (P.19)

International Deep-sea Passenger Shipping (P.19)

Could the ROK please provide us with more details of the criteria used by the Administrator of the Korean Maritime and Port Administration (KMPA) under Article 4 of the Maritime Transport Business Act (MTBA) for the approval of joint venture applications? Is the ROK prepared to negotiate on the requirements that foreign equity shall be less than 50% and that the juridical representative of the joint venture shall be a Korean national?

International Deep-sea Cargo Shipping (P.19)

Could the ROK provide details of what marine cargo transport is reserved for ROK shipping? Is the ROK prepared to negotiate to allow non Korean flag vessels to transport these marine cargoes? What other restrictions to the transport of marine cargo are contained in Article 16-1 of the Maritime Transportation Industry Fostering Act (MTIFA)?

Could the ROK please provide us with more details of the cargo preference system which is to be phased out by January 1995? Is the ROK prepared to negotiate concessions on the cargo preference system before that time?

Could the ROK please provide us with more details of the criteria used by the Administrator of the KNPA under Article 26-2 of the MTIFA for the approval of applications from foreign maritime cargo transporters to establish branch offices?

Could the ROK please provide us with more details of the criterion for licensing foreign investors for joint ventures on specific liners and specific cargoes? Is the ROK prepared to negotiate on the condition that the juridical representative of the joint venture shall be a Korean national?

Auxiliary Services (freight forwarding, ship brokering, ship management, ship leasing, shipping agency) (P.19)

Is the ROK prepared to negotiate on the requirements that foreign equity shall be less than 50%, that the juridical representative of the joint venture shall be a Korean national and that joint ventures of the shipping agency invested in by a foreign shipping company shall be an agent only for their own cargoes and vessels?

C. Road Transportation (P.20)

Freight Transport by Road (P.20)

Could the ROK please provide us with more details of the criterion for licensing foreign road freight transport providers for general local freight transport?

0235

/2-11

Storage and Warehousing (P.20)

Could the ROK please provide us with more details of the
criterion for licensing of foreign storage and warehouse
providers under the Storage and Warehousing Law?

8. Tourism (P.22)

Tourist Hotels, Youth-Hostel, Family Hotels, Korean
Traditional Hotels (P.22)

Could the ROK please provide us with more details of the
registration requirements contained in the Article 4 of the
Tourism Promotion Law?

Foreigner's Tourist Souvenir Shops (P.22)

Could the ROK please provide us with more details of the
registration requirements contained in the Article 4 of the
Tourism Promotion Law?

Professional Convention Organizers (P.22)

Could the ROK please provide us with more details of the
registration requirements contained in the Article 4 of the
Tourism Promotion Law?

Travel Agencies (P.22)

Could the ROK please provide us with more details of the
registration requirements contained in the Article 4 of the
Tourism Promotion Law?

doc:korean.offer

0236

12—12

경 · 제 · 기 · 획

봉조삼 10502-*백○*   503-9149   1991. 8. 17.

수신 수신처참조

제목 UR대책 서비스분야 실무소위원회 개최

　　1. 봉조삼 10502-529 ('91.8.5)와 관련입니다.

　　2. '91년 상반기중에 진행된 양허표작성방법에 대한 기술적인 토의결과를
바탕으로 각국은 Offer List를 수정하여 GATT에 제출해야 할 것으로 예상됩니다.
또한 서비스협상그룹의장은 각국이 MFN일탈을 필요로 하는 사항을 9.20일까지
GATT에 제출할 것을 요청한 바 있읍니다.

　　3. 이에따라 우리 Offer List의 수정작업과 MFN일탈 사항의 작성에 필요한
지침을 논의하고 각부처가 추진중에 있는 분야별 규제파악현황 및 양허협상대책
추진현황을 점검하기 위한 UR대책 서비스분야 실무소위원회를 다음과 같이 개최
하니 필히 참석해 주시기 바랍니다.

다   음

　　가. 일시: '91.8.20(화)   15:00-18:00

　　나. 장소: 경제기획원 대회의실 (과천청사 1동 727호)

　　다. 의제: ① Offer List 수정작업 및 MFN일탈사항 작성지침

　　　　　　　② 분야별 규제파악현황 및 양허협상대책 추진현황점검

　　라. 참석범위: 별첨참조

첨부: 참석범위 1부.   끝.

경 제 기 획 원 장

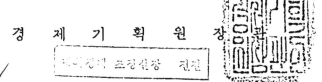

수신처: 외무부장관, 내무부장관, 재무부장관, 법무부장관, 교육부장관,
　　　　문화부장관, 상공부장관, 보건사회부장관, 건설부장관, 교통부장관,
　　　　노동부장관, 체신부장관, 체육청소년부장관, 과학기술처장관, 환경처
　　　　장관, 공보처장관, 특허청장, 해운항만청장, 대외경제정책연구원장,
　　　　한국개발연구원장, 대한무역진흥공사장.

0237   27235

(별첨)

參 席 範 圍

소속기관	참석대상자	비 고
경제기획원	제2협력관(회의주재) 통상조정3과장 산업3과장	* 분야별 연구기관 전문가참석
공정거래위원회	제도개선과장	
외 무 부	통상기구과장	
내 무 부	지적과장	
재 무 부	국제금융과장	
법 무 부	국제법무심의관실검사 입국심사과장	
교 육 부	교육협력과장	
문화공보부	영화진흥과장	
상 공 부	유통산업과장	
보건사회부	국제협력과장	
건 설 부	해외협력과장	
교 통 부	국제협력과장	
노 동 부	고용관리과장	
체 신 부	통신협력과장	
체육청소년부	체육시설과장	
과학기술처	기술협력2과장	
환 경 처	정책조정과장	
공 보 처	광고정책과장	
항 만 청	진흥과장	
특 허 청	지도과장	
K I E P	김태준, 성극제박사	
K D I	김지홍박사	
K O T R A	국제경제과장	

0238

UR 대책 서비스 분야 실무 소위원회 결과

1991. 8.21.
통상기구과

1. 회의 일시 : 1991. 8.20(화) 15:00-18:00

2. 장   소 : 경제기획원 회의실

3. 참 석 자 :

    ㅇ 경제기획원 대조실 제3협력관 (현황 보고 및 회의 주재)

    ㅇ 외무부, 재무부, 법무부, 교육부등 16개부처 및 대한무역진흥공사
       UR/서비스 협상 담당 실무자

    ㅇ 대외경제정책연구원, 한국개발원, 통신개발연구원 관련 연구관

4. 협의 내용

    ㅇ UR/서비스 협상의 91년 상반기 협상 동향 및 91년 하반기 협상 전망 보고

    ㅇ 양허표 수정, 보완 작업 및 Request List 작성 지침 설명
       - 관련부처는 소관 업종별 양허표 수정 시안을 8.31한 경제기획원에 제출
         (91.1월이후 추가 개방이 이루어진 분야 및 서비스 공급 유형 구분이
         변경된 사항 반영)
       - 관련부처는 국가별, 업종별 Request List를 8.31한 경제기획원에 제출
       - 91년 하반기중 UR/서비스 협상 진척상황에 따라 수정 양허표 및 아국의
         Request List 제출

    ㅇ MFN 일탈에 대한 아국 입장 수립 방안
       - 관련부처는 MFN 일탈 희망사항을 8.31한 경제기획원에 제출
       - 추후 UR 대책 서비스 분야 실무 소위원회를 재소집, 아국 입장 확정. 끝.

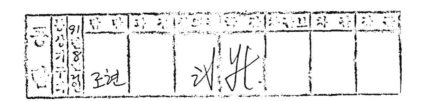

0239

경 제 기 획 원

통조삼 10502-    503-9149   1991. 8. 23.

수신 수신처참조   통상기주2

제목 UR대책 서비스분야 실무소위원회 결과통보

　　1. '91.8.20일 개최된 표제회의 결과를 별첨과 같이 통보하니 각부처
(및 기관)는 UR/서비스협상 대책추진에 만전을 기해 주시기 바랍니다.

별첨: UR대책 서비스실무소위 결과 1부.　　끝.

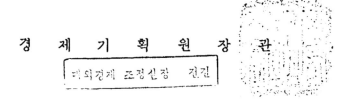

경 제 기 획 원 장 관

대외경제 조정실장   전결

수신처: 외무부장관, 내무부장관, 재무부장관, 법무부장관, 교육부장관,
　　　　 문화부장관, 상공부장관, 보건사회부장관, 건설부장관, 교통부장관,
　　　　 노동부장관, 체신부장관, 체육청소년부장관, 과학기술처장관, 환경처
　　　　 장관, 공보처장관, 특허청장, 해운항만청장, 대외경제정책연구원장,
　　　　 한국개발연구원장, 대한무역진흥공사장.

27964　　　　　　0240

UR對策 서비스實務小委 結果

I. 會議槪要

- 日　　時: '91.8.20, 15:00-18:00

- 場　　所: 經濟企劃院 大會議室

- 參 席 者: 經濟企劃院　第二協力官 (회의주재)
　　　　　　서비스協商關聯 16개部處의 課長 또는 事務官,
　　　　　　KOTRA, KIEP, KDI, KISDI, 해운산업연구원등
　　　　　　關聯機關의 專門家등 28명

- 會議議題

　○ 서비스協商關聯 主要推進課題 및 日程

　○ 讓許表 修正 方法

　○ MFN逸脫 希望事項 作成方法

　○ 各分野別 協商對策 推進狀況 점검

0241

Ⅱ. 會議結果

가. 서비스協商關聯 主要推進課題 및 日程의 再確認

作業推進課題	所管部處	日 程
① 우리 讓許表의 修正.補完作業		
- 所管業種別 各種規制制度를 EPB에 提出	各部處	~8.16
- 讓許表作成 方式에 대한 實務者 會議開催	E P B	8.20
- 各業種別 讓許表 修正試案作成	各部處	8.16~8.31
- 各業種別 讓許表에 대한 綜合檢討	E P B	9. 5~9.13
- 各業種別 勞動力移動 許容範圍을 勞動部 및 EPB에 提出	各部處	~8.31
② 讓許協商對策 推進		
- 各業種別 讓許表에 대한 說明資料 補完 內容을 EPB에 提出	各部處	~9.15
- 國家別.業種別 Request List를 EPB 에 提出 (GATT에 제출시한: 9.20)	各部處	~9. 5
③ MFN逸脫에 대한 我國立場整理		
- MFN逸脫希望事項을 EPB에 提出	各部處	~8.31
- UR對策 서비스實務小委員會 開催	E P B	~9. 5

0242

作業推進課題	所管部處	日 程
④ Framework 및 分野別 附屬書協商 對策推進		
- Framework 協商進展狀況 점검 및 향후 對應對策 樹立	E P B	~9.15
- 分野別 附屬書協商에 참여 ○ 海運(9.17), 通信(9.19), 金融(9.20)	各部處	~12월

0243

나. GATT分類表上의 各서비스業種에 대한 所管部處를 暫定的으로 決定

(異見이 있을 경우 EPB와 協調하여 調整)

GATT事務局의 서비스業種 分類	所管部處	韓國標準産業分類表上의 細部分類 (5단위)	備 考
1. 事業서비스			
A. 專門職서비스			
a. 法務	法務部		
b. 會計	財務部		
c. 稅務	財務部		
d. 設計	建設部		
e. 엔지니어링	科技處		
f. 綜合 엔지니어링	科技處		
g. 都市計劃 및 조경설계	建設部		
h. 醫師 및 齒科醫療서비스	保社部		
i. 獸醫師서비스	農産部		
j. 其他 保健關聯 專門서비스	保社部		
k. 其他			
B. 通信網을 통하지 않는 컴퓨터 關聯서비스			
a. 컴퓨터 하드웨어의 設置에 대한 諮問서비스	科技處		
b. 소프트웨어사용서비스	科技處		
c. 情報處理서비스	科技處		
d. 데이타베이스서비스	科技處		

0244

GATT事務局의 서비스業種 分類	所管部處	韓國標準産業分類 表上의　細部分類 (5단위)	備 考
e. 其　他			
C. R & D 서비스	科技處		
D. 不動産서비스	建設部		
a. Involving own or leased 　　property			
b. on a fee or contract 　　basis			
E. 乘務員이 없는 運送裝備의 　賃貸	交通部		
a. 배			
b. 航空機			
c. 기타 運送裝備			
F. 기타 事業서비스			
a. 廣告	公報處		
b. 프랜차이징	商工部		
c. 市場調査 및 輿論調査	公報處		
d. 經營컨설팅	科技處		
e. 製造業關聯 컨설팅	商工部		
f. 技術테스트 및 分析서비스	科技處		
g. 農業,狩獵,林業에 부수되는 　　서비스	農産部		
h. 漁業에 부수되는 서비스	農産部		

0245

GATT事務局의 서비스業種 分類	所管部處	韓國標準産業分類 表上의 細部分類 (5단위)	備 考
i. 鑛業 및 油田에 부수되는 서비스	動資部		
j. 人力配置 및 供給서비스	勞動部		
k. 탐정 및 警護	警察廳		
l. 科學 및 技術컨설팅	科技處		
m. 建設以外의 設置및 組立作業	商工部		
n. 裝備의 維持 및 修繕	科技處		
o. 建物淸掃서비스	警察廳		
p. 사진서비스	警察廳		
q. 포장서비스	內務部		
r. 飜譯 및 通譯	文化部		
s. 下水處理 衛生서비스	環境處, 保社部		
t. 印刷 및 出版	文化部		
2. 커뮤니케이션			
A. 郵便	遞信部		
B. 配達	交通部		
C. 通信	遞信部		
D. 視聽覺서비스			
a. 映畫,비디오製作 및 流通	文化部		
b. 映畫上映	文化部		
c. 라디오 및 TV放送	公報處		
d. 音盤錄音	文化部		
e. 其他			

0246

GATT事務局의 서비스業種 分類	所管部處	韓國標準産業分類 表上의 細部分類 (5단위)	備 考
E. 其他 커뮤니케이션 서비스			
a. 뉴스 및 新聞代行	公報處		
b. 圖書館서비스	文化部		
c. 其他			
3. 建設 및 建設關聯 엔지니어링			
A. 프로젝트디자인,契約,監督등	科技處		
B. 事業性 檢討	科技處		
C. 빌딩建築	建設部		
D. 土木建築	建設部		
E. 設置 및 組立	建設部		
F. 마무리作業	建設部		
G. 構造物의 維持 및 修繕	建設部		
H. 其他			
4. 流通	商工部		
5. 教育	教育部		
6. 環境서비스	環境處		
7. 金融	財務部		
A. 保險 및 保險關聯서비스			

0247

GATT事務局의 서비스業種 分類	所管部處	韓國標準産業分類 表上의 細部分類 (5단위)	備 考
B. 銀行 및 기타 金融서비스			
a. 預金			
b. 貸出			
c. 金融리스			
d. 送金에 따른 支給			
e. 支給保證			
f. 外換, 어음, 轉換證券등 각종 金融商品의 去來			
g. 證券發行의 參與			
h. 資金仲介			
i. 資金管理			
j. 金融資産의 淸算			
k. 金融諮問 및 부수서비스			
l. 金融情報의 提供 및 處理			
8. 健康關聯서비스			
A. 病院서비스	保社部		
B. 其他			
9. 觀光, 旅行, 레저서비스			
A. 호텔 및 레스토랑	交通部, 保社部		
B. 旅行斡旋 및 運營서비스	交通部		
C. 觀光가이드서비스	交通部		

0248

GATT事務局의 서비스業種 分類	所管部處	韓國標準産業分類 表上의 細部分類 (5단위)	備 考
D. 視聽覺서비스이외의 엔터테인 먼트서비스	文化部, 交通部, 保社部		
E. 스포츠 및 레크레이션서비스	體育部		
F. 其他			
10. 運送서비스			
A. 國內海運	港灣廳		
B. 內水路	內務部		
C. 國際航空	交通部		
D. 國內航空	交通部		
E. Space 運送	交通部		
F. 國際鐵道	鐵道廳		
G. 國內鐵道	鐵道廳		
H. 國際道路	交通部		
I. 國內道路	交通部		
J. Pipeline 運送	動資部		
K. 運送補助서비스	交通部, 港灣廳		
a. 貨物處理			
b. 貯藏 및 倉庫서비스			
c. 貨物周旋			
d. 其他			
11. 其他			

0249

다. 讓許表作成方法

- 修正讓許表를 作成하는 기준시점은 '91.8.31로 함.

- 신규로 作成된 市場接近條項 및 內國民待遇條項(회의자료에 첨부)
  에 따라서 所管業種에 대한 모든 규제를 기재한 分野別 修正讓許表
  試案(勞動力移動 許容範圍 포함)을 EPB에 8.31까지 제출

  ○ 各類型에 따라 規制制度를 구분하는 것은 2차적인 문제이고
    Top-down 方式에 의해서 讓許表를 作成하게 되어 있으므로
    서비스交易을 제한하는 모든 規制措置를 망라하는 것이 重要

  ○ 量的規制 또는 質的規制로 구분하는 問題, 差別的 規制, 또는
    無差別的 規制로 구분하는 問題, 市場接近란에 기재되야 하는
    규제 또는 內國民待遇란에 기재되야 하는 규제로 구분하는 問題,
    各供給形態別룰 구분하는 問題등에 대하여 불명확한 事項이
    있으면 EPB의 實務者 및 關係研究機關의 專門家로 구성된 總括
    作業班과 協議하여 決定 (연락처: EPB 503-9149, 9152,
    KIEP 519-3407, 3408)

- 修正讓許表 試案에 대하여 9.5-13간 各業種別로 일정을 정하여
  總括作業班과 各業種別 所管部處의 擔當者 및 專門家 참여하는
  關係部處會議를 개최하여 綜合檢討

- Offer List에서 除外시킨 業種에 대해서는 相對國家를 설득시킬수
  있는 理由와 論理를 EPB에 9.15까지 提出

- 修正讓許表의 GATT제출은 다른국가의 提出動向 및 協商動向을 勘案
  하여 소정의 節次를 걸쳐 追後決定

0250

분류기호 문서번호	통기 20644- /04	(2170, 2391)		결 재	담 당	담당관	심의관
시행일자	1991. 8.24.				조천		
수 신	총무과장	발 신	통상국장				
제 목	주재관 일시 귀국						

    1. 경제기획원은 주 제네바 대표부 이종화 경제협력관을

UR 협상과 관련한 부내 협의차 8.29-9.5간 일시 귀국시킬것을 요청하여

왔으니 필요한 조치를 취하여 주시기 바랍니다.

    2. 당국으로서도 UR/서비스 협상의 국내협상 대책 수립과

관련하여 상기 이종화 경협관의 일시 귀국<del>이 필요한 것으로 판단됨</del>을
에 이의가 없음을

첨언합니다.

    첨 부 : 경제기획원의 일시 귀국 협종 요청 공문 사본.   끝.

0251

경 제 기 획 원

통조삼 10502-591   503-9149   1991. 8. 23.

수신 외무부장관 (통상국장)

제목 주제네바대표부 경제협력관의 일시귀국 협조요청

　주제네바대표부 이종화 경제협력관을 다음과 같이 일시귀국시키고자
하니 협조하여 주시기 바랍니다.

다   음

가. 기간: '91.8.29-9.5 (7박 8일)

나. 사유

- UR/서비스협상과 관련하여 아국은 '91.1월 GATT사무국에 제출한
  Offer List의 수정작업을 하고 있는바 동 수정작업에 직접 참여

- 9월중순부터 본격화됨 분야별 UR협상의 동향 및 향후 전망과
  주요국협상전략등에 대하여 동 기간중 개최예정인 UR대책 실무
  위원회에 참석 직접 설명토록하여 협상대책의 수립.추진에 협조

끝.

경 제 기 획 원 장

0252

기록물종류	일반공문서철	등록번호	2019080105	등록일자	2019-08-14
분류번호	764.51	국가코드		보존기간	영구
명 칭	UR(우루과이라운드) / GNS(서비스협상그룹) 회의, 1991. 전5권				
생 산 과	통상기구과	생산년도	1991~1991	담당그룹	
권 차 명	V.4 9-10월				
내용목차					

0001

외 무 부

종 별 :

번 호 : GVW-1688   일 시 : 91 0906 1800

수 신 : 장 관(통기, 경기원)

발 신 : 주 제네바 대사대리

제 목 : UR/GNS 협상의제 송부

　　91.9.17-27 간 개최 예정인 UR/GNS 회의 의제를 별첨 송부함.

　　첨부: UR/GNS 의제 1부 끝

　　(GVW(F)-329)

　　(차석대사 김삼훈-국장)

─────────────────────────────
통상국　　　　　　경기원

GATT/AIR/3228   30 AUGUST 1991

SUBJECT: URUGUAY ROUND: GROUP OF NEGOTIATIONS ON SERVICES

1.   THE GROUP OF NEGOTIATIONS ON SERVICES WILL HOLD ITS NEXT MEETING ON
17-27 SEPTEMBER, STARTING ON TUESDAY, 17 SEPTEMBER 1991 AT 10 A.M. IN THE
CENTRE WILLIAM RAPPARD.

2.   THE FOLLOWING ITEMS ARE ON THE AGENDA:

     2.1 TELECOMMUNICATION SERVICES ANNEX:
          -   FURTHER WORK ON DRAFT ANNEX (IN MTN.TNC/W/35/REV.1);

     2.2 MARITIME TRANSPORT SERVICES
          -   DISCUSSION BASED ON THE FORTHCOMING COMMUNICATION FROM THE
              NORDIC COUNTRIES;

     2.3 FINANCIAL SERVICES ANNEX:
          -   DISCUSSION OF ANNEX BASED ON MTN.TNC/W/35/REV.1 AND
              SUBMISSIONS MTN.GNS/W/71; MTN.TNC/W/50; MTN.TNC/W/52;
              MTN.TNC/W/68;

     2.4 (i)   SUBSTANTIVE GUIDELINES: INCLUDING ARTICLES IV, RELEVANT
                 PARTS OF XVIII AND DRAFT DECISION ON SUBSTANTIVE
                 GUIDELINES FOR THE NEGOTIATION OF INITIAL COMMITMENTS;

          (ii)   SCHEDULING OF COMMITMENTS: INCLUDING ARTICLES VI, VII,
                 XIV, XVI, XVII, RELEVANT PARTS OF XVIII, XIX AND XX;

          (iii) M.F.N. (I.E. ARTICLE II);

          (iv)   OTHER DRAFT ARTICLES: INCLUDING ARTICLES V, XXII, XXIII,
                 ETC.;

          (v)   ANNEX ON MOVEMENT OF NATURAL PERSONS PROVIDING SERVICES
                 UNDER THE AGREEMENT: INCLUDING ARTICLE I;

          (vi)   DEFINITION OF TERMS: INCLUDING ARTICLE XXXIV;

          (vii) FURTHER WORK ON INITIAL COMMITMENTS;

     2.5 OTHER BUSINESS.

3.   THE AGENDA ITEM ON TELECOMMUNICATION SERVICES ANNEX WILL BE TAKEN UP
ON 17 SEPTEMBER AT 10 A.M., MARITIME TRANSPORT SERVICES ON 19 SEPTEMBER AT
10 A.M., AND FINANCIAL SERVICES ANNEX ON 20 SEPTEMBER AT 10 A.M.
DISCUSSION OF AGENDA ITEMS 2.4 AND 2.5 WILL COMMENCE ON MONDAY,
23 SEPTEMBER AT 10 A.M.

                                                              ./.

91-1198

0003

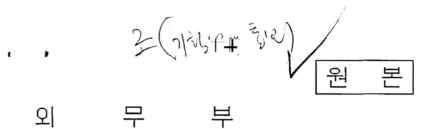

외 무 부

종 별 :

번 호 : GVW-1723 일 시 : 91 0911 1900

수 신 : 장관(통기, 경기원, 재무부, 상공부, 교통부, 체신부, 항만청)

발 신 : 주제네바 대사

제 목 : UR/GNS 비공식 협의

9.11(수) JARAMILLO 의장 주재로 개최된 표제협의(약 30개국 참석)는 9.17-27간 GNS회의 진행계획에 대하여 논의하였는 바 동결과 하기 보고함.

1. GNS 회의 진행계획

- 9.17(화): 통신분야 GNS 비공식 회의(GNS의장 및 ROBERT TRITT 공동주재)

0 의제

I) SCOPE/OBLIGATIONS(통신부속서 초안 2항 7항)

II) 기업내 통신(9항, 14항)

III) 정보에의 접근(14항, 15항)

IV) 통신망 사용과 조건부과와의 균형(11,12,13,16,17,18항)

0 미국의 수정제안: 금일 공식 제안으로 제출함(별도 FAX 송부)

- 9.19(목): 해운분야 GNS 비공식 회의

0 서면제안 제출 예정자이던 북구가 국내작업과정에 있다고 한바 다음주말까지 동 제안이 제출되지 않을 경우 회의를 취소키로 함.

- 9.20(금): 금융분야 GNS 비공식 회의(GNS의장 및 FRANK SWEDLOVE 공동 주재)

0 SWEDLOVE 공동의장이 작성한 주요 쟁점에 관한 비공식 문서(별도 FAX 송부)를 배부하였음.

0 공식 의제상 토의기초 문서는 TNC/W/50 과TNC/W/52 이나 상기 비공식 문서 위주로 토의가 진행될 것으로 예상됨.

- 9.23(월): GNS 비공식

0 양허협상의 실질적 기준, SCHEDULING OF COMMITMENTS

- 9.24(화) 오전: GNS 비공식

0 협정 초안상의 조문(제 5조, 22조, 23조등)

통상국	2차보	교통부	체신부	경기원	재무부	상공부	해항정

91.09.12 04:50 DQ

외신 1과 통제관

0004

- 9.25(수): GNS 비공석

0 인력이동 부석서, 용어의 정의(34조)

- 9.26(목) 오후: GNS 비공식

0 MFN

- 9.27(금) 오전: GNS 공식(필요시 오후에도 개최)

0 OFFER 제안 설명(헝가리등), 향후 작업계획에 대한 의장 제의

2. 기타 사항

- 수평적 협정

0 각국의 자료 제출이 불충분하여 사무국의 작업추진에 어려움이 있으나 다음주까지 추가 자료 제출이 없을 경우 기존 자료를 토대로 비공식 문서를 작성키로 함.

- MFN 일탈 관련 구체적 정보 제출

0 의장은 지금까지 제출 국가가 하나도 없음을 지적한바 호주가 다음주까지 제출하겠다고 발언함.

- REQUEST LIST 제출

0 의장이 지금까지 제출된 사례가 없음을 지적한바 호주가 9.20 또는 그 다음주까지 제출하겠다고 발언함.

0 호주는 또한 각국에 배부할 REQUEST LIST 를 요약본이 아닌 완전한 사본 형태로 사무국에도 제출할 계획임을 밝히고 다른 나라들의 계획을문의한바, 각국이 묵시적으로 동의함.

- 용어의 정의에 관한 비공식 문서 작성

0 의장은 사무국에서 동 문서를 작성중에 있다고 언급함.

- EC 는 협정 초안(TNC/W/35)을 법률적 관점에서 정비한 작업문서(WORKING DOCUMENT)작성문제를 제기하였으나 사무국은 내부작업중에 있으나 많은 국가가 시기가 적절치 않다는 의견을 가지고 있다고 언급함.

- EC 는 또한 10월중 AUDIO VISUAL 분야에 대한 토의를 제기하였는바, 추후 협의키로 함.

첨부: 1. 미국의 통신부속서 수정 제안 1부

2. 금융분야 비공식 문서 1부. 끝

(GVW(F)-337)   [서명]

PAGE 2

45444 기 안 용 지

분류기호 서번호	통기 20644-	(전화 : 720 - 2188)	시 행 상 특별취급	
보존기간	영구 . 준영구 10. 5. 3. 1.	장 관		
수 신 처 보존기간				
시행일자	1991. 9.13.			

보조 기관	국 장	전 결	협 조 기 관		문 서 통 제
	심의관				
	과 장	대결			
기안책임자		조 현			발 인

| 경수참유신조 | 수신처 참조 | 발신명의 | |

| 제 목 | UR/서비스 협상 정부대표 임명 |

91.9.17(화)-20(금)기간중 제네바에서 개최되는 UR/서비스 협상

부속서 회의에 참가할 정부대표단이 "정부대표 및 특별사절의 임명과

권한에 관한 법률"에 의거, 아래와 같이 임명 되었음을 통보합니다.

- 아   래 -

0006

- 1 -

1. 회의명, 개최일시 및 정부대표단 (괄호안은 출장기간)

가. 통신분야 부속서 회의(9.17)

    ㅇ 주제네바 대표부 경협관

    ㅇ 체신부 통신협력과 사무관 노영규 *(9.15-20)*

    ㅇ 통신개발연구원 연구위원 최병일 (자문)

나. 해운분야 부속서 회의(9.19)

    ㅇ 주제네바 대표부 경협관

    ㅇ 주영 대사관 해무관 최낙정 *(9.17-20)*

    ㅇ 해운산업연구원 주임 연구원 최동현 (자문)

다. 금융분야 부속서 회의 (9.20)

    ㅇ 주제네바 대표부 경협관, *재무관*

    ㅇ 재무부 국제금융과 사무관 최희남 *(9.18-23)*

    ㅇ 경제기획원 통상조정3과 사무관 주형환 *(9.18-23)*

2. 소요경비 : 소관부처 예산.   끝.

수신처 : 재무부, 경제기획원, 체신부장관, 해운항만청장

- 2 -

0007

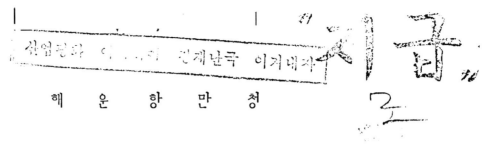

해 운 항 만 청

진흥 33700-**5950**   (744-4730)   1991. 9. 6

수신 외무부장관

제목   UR /해운분야 회의 정부대표 임명 요청

'91.9.17 스위스 제네바에서 개최예정인 UR/ GNS 해운분야
회의에 아래와 같이 참가코자 하오니 조치하여 주시기 바라며,
또한 주영한국대사관 소속 해무관이 동 회의에 참석할 수 있도록
훈령하여 주시기 바랍니다.

- 아   래 -

1. 회의명 : UR/ GNS 해운분야 부속서 회의

2. 회의기간 및 장소

   ㅇ 기 간 : '91. 9. 17(1일간) (19)
   ㅇ 장 소 : 스위스 제네바

3. 정부대표

   ㅇ 주영한국대사관 해무관 최낙정
   ㅇ 해운산업연구원 주임연구원 최동현(자문)

4. 출장기간 : '91. 9. 15 - 9. 18

5. 대책자료 : 별첨

6. 소요예산

   ㅇ 해운항만청 : 주영해무관 경비부담
   ㅇ KMI : 소속직원 경비부담

첨부 대책자료 1부. 끝.

0008   29916

진흥 33700-   1991. 9. 6

해 운 항 만 청

해 운 항 만 청

진흥 33700-8기   (744-4730)

1991 . 9 . 11.

수신 외무부장관

참조

제목   UR /해운분야회의 정부대표 임명요청내용변경

　　1. 진흥33700-5950('91. 9. 6)의 관련입니다.

　　2. 위 관련으로 요청한 UR /해운분야 주석서회의 정부

대표 임명 요청내용에 대하여 아래와 같이 변경 요청하오니

조치하여 주시기 바라며, 아울러 주영해무관이 동회의 참석에

차질 없도록 협조하여 주시기 바랍니다.

　　　　　　　　　- 아　　　래 -

	당　　초	변　　경	사　　유
회의개최일시	'91.9.17	'91.9.19	회의일시 변경
출장기간	'91.9.15-9.18	'91.9.17-9.20	

끝.

해 운 항 만 청

0010

통상기구 조변서기관님

해 운 항 만 청

진 흥 33700-**829**   (744-4730)   1991. 9.13

수 신   외무부 장관

제 목   UR / 해운분야 회의

1. 진흥 33700-5950 ('91.9.6) 및 진흥 33700-821('91.9.11)와 관련입니다.

2. '91. 9.12 제네바 대표부에서 송부한 전문(GVW - 173)에 의하면, 당초 서면 제안키로한 복구의 제안이 주말까지 제출되지 않을경우 '91.9.19 개최 예정인 UR/GNS 해운분야 회의를 취소키로 하였다 하오니, 동 회의 정부대표로 임명 요청한 바 있는 주영해무관으로 하여금 사전에 회의개최 여부를 확인한후 출국하도록 조치 히여 주시기 바랍니다.   끝.

해 운 항 만 청

0011

"질서앞에 혼란없고 협약앞에 가난없다"

체   신   부

모사전

통협 34475-6692   750-2343   91. 9. 13.

수신 외무부장관

제목 UR/GNS 통신분야 전문가회의 참가

    1. 경제기획원 통조삼 10502-590(91. 8. 23)관련.

    2. 위 관련 UR/GNS 통신분야 부속서 제정을 위한 전문가 회의 및 기본통신분야 시장개방문제를 협의하기 위한 비공식 회의가 91.9.18(수)-9. 19(목) 스위스 제네바에서 개최될 예정인 바, 동 회의에 대한 통신분야 전문가를 아래와 같이 참석하고자 하오니 적극 협조하여 주시기 바랍니다.

    가. 참가자 및 출장기간

소 속	직 위	성 명	출장기간	비 고
체신부	행정사무관	노영규	91. 9.15-9.20	기본통신시장 개방관련 비공식 회의 및 통신분야 전문가 회의
통신개발연구원	연구위원	최병일	"	

붙임 : 1. 훈령(안) 1부.

체   신   부   장

차 관 전 결

0012

훈 령 (안)

1. 기본훈령

o 금번 UR/GNS 통신분야 전문가회의는 지난 90.12월에 확정이
   보류된 통신부속서를 협의하는 중요한 회의이므로

   - 통신서비스 이용보장문제가 UR서비스 다자간협상을 통하여
     해결될 수 있도록 적극적으로 협의에 임할 것

o 미국이 주장하고 있는 기본통신분야의 최혜국대우 원칙적용
   일탈에 대해서는

   - 최혜국대우원칙은 다자간 규범의 초석으로서 기본통신분야
     에도 최혜국대우원칙이 적용되어야 한다는 입장을 견지할 것

2. 세부훈령

o 통신부속서상의 의무를 부과함에 있어 경쟁상태에 있는 민간
   공중통신사업자에게 부속서의 의무를 적용시키는 문제에
   대해서는

   - 부속서의 의무를 모든 공중통신사업에게 적용하여 각국
     사업자간 균형을 유지해야 한다는 입장을 견지할 것

o 기업내통신의 허용에 대해서는 기업내통신의 허용이 각국의
   공중통신사업자에게 미칠 영향을 충분히 고려하여 업무상긴밀
   관계자로 한정하여 허용해야한다는 입장을 견지할 것

o 공중통신사업자의 서비스 공공제공의무 수행을 위해 공중통신
   서비스의 접근 및 이용에 대한 제한을 허용하는 문제는

   - '서비스 공공제공의무'의 개념을 구체화할 필요는 있으나
     by-pass 방지등을 위한 규제는 필요하다는 입장을 표명할 것

0013

o 원가를 지향한 요금제도에 대해서는 요금결정시 각국의 국내
  정책이 고려될 수 있어야 하지만 기본적으로 공중통신서비스의
  요금은 원가를 지향해야 한다는 입장을 견지할 것

o 국경간 정보이동 및 정보접근을 위한 공중통신서비스의 이용
  보장문제는

  - 각국의 국내법에 따라 국가안보 등을 위해 필요할 경우
    이를 제한할 수 있는 권한이 각국에 부여되어야 한다는
    입장을 견지할 것

0014

경 제 기 획 원

봉조일 10520-646   (503-9144)   1991 . 9 .11

수 신 외무부장관

참 조 통상국장

제 목 UR관련 협상회의 참석자 추천

     스위스 제네바에서 개최되는 91년도 제7차 UR/금융서비스 협상 그룹
회의에 아국대표단의 일원으로 참석할 당원 소속직원을 다음과 같이 추천
합니다.

     1. 소   속 : 경제기획원 대외경제조정실 통상조정1과

     2. 직, 성명 : 행정사무관 주 형환

     3. 출장기간 : '91. 9. 18 ~ 9. 23.   끝

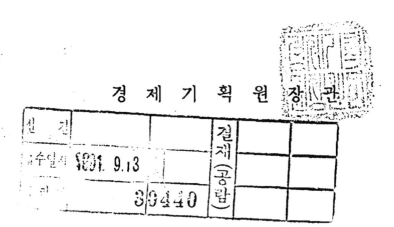

경 제 기 획 원 장 관

0015

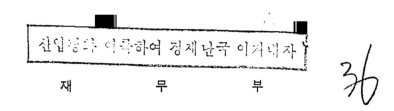

재　　　무　　　부

국금 22251-   (503-9266)   1991. 9. 13.

수신 수신처 참조

제목 UR 금융서비스 회의 참석

1. GVW-1418('91. 7. 26)와 관련입니다.

2. UR 서비스협상과 관련 스위스 제네바에서 개최되는 금융부속서
회의 (9.20)에 참석할 당부대표를 아래와 같이 파견코자 하오니 필요한
조치를 취하여 주시기 바랍니다.

- 아   래 -

소 속	성 명	기 간
국제금융과 사무관	최 희 남	9. 18 ~ 23

첨부 : 회의참석 대책   끝.

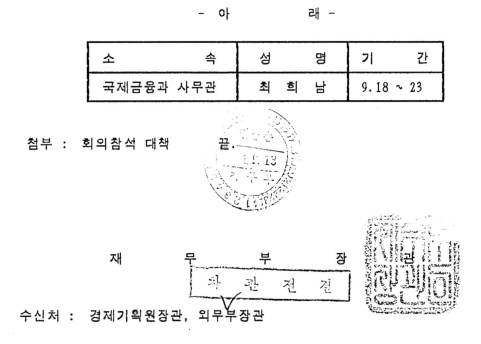

재   무   부   장

수신처 : 경제기획원장관, 외무부장관

0016

UR/금융서비스 협상 대책

'91. 9

재 무 부

0017

1. 협상동향

- 금융서비스의 특수성을 반영할 수 있는 금융부속서 제정을 목적으로
  하는 금융서비스 협상은 선·개도국간 의견대립으로 브라셀 각료회의
  에서 부속서 제정에 실패

    o 서비스 일반 협정(Framwork)보다 강화된 자유화를 주장하는 선진
      4개국안과 이에 반대하는 SEACEN안으로 대립

- 금융부속서에는 자유화 추진방식, 내국민대우, 시장접근 등을 규정할
  목적으로 협상이 진행중이며

    o 금년 4월, 7월등 2차례의 금융부속서 회의를 개최하여 선·개도국간
      의견 절충을 시도하였으나 별다른 진전이 없었음.

    o 다만, 지난 7월 회의시 선진국은 자유화 추진방식에 있어서
      개도국의 입장을 수용한 Two-Track Approach를 제안하였으며
      금년 9월 회의시 논의 예정임.

0018·

2. 주요쟁점 및 아국입장

┌─────────────────── < 아국 기본 입장 > ───────────────────┐
│   │
│   - 통화신용 정책 및 금융제도의 안정성과 건전성을 보장하기 위한   │
│   각국의 정책수행 권한이 존중되어야 함.   │
│   │
│   - 금융서비스의 자유화는 각국의 발전단계 및 금융구조의 특수성을   │
│   고려하여 단계적인 자유화가 되어야 함.   │
│   │
│   - 상기 아국입장이 반영된 SEACEN 공동안을 지지   │
│   │
└───┘

가. 자유화 추진 방식

(1) 선진국 입장

- Negative 방식에 의한 자유화 추진

   o 이는 시장접근 및 내국민대우에 대한 의무사항들을 열거하고, 동
     의무사항중 자유화가 불가능한 내용만을 명시토록하여 자유화를
     촉진하려함.

- 최근 선진국은 각국의 여건에 따라서 자유화추진방식을 선택할 수
  있으며, 자유화추진 방식의 선택으로 서비스협정상의 권리의무에
  영향을 미치지 않는다는 것을 명시하는 방안을 타협안으로 제안
  (Two-Track Approach)

0013

(2) SEACEN 입장

- Framework 규정에 따라서 각국이 자유화를 약속한 범위내에서만 적용할 것을 주장(Positive 방식)

  o 금융분야만 Framwork와는 상이한 자유화 방식채택은 부당

- 그러나 선진국이 제안한 Two-Track Approach는 각국이 자유화 추진 방식을 선택할 수 있도록 함으로써 Framework에 의한 자유화 추진이 가능하므로 수용 가능

  o 단, Framework 협상에서 논의중인 무차별적인 시장접근 제한조치를 양허계획표에 명시하는 것에는 반대

나. 내국민대우

(1) 선진국 입장

- 외국 금융서비스 공급자에게 자국내에서 수행하는 모든 업무를 할 수 있도록 하는 동등한 경쟁기회(Equal Competitive Opportunity) 까지 보장하도록 요구

  o 이를 통하여 각국의 실질적인 장벽을 제거함으로써 금융 서비스 교역 자유화 촉진

  o 증권 거래소, 결제기구, 선물거래소 등 자율규제 단체의 회원국 가입이 서비스 공급을 위하여 필요한 경우 내국민대우 대상임.

0020

(2)   SEACEN 입장

   - 내국민 대우 개념은 법적, 제도적 내국민 대우인 "보다 불리하지 않은
     대우" (No less favorable than)로 한정할 것을 주장
       o ECO의 판단기준이 불명확하고 결과를 예측할 수 없으며 불필요한
          분쟁을 야기

   - 그러나 Framework 협상에서 ECO와 유사한 사실상의 내국민대우 개념이
     채택될 가능성이 높음을 고려하여 이에 대한 대응방안 모색

다.   금융감독 관련 국내규제(Prudential Regulation)

(1)   선진국 입장

   - 예금자, 투자자 보호 및 금융제도의 안정성 보장등을 이유로한 금융
     감독 규제권한을 인정하였으나
       o 금융감독 규제권한의 남용을 방지하기 위하여 예외조항에 포함시켜
          제한적이며 객관적 기준하에 운용하도록 제한해야 함.

(2)   SEACEN 입장

   - 금융질서 및 금융제도의 안정을 위하여 광범위한 포괄범위 인정이
     필요하므로 이를 일반적 원칙으로 규정해야 하며
       o 예외조항 포함시 예외적인 경우에만 동조항을 원용해야 하며 이를
          통보하여야 하는 부담이 있음.

   - 다만 일반적원칙으로 규정할 경우 규정 남용으로 금융서비스 교역
     자유화가 무의미해질 수 있음을 감안 동 조항의 남용방지 방안을
     모색키로 함.

0021

라. 제도조항

  (1) 금융서비스 기구

    - 대부분의 국가가 동기구의 필요성과 금융전문가로 구성할 것을 인정
      하였으나, 구체적인 기능에 대하여는 논의 진전이 미비

  (2) 서비스분야간 보복

    - 금융분야의 특수성과 민감성을 고려하여 서비스 분야간 보복 금지에
      대체로 합의하고 있으나, 같은 분야내에서 보복이 불가능한 경우 등
      추가 논의가 필요

4. 금융서비스 Offer 현황

  - 금융서비스에 대한 자유화 대상이 되는 구체적 약속사항(Initial
    Commitment)을 아국 포함 17개국 제출

  - 아국 Offer(1991. 1)

    o 은행, 증권, 보험분야에 대하여 현존시장 개방 수준을 동결하는
      Commitment 제시
    o 동 Commitment에 대하여 '91. 4 주요국과의 협의가 있었는 바,
      비교적 긍정적 평가

0022

5. 향후 협상전망 및 대응방안

```
┌───────────────────< 협 상 전 망 >───────────────┐
│                                                              │
│  - UR 서비스협상의 논의가 Framework 및 부속서 등 Rule Making │
│    작업보다는 실질적인 양허협상 단계로 이전되고 있으며,      │
│                                                              │
│    o 금융분야도 금융부속서에 대한 논의보다는 전체 서비스협상 │
│      그룹에서 양허협상 위주로 진행될 것으로 전망.            │
│                                                              │
│  - 따라서 양허협상에 대한 준비작업 위주의 협상대응이 필요    │
│                                                              │
└──────────────────────────────────────────────────────────────┘
```

- 아국의 적극적인 참여로 UR 서비스협상 타결에 기여함으로서 미국
  등으로부터의 비협조적 국가라는 인식을 받지 않을 필요가 있음.

  o UR 협상은 전체적인 협상 Package로 타결되므로 특정분야에 대한
    불참은 불가능하며, 만일 협상 불참시 향후 개별적으로 금융서비스
    협상에 임하여야 하므로 개방압력이 더욱 과중될 우려가 있음.

- UR 서비스협상에 의한 금융산업에 대한 영향은 금년중에 있을 양허
  협상에 따른 결과에 달려 있으므로 이에 대한 사전 준비작업이 필요

  o 기제출한 Offer List의 수정작업을 준비하고, 그간 수집된 자료를
    중심으로 각국에 대하여 개방을 요구할 Request List 작성

0023

- UR 금융서비스 협상에서의 금융시장 개방은 현존 개방수준 위주로
  협상하되 협상과정에서 제기될 추가 개방요구는 협상전략 차원에서
  검토

  o 증권거래소 회원가입, 금융전산망 가입 등 지난 5월 한·미 금융
    회의에서 약속한 개방수준을 고려할 때 큰 문제가 없을 것으로
    예상됨.

0024

발 신 전 보

	분류번호	보존기간

번   호 :   WGV-1227   910914 1044 BE 종별 :

수   신 : 주 제네바 대사. 총영사

발   신 : 장 관 (통 기)

제   목 : UR/GNS 부속서 협상

1.   귀지에서 9.17-20 기간중 개최되는 UR/GNS 분야별 부속서 협상에 참가할 본부대표가
      아래 임명 되었으니 귀관 관계관과 함께 참석 조치바람.

   O 통신 부속서

      - 체신부 통신협력과 사무관   노영규

      - 통신개발연구원 연구위원   최병일 (자문)

   O 해운 부속서

      - 주영 대사관 해무관   최낙정

      - 해운산업연구원 주임 연구원   최동현 (자문)

   O 금융 부속서

      - 재무부 국제금융과 사무관   최희남

      - 경제기획원 통상조정3과 사무관 주형환

2.   훈령 : UR 대책 실무회의(9.12)에서 결정된 대책자료 참고(별도 송부) 예정.

                        끝.   (통상국장 김 용 규)

	보안통제	

앙고재	91년 7월 13일	통기과	기안자 성명 조현		과 장	심의관 최	국 장 전결		차 관	장 관	

외신과통제

0025

발 신 전 보

	분류번호	보존기간

번   호 : WUK-1691   910914 1043 BE 종별 : _____

수   신 : 주   영국   대사. 총영사

발   신 : 장   관 (통 기)

제   목 : UR/GNS 해운 부속서 협상

1. 제네바에서 9.19 개최되는 표제 회의에 귀관 최낙정 해무관이 정부대표로 임명
되었음. ~~다 등 회의에 참과토록 조치바람.~~

　　o 출장기간 : 9.17-20

　　o 출 장 비 : $1,028 (해운항만청에서 귀관에 송금 예정)

　　~~o 동 회 의 복부대표 (해 운산업연구원 최동현 연구원)과 지참 예정.~~

　　　　　　　　　　　끝.　　　　　(통상국장 김 용 규)

2. 다만 주제네바 대표부 보고에 의하면 동회의 개최 일자가
변경될 가능성이 있다하니, 출장전에 제네바 대표부와
연락, 정확한 회의개최일자를 확인바람.

	보 안 통 제	Ur

앙고재	년 월 13일 통 기 과	기안자성명 조현	과장 Ur	심의관 최	국장 전결		차관	장관 Ur	

	외신과통제

0026

37-3

UR/해운분야 부속서 회의대책 자료

'91. 9

혜 운 항 만 청

UR/해운분야 부속서 회의대책 자료

1. 회의 개요

가. 일시 및 장소

o 일 시 : '91. 9. 17 (1일간)

o 장 소 : 제네바 GATT 본부

나. 회의내용 : 해운분야 부속서 협의

다. 대 표 단

o 주영대사관 해무관 최 낙 정

o 해운산업연구원 주임연구원 최 동 현

라. 소요예산

o 주영해무관

- 출장기간 : '91. 9. 15 ～ 9. 18

- 출 장 비 : $1,028 (항공료 : $582, 체재비 : $446)

o 최동현 : KMI에서 부담

0028

2. 해운분야 부속서 협상경위 및 동향

  가. 경위

    o '90. 5 제4차 GNS 회의시 분야별 부속서 작성 작업반 구성

    o '90. 9.24 - 25 ───┐
                        │ 해운분야 부속서 회의 개최
    o '90.10.29 - 31 ──┘ - 부속서 작성의 필요성 인식

    o '90.11.17 해운분야 비공식 회의 개최
                - 부속서 초안에 규정할 사항 확인 및 협의

  나. 진전상황

    o '90. 10월까지 해운분야 회의를 몇차례 개최 하였으나 각 국별 입장
      차이 심화
      - 기본적인 입장만 표명 하였을 뿐 합의사항 없음

    o '90.11월 사무국에서 부속서 초안 작성 및 비공식 회의 개최

    o 현재까지 합의에 도달하지 못하고 몇가지의 대안을 동시에 표기해 놓고
      있는 실정임

  다. 주요 국가동향

    o 해운분야 MFN 일탈 및 인인분야외의 협상 적용 관란 (미국)

    o 현존하는 쌍무협상 및 다자간 협정에 대하여는 일정기간 유예후 점신적
      으로 GNS 체제로 흡수 (EC, 유고, 맥시코)

3. 금번 회의시 주요 생심사항 (예상)

  o 금번 회의시에는 그동안 추진하여온 해운분야 부속시 내용에 대한 각국의
    의견을 조정할 것으로 예상되며

  o 기타 사항이 논의될 경우에는 각국의 입장 표명선에서 회의가 마무리될
    것으로 예상됨

4. 대 책

기. 기본입장

  o 해운산업은 국제적 특성으로 국제간 협력 및 국제질서 확립이 불가피한
    분야이므로 UR 협상에 능동적으로 대응

  o 특히, 우리나라는 미국, EC등 선진국과의 쌍무협의를 통해 상당히 개방
    되어 있어 UR 협상 시행에 따른 영향이 적은 분야임

  o 따라서 금번 회의에 적극 참여하여 우리나라의 입장을 반영함과 동시에
    협상내용 및 추이와 각국의 동향을 파악하여 향후 UR 대책에 활용

0030

나. 해운분야 부속서 주요내용 및 입장

구 분	부 속 서 주 요 내 용	아 국 입 장
적용범위 ㅇ 제 1 조	ㅇ 관련 보조 써비스를 포함한 해운써비스에 적용	ㅇ 연안해운 제외 - 아국 연안 해운의 영세성 및 안보와의 관련성
M F N ㅇ 제 2 조	〈 안 〉 ㅇ 적용배제 〈 안 〉 ㅇ 기존 또는 장래의 쌍무협정 및 협약에 의한 화물배분 및 유보조치는 다음 조건으로 적용 배제 - Liner Code 및 비통행 선사에 관한 등 협정의 결의안 2호의 규정과 일치하는 조치들로서 기본 협정 제2조 1항 (최혜국대우 조항)의 규정에 반하는 사항은 199x. 1. 1까지 철폐	ㅇ UN Liner Code에 일치하는 기존 협정은 계속 존치 - 해운산업의 특정 다기성 및 국제성을 고려 기존 국제협약 존중 필요 ㅇ 기존 쌍무협정의 MFN 적용 곤란 - 쌍무협정은 양국간 give and take 형태로 이루어 진 것임 - MFN 적용시 상당기간의 유예기간 부여후 적용 바람직

0031

구 분	부 속 서 주 요 내 용	양 국 입 장
○ 제 6 조	○ 항만·부두·선석·창고·하역시설 등의 기간 시설에의 접근과 시설 사용에 대해 기본협정 제16조 및 제17조 (시장접근, 내국민 대우)에 의거 약속한 사항은 취소 또는 손상금지 - 단, 기간 시설의 부족으로 불가피한 경우는 예외	○ 부속서 내용 지지
재 검 토 ○ 제 7 조	○ 기본협정 발효후 X 년에 재검토하고 이후 정기적으로 재검토	○ 기본협정 발효후 5년 내에 재검토 - 해운분야의 기존 협정등 고려 (Liner Code 등)
부 록	○ 본 부속서 제3항에 의거 목록 추가	

다 . 기타사항

○ 기타사항은 우리나라 해운실정을 고려하여 국익이 되는 방향에서 적절히 대응

구분	부속서 주요 내용	이견 · 입장
	- 상기 이외의 조치들로서 기본협정 제2조 1항(최혜국 대우 조항)의 규정에 반하는 조치는 199X.1.1까지 철폐 - 상기 내용을 회피하기 위한 신규조치 금지	
o 제 3 조	o 본 부속서 부록에 열거된 특별조치나 연안해운에는 적용 배제	o 적용대상 및 범위(제1조)에서 연안해운이 제외될 경우 연안해운의 기재 불필요 o 제외되지 않을 경우 부속서안 지지
기타 조항		
o 제 4 조	o 기본협정 제3조는 해운동맹과 관련된 모든 사항에 적용(기본협정 제3조 : 공개주의)	o 국가안보와 관련된 사항 공개 유보
o 제 5 조	o 보조금에 관한 협상 및 결과가 시행될 때까지 체약국은 운임 동맹 관행에 대한 현행 제정 및 적용 가능	o 삭제 또는 보조금에 대한 개념 명확화 필요 - 보조금에 대한 개념 불명확으로 규제 수단으로 외국 시행 가능 - 산업구조 조정 등 특별한 상황 발생시 한정적으로 허용할 수 있다는 내용 추가

종 별 :

외 무 부

번 호 : GVW-1775   일 시 : 91 0918 1730

수 신 : 장 관(통기,경기원,재무부,법무부,상공부,건설부,보사부,노동부,교통부,

발 신 : 주 제네바 대사대리   체신부,문화부,공보처,과기처,항만청)

제 목 : UW/GNS 협상표제 협상 관련

 '91 하반기 협상 진행 계획에관한 GNS 의장의 비공식 문서를 별첨 송부하니 참고
바람.

 첨부: UR/GNS 협상 계획 1부(GVW(F)-352).끝

 (차석대사 김삼훈-국장)

통상국	2차보	법무부	보사부	문화부	교통부	체신부	경기원	재무부
상공부	건설부	노동부	과기처	해항청	공보처			

PAGE 1

91.09.19   09:29 WG

외신 1과 통제관

0034

WORK PROGRAMME FOR THE GNS

Note by the Chairman

1.   I have received requests from several delegations to present my views on the GNS work programme for the remainder of this year. This note outlines my views on this matter.

2.   The agreed assumption is that the GNS should complete its work by the end of this year. This would allow four formal meetings during which work should proceed in a parallel fashion on the three main areas -- the GATS draft text, the annexes and initial commitments. The amount of work that remains to be done is enormous and the time available is short. In order to conduct our work in the most efficient way, this note lays out a programme which attempts to divide the outstanding issues among the remaining four meetings in a logical manner. It does not present an exhaustive listing of the work before the group.

3.   This programme is not meant to be followed in a rigid manner, nor is it meant to be the subject of a discussion on which valuable negotiating time would be spent. Adjustments almost certainly would have to be made as we go along. This note is divided in terms of meetings of the GNS, although this autumn it may be necessary for negotiators to meet almost continuously. At this time it is possible to see in some detail how work could proceed on the outstanding issues in the GATS draft text, while in the other two areas -- the Annexes and initial commitments -- it is difficult to present that same level of detail.

7-1

0035

4. The note presents three categories of issues in the GATS draft text on which work would proceed in each of the four meetings. These are: issues to be resolved; issues on which work would continue; and issues on which work will recommence.

September meeting

5. Issues to be resolved:

(a) The scheduling group of Articles (VI, XVI, XVII, XVIII, XIX and XX).

(b) Substantive guidelines for the negotiation of initial commitments, with the relevant parts of Articles IV and XVIII.

(c) MFN, attempting to reach agreement on the techniques to be followed in dealing with problems in this area (Article II).

6. Issues on which substantive work should continue:

(a) MFN, on the basis of the agreement reached in 5(c), measures subject to such techniques, and the conditions to be attached (time limits, periodic review, etc.).

(b) Definition of terms (Article XXXIV).

0036

7. Substantive work would recommence on:

   (a) Exceptions (Article XIV).

   (b) Dispute settlement (Articles XXII and XXIII).

   (c) Economic integration (Article V).

8. With respect to Annexes:

   (a) Work should be advanced, to the maximum extent possible, on the Annex on the movement of natural persons. It is, of course, understood that progress on some issues in this Annex will depend on the resolution of other issues in the GATS itself (Articles II, V and XIV).

   (b) On financial services, the group should continue to work towards arriving at a common draft Annex.

   (c) On telecommunications services the group should work towards resolving outstanding issues.

   (d) Other sectoral issues could be raised.

9. Negotiations on initial commitments should be intensified at this stage. Progress achieved on relevant Articles of the GATS, negotiating guidelines and the Annex on the movement of natural persons should provide the basis for substantial progress in this area including revision of offers, submission of new ones as well as submission of requests. Decisions are

9—3

0037

necessary on approaches and techniques to be followed in this area. It is understood, of course, that the process of negotiations on initial commitments may not be confined to periods of the GNS meetings.

10. A proposal by the Nordic countries on maritime transport is scheduled for discussion in the September meeting (MTN.GNS/W/135)

October meeting

11. Issues to be resolved:

    (a) MFN, measures for which derogations from MFN are sought (Article II).

    (b) Definition of terms (Article XXXIV).

    (c) Exceptions (Article XIV).

12. Issues on which work should continue:

    (a) MFN, legal solutions on requests for derogations, conditions applying to derogations (Article II).

    (b) Dispute settlement (Articles XXII and XXIII).

    (c) Economic integration (Article V).

13. Issues on which work would recommence:

7-4

0038

- 5 -

(a) (Begin work on) Rules of origin.

(b) Harmonization and recognition (Article VII).

(c) Non-application (Article XXX).

(d) Payments and transfers, and restrictions to
safeguard balance of payments (Articles XI and XII).

14. Work on Annexes should proceed in the light of progress
achieved at the September meeting.

(a) Outstanding issues in the Annex on the movement of
natural person should be resolved.

(b) On financial services, the group should arrive at a
common draft Annex on the basis of which
negotiations would continue in the November meeting.

(c) On telecommunications services, the group should
continue to work towards resolving outstanding
issues in the draft Annex.

(d) Decisions with respect to the need for other
annexes.

15. Negotiations on initial commitments should be further
intensified in the light of progress achieved in different
areas.

7-5

16. A legal drafting group should be convened, consisting of legal experts and negotiators, to begin work at the close of the October meeting.

November meeting:

17. Issues to be resolved (or options clearly identified for final December meeting):

  (a) MFN (Article II).

  (b) Dispute settlement (Articles XXII and XXIII).

  (c) Economic integration (Article V).

  (d) Harmonization and recognition (Article VII).

  (e) Non-application (Article XXX).

  (f) Any other issues which might have arisen.

18. Issues on which work would continue:

  (a) Rules of origin.

  (b) Payments and transfers, and restrictions to safeguard the balance of payments (Articles XI and XII.

7-6

0040

19. Work on the Annexes should be completed. This is necessary to facilitate concluding negotiations on initial commitments.

20. Negotiations on initial commitments should be nearing conclusion. The GNS should carry out a multilateral review.

21. Legal drafting group continues its work.

December meeting

22. Work should be completed in all three areas and the final package should emerge. The legal drafting group should complete its work and prepare the final texts for adoption.

23. Finally, I would like to stress that, from the September meeting onward, negotiations will be at a stage where participants have to be prepared to take decisions on specific issues, recognizing of course that nothing is finally agreed until everything is agreed.

발 신 전 보

분류번호 보존기간

번 호 : WGV-1274　910920 1934　FN　종별 :

수 신 : 주 제네바　대사. 총영사

발 신 : 장 관 (통 기)

제 목 : UR/GNS 부속서 협상(정부대표 출장기간 연장)

연 : WGV-1227

　　　금융부속서 공식 회의(9.20)에 참석차 귀지에 출장중인 최희남 사무관의 출장기간을
9.26까지로 연장 하였으니 9.21-24간 개최되는 UR/GNS(금융) 비공식 회의에도 계속
참석토록 조치바람. 　　　　　　　끝. 　　　　　　　　(통상국장 김 용 규)

보 안 통 제

앙고재	91년 9월 20일	통기 과	기안자 성명	과 장	국 장	차 관	장 관
			조현	대결	전결		

외신과통제

0042

주 제 네 바 대 표 부

제네(경) 20644-*794*   1991. 9. 20

수신 : 외무부장관

참조 : 통상국장, 경제기획원장관

제목 : UR/서비스 협상

     '91.7.24 한.북구간 양자협의시 스웨덴 Offer에 관한 아측 질문에 대한 스웨덴의 서면 답변을 별첨 송부합니다.

     첨부 : 스웨덴의 서면답변 1부.   끝.

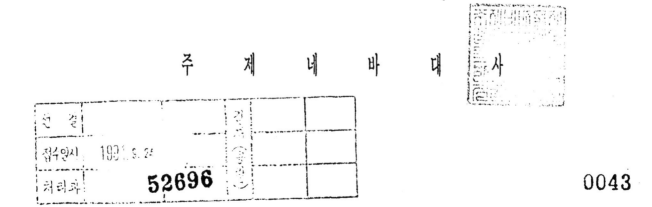

Geneva, 17 September 1991

Mr. Chol Soo Han
Permanent Mission of the
Republic of Korea
20, route de Pré-Bois
1215 Geneva

Dear Mr. Han,

Enclosed please find written answers to the
questions your country posed to Sweden at our
bilateral meeting in July on our offers in the
services negotiations within the GATT.

With regard the telecommunication services, I hope
that our experts get an opportunity to discuss your
questions in the margins of the GNS meeting on
telecommunications this week.

Yours sincerely,

Anders Ahnlid
First Secretary

/Gunilla Sandberg
Secretary

Encl. 1

0044

Postal Address	Street Address	Telephone	Telegrams	Telex
Délégation Permanente de Suède	9-11, Rue de Varembé	022/34 36 00	Svensk	22 112
Case Postale 190				
CH - 1211 GENÈVE 20				

302　우루과이라운드 서비스 협상 2

GATT/UR/SERVICES: Replies to the Korean questions on the Swedish
offer, forwarded to the Swedish Delegation in Geneva at the
bilateral consultation, July 24th, 1991.

GENERAL

Q.1: Does Sweden have any regulations on the equity-participation
at foreign investments? What does the foreign ownership clause
mean?

A.1: Yes, the equity-participation at foreign investments is
regulated in the "Law on foreign acquisition of Swedish firms"
./1   (SFS 1982:617). We enclose an _informal_ translation (enclosure 1)
of this law. In section 4 of this law the foreign ownership
clause is explained.

Q.2: Are there two different authorisation needed; one under
"Establishment" on page 4 and one under "Conduct of commercial
operations" on page 5?

A.2: Yes.

Q.3: What does Sweden mean by "independent" branch on page 5 (8
lines from the bottom)? Does this relate to cross-border supply?

A.3: The text on page 5, regarding the "independent" branch,
relates to establishment and the law about the requirement for
foreign legal entities and persons with foreign citizenships, to
have (at least) a branch in Sweden in order to be permitted to
conduct business here. These regulations aim at giving an
established business a certain degree of connection to Sweden.
The branch should have a managing director with residency in
Sweden. Thus, this regulations do not relate to "cross-border
supply", instead it relates to "commercial presence".

0045

Q.4: On page 6, first paragraph, what regulations are adressed in the brackets - (Regulations to be liberalized) - in the market access column? And what kind of conditions may be specified in individual licences (see national treatment column)? Are these conditions the same for locals and foreigners?

A.4: Below we give you an <u>informal</u> summary of the relevant regulations:

The "Law on temporary trade, L 1975:985", was been replaced by a new law on the 1st of April, 1991, the "Law on temporary trade, L 1990:1183"; These laws concerns trade, conducted in a temporary sales place including markets, fairs, exhibitions, etc., and are the same for foreigners and locals. The new law means a liberalization, as it normally does not require an authorization for the conduct of temporary trade and as the old law required a permit for all temporary trade except for food, flowers, handicraft and printed matters.

L 1990:1183 (the new law); When conducting temporary trade, the salesperson must clearly post his name, address and telephone number. If the price that the consumer totally pay exceeds 300 SEK, this information should also be given to the consumer in writing.

Authorization for temporary trade in clothing, shoes or food (which is not intended for immediate consumption) might be required by the government in special cases, when it is considered necessary regarding the supply of goods in a certain area. Such authorization is given by the local authorities and shall be granted, if the sale is not expected to cause disturbance for the supply of goods in the area.

LAND TRANSPORT

Q.1: Korea would like to get more information about our bilateral agreements under the section "International Road Transport".

A.1: Sweden has bilateral agreements about international road transports with 29, mainly European, countries.

The number of permits for bilateral traffic as well as for third-country traffic is negotiated every year.

0046

AIR TRANSPORT

Q.1: What does Sweden mean by "authorized services" under Sales and Marketing on page 27?

A.1: This refers to the fact that a company is only allowed to sell and market air transport services from the very moment that they have obtained the concession for the same services, and not beforehand.

DISTRIBUTION SERVICES

Q.1: Sweden states that "Rules on comissions, licenced agencies and travelling salesmen" are under review. What regulations?

A.1: The rules on commissions, licenced agencies and travelling salesmen (L 1914:45) have been replaced by two new laws which will enter into force on January 1st, 1992. A translation of the old law into English exists, but not yet for the new ones.

./2 We enclose a translation of the old law (enclosure 2) and explain the differencies between it and the two new ones here below. If you desire the exact formulations of the new laws, we will be glad to return to you, once the new laws have entered into force and a translation into English exist.

The first new law, SFS 1991:352, is titled "Law on commission" and is largely the same as the old L 1914:45, with the following changes;
- chapter 3 and 4 are abolished,
- 27 § is replaced in order to strengthen the possibility for an agent to get commission on goods sold after the end of his contract but as a result of his sales efforts under the contract's duration,
- some minor editorial changes.

The second law, SFS 1991:351, is a new law titled "Law on licenced agencies" which only deals with the rights and obligations of licenced agencies, previously stated in the old L 1914:45, chapter 3 and 4. The new law entails a strengthened position for the licenced agency towards his principal and is compatible with the EEC directive, dealing with the same issue. The regulations about travelling salesmen are abolished and instead normal employment regulations apply for this category.

0047

Informal Embassy translation

SWEDISH STATUTES AT LARGE   (SFS)

SFS 1982:617
Printed June 29, 1982

Law
On Foreign Acquisitions of Swedish Firms, Etc;

promulgated June 17, 1982.

In accordance with the decision of Parliament 1/, the following is
stipulated.

Introductory Regulations

Section 1. This law contains regulations limiting the right of foreign
legal entities and certain Swedish legal entities to acquire shares in
Swedish corporations, holdings in Swedish trading partnerships, or
business operations conducted in the country. The law also restricts the
right to participate in a Swedish trading partnership.

Section 2. This law does not apply to Swedish banking or insurance
corporations or to the stock of such corporations.

Control Subjects

Section 3. Control subjects according to this law are:
    1. aliens and other foreign legal entities,
    2. Swedish corporations which lack a foreign-ownership restriction
clause in their articles of incorporation,
    3. Swedish trading partnerships if one of the partners is a control
subject,

1/ Bill 1981/82 No. 135, Economics Committee Report No. 56,
     Parliamentary Decision No. 378.

0048

4. Swedish foulldations,

5. Swedish incorporated associations whose activities are regulated by the law (1951, No. 308) on incorporated associations, the tenancy rights law (1971, No. 479), the law (1975, No. 417) on collective farming associations, or by older legislation corresponding to the law on incorporated associations or the tenancy rights law.

The first paragraph of subsection 5 does not apply to

a) associations--excepting collective farming associations--whose main object is to promote the economic interests of its members by

obtaining foodstuffs or other supplies for its members,

selling the produce of its members' operations,

selling the transportation services provided by its members,

obtaining housing other than recreational housing for its members, or obtaining loans for its members,

b) associations formed into a group which is not a control subject.

A Swedish foundation or Swedish incorporated association may be freed of the appellation 'control subject' by dispensation. Such dispensations may be limited in time and can be withdrawn should there no longer exist any prerequisites for dispensation.

Foreign-Ownership Restriction Clauses

Section 4. For the purposes of this law, the term 'foreign-ownership restriction clause' shall mean a clause included in the articles of incorporation of a Swedish firm whereby a control subject, by subscription or by transfer, may only acquire a certain portion of shares in the company: at any one time corresponding to less than forty percent of the entire share capital and less than 20 percent of the voting strength of all shares in the company. The term 'foreign-ownership restriction clause' shall also apply to clauses imposing stricter conditions of this kind.

Special permission may also be granted for other clauses than those in the first paragraph to be regarded as foreign-ownership restriction clauses.

Section 5. A foreign-ownership restriction clause does not prevent the acquisition of stock belonging to a share investment fund as defined in the Share Investment Fund Law (1974, No. 931) or of portions of such a fund.

Alteration of a foreign-ownership restriction clause

Section 6. A foreign-ownership restriction clause may not be altered without permission.

0049

Acquisition permits

Section 7. Without permission (an acquisiton permit) in each separate instance, a control subject may not acquire
   1. so many shares in a Swedish corporation as to make the purchaser's holding of the share capital or voting strength of all shares in the corporation, through the acquisition, exceed any of the ceilings of ten, twenty, forty, or fifty percent,
   2. holdings in a Swedish trading partnership,
   3. the rights of ownership or rights of use of business operations conducted in the country or portions of such operations.

Section 8. When assessing the number of shares in accordance with Section 7, each share shall be counted if it belongs to
   1. a firm which is part of the same group as the acquirer,
2. a firm over which the acquirer exerts a controlling interest, if the acquirer is an alien,
   3. the acquirer's spouse, children, parents, or siblings, or to a firm over which one of these relations exerts a controlling interest.

Section 9. An acquisition permit is not required for acquisition
   1. through estate distribution, inheritance, or bequest,
   2. through merger in accordance with Chapter 14, Section 8 of the Corporation Law (1975, No. 1365),
   3. of shares belonging to a share investment fund in accordance with the Share Investment Fund Law (1974, No. 931) or of holdings in such a fund,
   4. of shares which on new issue or stock dividend issue are acquired with preference in relation to the number of shares previously held by the acquirer,
   5. of shares which the acquirer has the right to purchase by reason of a proviso in accordance with Chapter 3, Section 3 of the Corporation Law, if the acquirer has received permission, notwithstanding the provisions of Section 7, to acquire shares in the firm by reason of the proviso.

Section 10. If an acquisition permit has not been sought before the acquisition, the acquirer must do so after no more than one month has elapsed from the date of acquisition.

Section 11. If an acquisition permit is not applied for within the prescribed time and in the prescribed manner, or if a permit is refused, the acquisition shall be invalid.
   If an acquisition of shares which are not restricted by a foreign-ownership restriction clause has been effected on the Stockholm Stock Exchange or by bid at a court-enforced auction, the first paragraph shall not apply. Instead, the permit authority shall direct the acquirer to sell the shares within six months or within a longer period should the authority so decide. :·

Permission to Participate in a Trading Partnership

Section 12. A control subject may not contract to participate in a Swedish trading partnership without permission.

Agreements signed in contravention of the first paragraph shall be invalid.

Acquisition of Shares in Contravention of Foreign-Ownership Restriction Clauses, Etc.

Section 13. The acquisition of shares in contravention of a foreign-ownership restriction clause shall be invalid. A person holding convertible bonds or option certificates as defined in Chapter 5 of the Corporation Law (1975, No. 1385) may, however, acquire unrestricted shares through exchange or new subscription if the convertible bond or option certificate grants this right, even though the proportion of restricted to unrestricted shares may thereby be altered or already have been altered in contravention of the restriction clause.

Section 14. Should an individual acquire, by subscription or transfer, shares which are restricted by a foreign-ownership restriction clause and that individual become a control subject after the acquisition, the individual must have permission in order to keep the shares.

Such permission must be sought by the shareholder no later than three months after his or her becoming a control subject. If permission is not sought within the prescribed time and in the prescribed manner, or if permission is refused, the permit authority shall direct the shareholder to sell the shares within six months or within a longer period should the authority so decide.

Permit Examination

Section 15. Questions relating to permits under this law shall be assessed by the Government or authority designated by the Government.

Section 16. A permit in accordance with this law shall be granted if it does not conflict with any key public interest.

Decisions on acquisition permits shall record any undertakings which the acquirer or, regarding the acquisition of shares or a part of a business, the firm involved in the acquisition may have made in connection with the transaction and which have been accorded importance in the permit examination.

Section 17. If the permit concerns some future acquisition, a certain duration for the validity of the permit shall be stated in the permit decision.

0051

Section 18. Permission to participate in a trading partnership or to acquire holdings in a trading partnership will be granted only if there exists an agreement by which the partnership has undertaken to be formed or participation to be allowed when permission is granted.

Responsibility, Etc.

Section 19. A fine or maximum imprisonment of six months will be imposed on anyone who wilfully or through gross negligence submits incorrect information in cases involving this law.

Criminal proceedings will only be instituted on the instructions of the Government or authority designated by the Government.

Section 20. Injunctions issued under this law may be combined with the penalty of a fine. Proceedings to impose a fine may only be initiated on the instructions of the Government or the authority designated by the Government.

Appeals

Section 21. If a decision involving this law has been made by some other body than the Government, appeal against the decision may be lodged with the Government.

Secrecy

Section 22. Whoever has come to learn about the business dealings or operating status of an individual by reason of the regulations of this law shall not improperly divulge or make use of what he or she has thus learned.

The activities of publicly-owned enterprises, on the other hand, will be subject to the provisions of the Secrecy Law (1980, No. 100).

———————————————————————

The implementation of this law is decreed in a separate law.

On behalf of the Government

    THORBJÖRN FÄLLDIN

                      CARL AXEL PETRI
                     (Ministry of Justice)

(SWEDISH) ACT OF APRIL 18, 1914, REGARDING FACTORS, COMMERCIAL AGENTS AND COMMERCIAL TRAVELLERS*

Chapter 1
General provisions

Article 1

The rules of this Act shall be applied only in so far as no provision to the contrary has been agreed upon by the parties or follows from the customs of trade or other usages.

It is stated in Article 45 that in certain cases a contract or custom cannot be invoked against the provisions of this Act.

Article 2

For the purposes of this Act "merchant" shall mean anyone who has a statutory duty to keep books.

Article 3

Where this Act provides that unless a party gives due notice to another party, the former forfeits his right of action or shall be deemed to have accepted an offer, a contract or a payment, and where a message containing such notice is duly delivered to a post or telegraph office or otherwise dispatched in an expedient manner, the fact that such message is delivered too late or lost shall not be held to imply that the sender has not fulfilled his duties as set out above.

Chapter 2
On commission
Introductory provisions

Article 4

For the purposes of this Act "factor"[1] shall mean a person who has accepted a commission to sell or to buy goods, securities or other personal property on behalf of another person but in his own name. The person on whose behalf such sale or purchase is to be effected is called "principal"[2].

If the factor is a merchant, and the commission entrusted to him refers to a sale or purchase within the customary course of his business, he is called "mercantile factor"[3] and such commission is called "mercantile commission"[4].

Article 5

Where a person whose regular business is to sell or buy goods as a mercantile factor is invited by anyone with whom he stands in a business relationship to undertake a commission regarding a sale or purchase falling within the customary course of his business and such factor does not wish to accept the commission, he has a duty to inform the other party without unreasonable delay. Should he neglect to do so he shall be deemed to have accepted the offer.

---

* Translation (supplemented in the Institute) from: Unification of Law. Yearbook 1961, ed. Unidroit (Rome 1962) 225.—Similar Acts have been enacted in Denmark (8/5/1917) and Norway (30/6/1916).
[1] The term used in the Swedish law is: "Kommissionär".
[2] The term used in the Swedish law is: "Kommittent".
[3] The term used in the Swedish law is: "Handelskommissionär".
[4] The term used in the Swedish law is: "Handelskommission".

220

Article 14

.Where, under a contract or by trade custom or other usage, the factor stands *del credere*, he answers to the principal as for his own debt for the fulfilment of a contract concluded by him for the principal's account with a third party.

Likewise, even where a mercantile factor does not stand *del credere*, the principal has a right to demand from him the performance of a contract if, in his report to the principal on the fulfilment of the commission concerned, the factor does not disclose the name of the party with whom such contract has been concluded.

Article 15

Where a factor who has concluded an agreement for the principal's account has shown neglect in the fulfilment of his commission either when concluding such agreement or subsequently, the principal has a right to repudiate such contract, provided his interests have been essentially neglected or the factor has acted fraudulently against him.

Where a principal has thus repudiated a contract, but is barred by the provision in Article 54 from recovering goods sold by the factor, such factor shall be liable for the value of the goods.

Article 16

Where a factor has bought at a higher price or sold at a lower price than that which the principal has fixed or it should otherwise have been the factor's duty to determine but such factor repays without unreasonable delay the price difference to the principal or provides satisfactory security for it, the principal is not entitled to repudiate the contract, unless the factor has acted fraudulently against him or the factor's conduct has caused him damage or inconvenience which is not repaid through the price difference and which is of such character as to provide a cause of action under Article 15, paragraph 1.

222

Article 17

.Where a factor has shown neglect in the fulfilment of his commission, the principal is entitled to compensation for damage arising from such neglect.

Article 18

Where goods are sold at a lower price or bought at a higher price than the principal has stipulated owing to a factor's neglect, and where such contract is not repudiated, the principal, *if unable to prove* greater damage, is entitled to receive from the factor the difference between the stipulated price and the price obtained or, where a deviation from the price was called for by the circumstances but the factor made a greater deviation than demanded, the difference between the price obtained and that which should rightly have been fixed by the factor.

Article 19

Where a sales factor has shown neglect by unjustifiedly permitting a delay with the payment of the purchase money, and where such contract is not repudiated by the principal, such factor has a duty to pay the purchase money, even though he is not a *del credere* agent, and also to account for the same on the date when the commission should have been accounted for, if no delay had been granted.

If the factor can prove that the goods would have realized a lower price if no delay of payment had been granted, he is not obliged to account for more than such lower price.

Article 20

If a principal considers that a factor has shown neglect in the fulfilment of his commission, and if he therefore wishes to repudiate a contract concluded for his account, to claim damages from the factor or to make use against him of the remedy provided for in Article 19, such principal has a duty to notify the factor that he will

0054

delivery in instalments and payment shall be effected separately for each consignment, the fact that the contract has not been performed with regard to any one particular consignment shall not affect the factor's right to commission for the remaining consignments.

Where a contract is not performed by the third party, the factor should nevertheless receive a commission, where such non-performance is due to the principal or to any event which he, if he had himself concluded the contract with the third party, would not have been able to plead against the latter.

Article 28

A sales factor is not entitled to any commission where the purchase money is only partly paid, unless that fact is due to an event of the kind referred to in Article 27, paragraph 2. However, if the commission which would be due if the whole purchase money had been paid exceeds the deficit, in the full payment, the factor is entitled to the difference.

The rule set out in paragraph 1 above shall be applicable also with regard to a buying factor's right to a commission where a contract is only partly performed by the vendor.

Article 29

Expenses for postage, telegrams and telephone calls, insurance premiums for the goods and other costs which a factor has incurred shall be paid to him separately provided that such expenses are reasonable and that the commission or other compensation to which he is entitled is not meant also to include payment for them. The factor is entitled to reimburse himself for carriage, warehousing or other similar charges for the goods, even though he has not had special outlays therefor.

Article 30

If a factor has had to perform by his own means a contract concluded by him

224

with a third party for the principal's account he has a claim of reimbursement against the principal.

A principal is not liable to repay an advance payment, which a buying factor has granted the vendor without the principal's permission, unless the vendor performs the contract to a corresponding extent.

Article 31

A sales factor who has granted the principal an advance of the purchase money, or who has any other claim against the principal in connection with the commission has a lien for such claim on goods consigned to him for sale, where he himself, or through a third party, is in possession of the goods, of a bill of lading or of such way-bill thereto as the sender must produce in order to be entitled to dispose of the goods.

Article 32

Where the principal is a merchant, a mercantile factor has a lien as set out in Article 31 on goods which he has been commissioned to sell, also for claims arising from any other commission for the principal's business.

Article 33

Where a sales factor's security would otherwise be imperilled, he is entitled, on the strength of the lien granted to such factors under Articles 31 and 32, to retain goods which the principal claims back, and also otherwise to disregard the principal's instructions. If such instructions include prohibition of sale, however, the factor may deviate from them only under the conditions set out in Article 34.

Article 34

When a claim for which a sales factor has a lien on the principal's goods is due for payment, the factor is entitled to sell such goods to make himself paid. Where

0055

The provisions of paragraphs 1 and 2 above shall also be applicable with regard to goods which a factor has in his possession for sale but which he is no longer bound to have in his charge: where such goods are sold, however, the factor has the same right to commission as he would otherwise have had.

Article 39

Where, for the fulfilment of his commission, a factor has received samples, patterns, etc. belonging to the principal and not intended for sale, such factor is entitled to retain what he has received, provided that his security for any claim founded upon his commission would otherwise be jeopardized, and only until the principal pays the claim concerned or gives satisfactory security for its payment.

Sales and purchases for the factor's own account

· Article 40

A factor is entitled to execute commissions entrusted to him by acting as buyer or vendor of the goods for his own account only where such right follows from contract, trade, or other usages.

Article 41

A factor is deemed to act for his own account where, in his notice relative to the discharge of the commission, he expressly informs the principal that he himself is the buyer or vendor of the goods.

Where a principal wants to assert that the factor was not entitled to act as buyer or vendor for his own account under Article 40 above, the principal shall give notice of such claim to the factor without unreasonable delay after the principal has been informed by the factor that the latter has acted as buyer or vendor for his own account. If the principal fails to give such notice, he forfeits his right to repudiate the factor's acting for his own account on the grounds set out in the present Article.

226

Article 42

When acting as buyer or vendor for his own account, a factor shall protect the principal's interests with the same care and diligence as required of him when discharging commissions for the principal by entering into agreements with third parties.

The following particular rules shall be observed with regard to the price at which a factor may buy or sell the principal's goods for his own account. The principal shall always be entitled to a price no less favourable than that current at the time when the factor dispatched his notice in respect of a transaction for his own account or when he gave such notice verbally. Where a sales factor has previously, for his own account, disposed of goods received by him for sale, he must not render accounts in respect of such goods showing a price lower than that current at the time when he disposed of the goods. Where a buying factor, after having received a request to undertake a commission, but prior to acting for his own account, has bought such goods to which the commission refers, the principal is entitled to claim that account be rendered in conformity with the price to which the factor has himself offered, unless the latter can show that he did not make the purchase in consequence of the principal's request. If a factor fails to perform the duties incumbent upon him with regard to the calculation of the price, the rules of Articles 15 to 17, 20 and 24 shall be observed, so far as applicable.

Article 43

After a factor has purchased or sold the principal's goods for his own account, such factor has, in relation to the principal, all the privileges and duties of a buyer or vendor respectively.

Where a factor has bought or sold for his own account, he has the same right to a commission as he would have been entitled to if he had discharged the commission by entering into an agreement with a third party. The factor is also entitled to receive

0056

Article 63

Where a principal is not entitled to make, against a third party, a claim on the strength of a contract of the kind referred to in Article 56, but the third party pays money or delivers goods to the principal, such third party is nevertheless bound to perform his obligations under the contract to the factor unless it is shown that the latter does not suffer any damage as a result of the payment being made or the goods being delivered directly to the principal.

Article 64

Where a sales factor makes use of his right to demand payment for goods sold from a third party and the third party wishes to deduct such claim as he may have upon the factor from the debt, such deduction may take place notwithstanding the fact that when concluding the contract or, where his claim on the factor has arisen later, at the time when such claim arose, the third party knew that the factor entered into the contract for the account of another. A claim on the principal may be invoked against a factor as a ground for deduction only in so far as it is shown that the factor will not suffer any damage through such deduction.

Should the claim be enforced by the principal, a third party is entitled to make deductions not only for such claims as he may have on the principal but also for such claims on the factor as have arisen for the third party at a time when he neither realized nor ought to have realized that it was the principal who had the right to make the claim against him.

Chapter 3
On commercial agency

Article 65

For the purposes of this Act, "commercial agent"[1] shall mean a person, who has accepted a commission for the account of another (the principal) to work for the sale of goods by soliciting orders for the principal or concluding contracts of sale in his name, provided that such agent is not in the principal's service but conducts his activity as an independent business with his own office or other accommodation of his own for such business, to which communications concerning the business may be sent.

Article 66

A commercial agent has a duty to protect the principal's interests when performing the commission. He should supply necessary information; in particular he should send to the principal without delay such offers as are worthy of consideration, and report upon contracts of sale which he has concluded for the principal's account.

Article 67

Where a commercial agent has caused damage to his principal by neglect in the fulfilment of the commission, the principal is entitled to compensation.

If the principal wishes to make such a claim, it is his duty to inform the agent that he will take action regarding such neglect without unnecessary delay after he has been informed by the agent about the matter in question. Should the principal omit to do so, he forfeits his right of action provided that the agent has not acted dishonestly against him or has shown gross negligence, from which the principal has suffered considerable loss.

Article 68

A commercial agent is entitled to a commission on contracts of sale concluded by him or otherwise brought about through his efforts, provided that the buyer fulfils his undertaking to pay. Where goods are sold for delivery in instalments and payment is to be made separately for each

[1] The term used in the Swedish law is: "handelsagent".

230

0057

consignment, the fact that payment does not forthcome for any one particular consignment shall not affect the agent's right to a commission for the remaining consignments.

Where a contract is not performed by the purchaser, the agent shall nevertheless receive a commission where such non-performance is due to the principal or to any event which the principal could not plead against the purchaser. If the principal has agreed with the purchaser that the contract shall be rescinded or if he has granted him a respite with the payment of the purchase money, with the result that the purchaser fails to pay, the agent's right to a commission is not affected unless he has agreed to the measure.

Article 69

Where the purchase money is paid only in part, the agent is not entitled to any commission otherwise than as follows from Article 68, paragraph 2. If the commission which would have been due to the agent if the whole purchase money has been paid exceeds the deficit, the agent is nevertheless entitled to the difference.

Article 70

Where a commission agent has an exclusive right to receive orders or to conclude contracts of sale for the principal's account at a specified place or within a specified district, such agent is entitled to a commission on contracts concluded with buyers resident within that district even though he has not taken part in the conclusion of such contracts.

Article 71

A commercial agent who permanently represents his principal has the right to receive a commission note from his principal twice a year—at the beginning of January and July—concerning sales which have come about through the intermediary of the agent or under such circumstances as are referred to in Article 70.

All sales contracts which have been, or should have been, performed by the vendor during the preceding six months' period counted from the 1st January and the 1st July should be included in the commission note as well as particulars of the amount of commission due to the agent under every contract, or, where no commission is credited to him, the reason therefor. Where contracts of sale have been concluded during the same period, which should be performed at a later date, the existence of such contracts should be mentioned in the commission note without crediting the corresponding commission. Where the commisson due under a contract has not been credited to an agent for any reason of a temporary nature, the contract shall be enlisted or mentioned also in a subsequent commission note.

Where, after a commission has been credited to an agent, such circumstances are revealed that the commission is found not to be due to him, the principal is entitled to reimburse himself for the amount in a subsequent commission note.

Article 72

A commercial agent who does not permanently represent the principal, has a right to receive a commission note with regard to every sale which has come about through his intermediary, stating the amount of commissions credited to him or, where no commission is credited, the reason therefor.

Article 73

Expenses for postage, telegrams and telephone calls and other costs which a commercial agent has incurred, should be paid to him separately provided that such expenses are reasonable and that the commission or other compensation to which he is entitled is not meant also to include payment for them.

Article 74

Where, for the fulfilment of his com-

231

0058

mission, a commercial agent has received samples, patterns, etc. belonging to the principal and not intended for sale, such agent is entitled to retain what he has received, provided that his security for any claim founded upon his commission would otherwise be jeopardized, until the principal pays the claim concerned or gives satisfactory security for its payment.

Article 75

Where a commercial agent holds goods for sale in stock for the principal's account, the rights and duties of such agent respecting such goods shall be governed by the provisions in the second Chapter of this Act relating to the rights and duties of a factor respecting goods entrusted to him for sale.

Article 76

The provisions in Articles 46 to 52 relating to factors are also applicable to the termination of commissions of commercial agents.

Article 77

Although a commercial agent permanently represents the principal, such agent is not entitled to conclude contracts of sale binding upon the principal without the latter's permission.

Article 78

Where a commercial agent reports a contract of sale which he has concluded for the principal's account, and where, in concluding such contract, the agent acted without authorization or exceeded the limits of a given authorization, the principal, if he wishes to repudiate the contract, has a duty to inform the buyer thereof, either himself or through the commercial agent, without unreasonable delay after receipt of the report. Failure to do so will be regarded as acceptance of the contract by the principal. ·

232

Article 79

If a principal is not willing to accept an offer of purchase forwarded to him by a commercial agent, he shall inform the buyer, either himself or through the commercial agent, without unreasonable delay after receipt of the offer. Failure to do so will be regarded as acceptance of the offer by the principal.

The rules set out in paragraph 1 above shall not apply where it is expressly stipulated during the negotiations between the agent and the person making the offer that the offer shall not be binding unless it is expressly accepted.

Article 80

The provisions in Articles 78 and 79 relating to a principal's duty to give notice if he is unwilling to accept a contract of sale reported by an agent or to accept an offer of purchase forwarded by such agent shall also apply where the principal is informed by the buyer, or the person making the offer of purchase, that the agent has concluded a contract or received an offer for the principal's account; in such cases, however, the principal's notice shall always be sent directly to the buyer or to the person making the offer.

Article 81

Where nothing to the contrary follows from the negotiations between a commercial agent and a person making an offer of purchase, the fact that such offer has been made to an agent and has been forwarded by him to the principal, shall not debar the offeror from the same right to inform the principal of the revocation of his offer as he would have been entitled to if he had sent the offer to the principal himself.

Article 82

Where a merchant who has negotiated with a commercial agent respecting a contract of purchase for his business receives

0059

notice from the principal of such agent referring to the negotiations and containing a declaration that the principal is willing to accept an offer made to the agent in the course of the negotiations or confirms the contract concluded in the course of such negotiations, it is the duty of such merchant, if he wishes to plead that he has not made any offer or concluded any contract or that the contents of the offer or of the contract are not correctly reproduced in the notice, to inform the principal of such fact without unreasonable delay. Failure on the part of the merchant to do so will be regarded as acceptance of the contract as notified by the principal provided, however, that the merchant reasonably ought to have understood from such notice that in the principal's opinion, such contract had been concluded, and provided also that the merchant cannot show that the notice was incorrect.

Article 83

A commercial agent is not entitled to receive payment for any goods sold, to grant a respite with payment after the sale, to agree to any reduction of price or to admit any other change or alteration of the contract without the principal's authorization. This rule is applicable notwithstanding the fact that the agent is empowered to enter into contracts of sale binding upon the principal.

Where a principal, who receives information from an agent or from a buyer that the agent has received payment in respect of goods that have been sold by, or with the assistance of, the agent or under circumstances of the kind contemplated by the provision in Article 70, considers that the agent was not entitled to receive payment and therefore is unwilling to recognise that the buyer is discharged through such payment, the principal shall give notice of such fact to the buyer without unreasonable delay. Failure to do so will be regarded as approval of such payment.

Article 84

If a buyer wishes to protest against defects or deficiencies in goods or delay in delivery, or if he wishes to give the vendor any other notice respecting the performance of a contract of purchase, such notice is valid if directed to the vendor's agent provided that the contract was concluded by, or with the assistance of, the agent, or under circumstances of the kind contemplated by the provision in Article 70.

Even where an agent is authorized to enter into contracts binding upon the principal, he is not entitled to make any decision binding upon the principal in respect of such notices from the buyer as are referred to in paragraph 1 above without authorization from the principal.

Chapter 4
On commercial travellers

Article 85

For the purposes of this Act, "commercial traveller"[1] shall mean a person who accepts the charge to travel from place to place for a merchant's account and to promote the sale of goods that are not carried on the journey, by soliciting offers of purchase (orders) for the principal or by entering into contracts of sale in his name.

Article 86

Where a commercial traveller holds an employment in the principal's service, the contract concluded by the parties or the custom of the trade shall govern the commercial traveller's rights and duties towards the principal.

A commercial traveller who holds an employment in the principal's service shall not be dismissed from his employment nor shall he himself leave his employment without prior notice, unless such right for either party follows from the terms of the contract or there is a valid reason therefor.

[1] The term used in the Swedish law is "handelsresande".

If notice of the termination of the contract is given by either party, such contract shall cease to operate at the end of the third calendar month after the month during which notice was given.

Without. the principal's agreement a commercial traveller to whom this Article is applicable is not allowed, in the course of his journeys, to take offers of purchase or conclude contracts of sale for the account of any person other than the principal.

Where a commercial traveller of the kind referred to herein is entitled to receive his salary wholly or in part by way of commission, the provisions in Articles 68 to 70 relating to commercial agents are applicable to the conditions upon which such commercial traveller may claim the payment of such commission.

Article 87

Where a commercial traveller is not in the principal's service the following rules shall apply: unless anything to the contrary follows from Article 1, his rights and duties towards the principal shall be governed by the provisions in Articles 66 to 74 relating to commercial agents, and the termination of the legal relationship between such commercial traveller and the principal shall be subject to the provisions in Articles 46 to 52 relating to factors.

Article 88

A commercial traveller is not entitled to conclude contracts of sale without the principal's permission authorization.

Where a commercial traveller has been furnished by the principal with order forms embodying the principal's name and drawn in such manner that they may be assumed to serve after the completion by the commercial traveller the purpose of proving that a contract has been concluded for the principal's account, then contracts of sale concluded by the commercial traveller through the completion of such form shall be binding upon the principal as if he had expressly authorized the commercial traveller to conclude the contract.

Article 89

The provisions in Articles 78 and 79 relating to a principal's duty to give notice if he is not willing to accept a contract of sale concluded by an agent or to accept an offer of purchase made to such agent are also applicable where a commercial traveller reports to the principal that he has concluded such contract or transmits to him an offer of purchase, with the exception, however, that where such message is sent by a commercial traveller, the principal shall send his notice directly to the buyer or the person making the offer.

The same rule shall apply where a principal is informed by a buyer or a person who has made an offer that the commercial traveller has concluded a contract of sale or accepted an offer of purchase for the principal's account.

Article 90

The provisions in Articles 81 and 82 are applicable with regard to the revocation of offers of purchase forwarded by a commercial traveller and to the duty of a merchant who has negotiated with such traveller regarding a purchase to give notice to the principal in certain cases.

Article 91

Notwithstanding the fact that a commercial traveller is authorized to enter into contracts of sale binding upon the principal, such traveller is not entitled to receive payment for goods sold. to grant a respite with payment after the sale, to agree to any reduction of price or to admit any other change or alteration of the contract without the principal's authorization.

Where a principal, who receives information from a commercial traveller or from a buyer, that the commercial traveller has received payment in respect of goods sold by, or with the assistance of, the

234

0061

commercial traveller, or under circumstances of the kind contemplated by the provision in Article 70, considers that the commercial traveller was not entitled to receive payment and therefore is unwilling to recognise that the buyer is discharged through such payment, the principal shall give notice of such fact to the buyer without unreasonable delay. Failure to do so will be regarded as approval of such payment.

Article 92

If a buyer wishes to protest against defects or deficiencies in goods or delay in delivery, or if he wishes to give the vendor any other notice respecting the performance of a contract of purchase, such notice is valid if directed to the vendor's commercial traveller provided that such traveller is staying at the buyer's place of residence or business at the time when such notice is given and that the contract was concluded by, or with the assistance of, the commercial traveller, or under circumstances of the kind contemplated by the provision in Article 70.

Even where a commercial traveller is authorized to enter into contracts of sale binding upon the principal, he is not entitled to make any decision binding upon the principal in respect of such notices from the buyer as are referred to in paragraph 1 above without authorization from the principal.

Article 93

Where a person accepts the charge to call upon customers for a merchant's account in the place where the latter conducts his business and to promote the sale of goods that he does not carry with him by soliciting offers of purchase (orders) for the principal or by entering into contracts of sale in his name, the provisions in Articles 88 to 92 shall also apply to such local salesman. Furthermore, where a local salesman has an employment in the principal's service, the provisions in Article 86 are applicable; in other cases, those set out in Article 87 shall apply.

This Act shall come into force on the first day of January, 1915.

By this statute it is abolished the ordinance of October 6, 1948, on the security interest in goods which have been entrusted for sale and for which payment in advance has been granted.

235

0062

외 무 부

원 본

외 무 부

종   별 :

번   호 : GVW-1794   일   시 : 91 0920 1100

수   신 : 장 관(통기,경기원,상공부,교통부,항만청)사본:주영대사(직송필)

발   신 : 주 제네바 대사대리

제   목 : UR/GNS (해운 분야) 회의(2)

    9.19(목) 개최된 표제회의는 JARAMILLO 의장주재로 해운분야 COMMON APPROACH 에 대한 북구제안 (GNS/W/135: 별도 FAX 송부)에 대하여 토의하였는 바 주요내용 하기 보고함.

    1. 일반논평(공식회의)

    - 캐나다, 이씨, 홍콩, 뉴질랜드, 호주, 멕시코, 스위스, 오지리등 많은 나라들이 북구제안을 지지하였으며

    0 특히 캐나다는 북구제안에 대하여 보다 더 많은분야에 COMMON APPROACH 를 적용할 것을 주장하였고, 호주 및 뉴질랜드는 동결 약속뿐만아니라 규제 조치 철폐에 관한 COMMITTMENT가 필요하다고 발언함.

    - 종전에는 회의에 참석치 않던 가나, 콩고등많은 아프리카 국가들과 인도, 이집트 및 알젠틴, 페루, 콜롬비아, 칠레등 중남미 국가와 말련, 인니등은 다음과 같은 이유를 들어 반대의사를 표명함.

    0 개도국들은 해운산업이 미비하여 운임수지가 적자상태에 있음.

    0 짧은 기간(3년) 내의 일괄 자유화는 개도국의개발 목적 추구와 상치됨

    0 COMMON APPROACH 는 점진적 자유화와 배치되는개념으로서 수용 곤란

    0 북구제안이 서비스 협정과 일체를 이루는 것은법률적 관점에서 곤란

    - 이에대하여 스웨덴은 해운분야 자유화는 운송비용의 절감을 통하여 수출지향국가 및 개도국경제에 유리하다고 전제하고

    0 제한조치 철폐기간 (3년)에 대하여는 다른 대안에 대하여 토의할 용의가 있으며

    0 자국은 TNC/W/35상의 해운 부속서 초안에 대하여 전적으로 불만이기때문에 동 초안을 협상 기초로 삼을 수 없으며 자국제안이 동 초안을 대체하기 위한 것이나 일반 협정에 반영하는 구체적 절차는 추후 토의할 수 있을 것이라고 함.

통상국   2차보   교통부   경기원   상공부   해항청

PAGE 1

91.09.21   10:42 WG

외신 1과 통제관

0063

2. 쟁점별 토의(비공식 회의)

가. 국제해운(3항)

- 아국은 동결 약속 및 3년이내 제한조치 철폐에별 문제가 없으나 UN LINER CODE하의 양자협정에 따른 조치는 존중되어야 한다고 언급하였는바 북구는 자국제안상의 자유화 약속에는 모든 조치가 포함된다고 답변함.

- EC 는 북구제안상의 '제한적이거나 무역왜곡효과 있는 조치'의 정의가 FRAMEWORK상의 제한조치와 일치하는 것인지 질의한바

0 북구는 FRAMEWORK 에서 동 문제가 완결되지않은 상태에서 구체적 답변을 하기는 어려우나 일반적 관점에서 보조금도 무역왜곡 효과가 있으므로 포함된다고 답변

- EC 는 근해 해운 (OFF-SHORE SUPPLY)가 국제해운에 포함되는지 질의한바

0 북구는 한 국토내의 항구간 운송이기 때문에 CABOTAGE에 포함된다고 답변

나. CABOTAGE(4항)

- 아국은 각국의 CABOTAGE 개방여부는 FRAMEWORK에 따라 국가간 양허 협상에 의하여 정해질 사항인바 북구제안의 법률적 가치가 무엇인지 질의한바

0 북구는 자국 제안이 새로운 것은 없으며 FRAMEWORK 에서 합의된 사항을 다시 써 놓은것에 불과하나 예시 목적으로 분명하게 하기위한 것이라고 함.

다. 해운 보조 서비스의 공급 (5항) 및 동 서비스에대한 접근 및 사용(6항)

- 홍콩, 폴란드, EC등이 5항과 6항의 보조서비스의정의 및 범위를 명확화할 필요성을 지적하였는바

0 북구는 5항과 6항의 보조서비스의 정의를 당분간 똑같은 용어로 사용하고 있으나 자국도 최종정의 규정을 마련한 것은 아니며 추후 토의할 용의가있다고 함.

- 인도는 보조서비스에의 접근 및 사용문제는 별도로 규정하지 않더라도 FRAMEWORK 의 무효화 규정으로 처리할 수 있다고 지적한바 (제 23조상 어떤 조치로 인하여 시장접근 약속이 무효화된 경우 분쟁해결 의뢰가 가능하다는 의미)

0 북구는 인도지적의 근본 취지는 이해하나 향후 분쟁해결관련 법률적 어려움을 피하기 위한것이라고 함.

3. 향후 진행계획

- 의장은 다음주 GSN 회의 종료전에 향후 진행계획을 밝히겠다고 언급함.

4. 건의

- 다음과 같은 이유에서 북구가 제안한 COMMONAPPROACH 의 긍정적 검토가

필요하다고 판단되는바 입장 검토 회시바람.

　O 북구 제안상의 COMMON APPROACH 는 CABOTAGE와 보조서비스에 관한한 실제 아무런 의무 규정이없으며 국제해운 분야에만 3년 이내 제한조치철폐 의무를 규정하고있는 바 아국의 경우 95.1.에 화물유보제도 폐지를 이미 OFFER 했다는 점

　O UN LINER CODE 의 경우도 동 CODE 가 실제로 적용되지 않고 있으며 아국이 맺은 양자협정들에도 실제 화물 분할 규정이 이행되고않고 있을 뿐만 아니라 만약 MFN 예외를 인정받아야 할 양자 협정하의 조치가 있는 경우에는 기합의된 방식대로 구체적 조치 목록을 제출하여 MFN 일탈을 허용받아야 하는것이므로 국제해운에 대한 COMMON APPROACH 채택여부와는 별개 문제라는 점.

　첨부: 북구제안 1부(GVW(F)-0356).끝

　(차석대사 김삼훈-국장)

MULTILATERAL TRADE
NEGOTIATIONS
THE URUGUAY ROUND

Group of Negotiations on Services

GVW(元)-0356 10户20 1/00
//GVW-1194 첨부

RESTRICTED

MTN.GNS/W/135
17 September 1991

Special Distribution

Original: English

COMMUNICATION FROM SWEDEN ON BEHALF OF THE NORDIC COUNTRIES

Proposal for a common approach to Maritime Transport Services under the GATS Agreement

The attached communication is circulated at the request of the permanent delegation of Sweden on behalf of the Nordic countries to the members of the Group of Negotiations on Services.

This communication contains a proposal for a possible approach to Maritime Transport Services. It is based on the present draft version of the GATS Agreement (contained in MTN.TNC/W/35/Rev.1) and should not be viewed as the final position of the Nordic countries.

9900

1991-09-20 16:33 KOREAN MISSION GENEVA 2 022 791 0525 P.05

PROPOSAL FOR A COMMON APPROACH TO MARITIME TRANSPORT SERVICES UNDER THE GATS AGREEMENT

(to form an integral part of the Agreement and be binding for all Parties)

1. Objectives

   Recognizing the special characteristics of the maritime transport services sector, the purpose of this text is to confirm the liberalization already achieved and to facilitate further liberalization of trade in maritime transport services.

2. Scope

   This text shall apply to measures of a Party affecting trade in the maritime transport services sector.

3. Common approach to specific commitments on international shipping

   (a) All Parties shall make a binding commitment not to impose any new restrictive and/or trade-distorting measures affecting international shipping services or suppliers of such services of other Parties.

   (b) All Parties shall make a binding commitment to remove existing restrictive and/or trade-distorting measures affecting cross-border supply of international shipping services and suppliers of such services of other Parties, within three years after the entry into force of this Agreement.

4. Common approach to specific commitments on cabotage

   In accordance with Articles XVI, XVII and XVIII of the Agreement Parties may negotiate specific commitments to bind, reduce or remove existing restrictions affecting cabotage services and suppliers of such services of other Parties.

5. Common approach to specific commitments on maritime transport auxiliary services

(a) All Parties shall make a binding commitment not to impose any new restrictive and/or trade-distorting measures affecting maritime transport auxiliary services or suppliers of such services of other Parties.

(b) In accordance with Articles XVI, XVII and XVIII of the Agreement Parties may negotiate specific commitments to reduce or remove existing restrictions affecting maritime transport auxiliary services and suppliers of such services of other Parties.

6. Access to and use of maritime transport auxiliary services

Each Party shall ensure that access to and use of maritime transport auxiliary services, offered within or from its territory, is accorded to maritime transport services and suppliers of such services of other Parties on reasonable and non-discriminatory terms and conditions.

7. Definitions

Maritime transport services = all services described in this paragraph.

International shipping = transportation of passengers or goods between ports located in different states, including passenger cruise traffic outside a Party's territorial waters.

Cabotage = transportation of passengers or goods between two ports located in the territory of the same Party, including passenger cruise traffic inside a Party's territorial waters.

Maritime transport auxiliary services = all services provided from port facilities or to assist vessels in ports (to be defined).

0068

FINANCIAL TIME (91. 9. 20. 금 .)

GIஐ(五)-0361
10/20 1730
" GVW-1800 첨부 "

Nordic shipping plan may help Uruguay Round

By William Dullforce in Geneva

THE NORDIC countries yesterday tabled a proposal for the liberalisation of maritime transport which they hope will remove an important stumbling block to the completion of an international agreement on services in the Uruguay Round trade talks.

Their move challenges the US to drop its opposition to having the General Agreement on Tariffs and Trade's most-favoured-nation (MFN) rule extended to shipping. Other participants in the Round, including the European Community, are refusing to accept a General Agreement on Trade in Services (Gats) that exempts

미외.MFN
예외 주건
block

GATT

maritime services. Finland, Iceland, Norway and Sweden propose that Gatt's members adopt a "common approach" to maritime transport that would be binding on all parties to a Gats.

Governments would undertake to impose no new restrictive or trade-distorting measures affecting international shipping services and to remove existing restrictions within three years of the agreement coming into force.

Cabotage or coastal shipping regulations, under which most countries confine transport between two home ports to vessels carrying their own flags, would not be affected but would be negotiable. Governments could agree between themselves to reduce or remove restrictions.

Port facilities and auxiliary services would be dealt with in the same way. Countries would agree not to impose any new restrictions and could independently negotiate the removal of existing restraints. In the meantime, they would ensure

Cabotage
연안해운

access to auxiliary services for other countries' shippers "on reasonable and non-discriminatory terms".

Shipping conferences – the cartel-like mechanisms under which companies fix freight rates and co-ordinate services on most international routes – would not be touched; these are seen as private arrangements subject to national regulations on restrictive business practices, but not to trade agreements between governments.

The Nordic proposal takes no position in the conflict between governments, such as the US, which maintain that conferences should be open to new members and those, including the EC, which allow closed conferences to operate.

Effectively, the Nordic proposal would require the US to accept the application of the MFN rule to all maritime services; countries could even ask Washington to negotiate on cabotage rights.

US shipping companies have so far succeeded in prodding their administration into rejecting the application of the MFN rule.

They have argued that application would have a de-liberalising effect in that it would prevent the US from using its right under domestic legislation to impose trade sanctions on countries it regarded as operating unfair shipping regimes. However, the Nordic proposal would ensure a fair measure of liberalisation within three years.

Opposition to the Nordic proposal can be expected from developing countries. African negotiators quickly voiced concern about the effect the proposal would have on cargo-sharing agreements concluded under the United Nations liner code, which is designed to stimulate developing countries' share of world shipping.

Under the code two countries can decide to reserve 40 per cent each of the maritime trade between them for their own flag carriers, leaving 20 per cent for vessels from other nations.

개도국반대
UN liner code 무효화우려

3—/0069

외 무 부

원 본

종 별 :

번 호 : GVW-1816

일 시 : 91 0923 1830

수 신 : 장관(통기, 경기원, 재무부, 상공부)

발 신 : 주제네바대사대리

제 목 : UR/GNS 금융분야 비공식협의

1. FRAMK SWEDLOVE 금융분야 공동의장은 금융부속서 주요쟁점에 대하여 그룹별로(선진국, SEACEN, 개도국) 비공식 협의를 개최하고있는바 9.21(토) 오전 및 9.23(월)오전에는 아국을 포함한 SEACEN 과 협의하였음.

2. 동 협의에서는 의장 비공식 문서상의 각쟁점별로 토의하였으나 PRUDENTIAL REGULATION에 대하여는 전혀 의견을 좁히지 못하였음.

0 다만 개별결정의 분쟁해결 의뢰와 관련 싱가폴은 지속적 처리관행(PATTERN OF PARCTICE)이 협정상의 의무 또는 시장접근 약속에 어긋난 경우나, 의무등에 어긋나는개별결정이 PRUDENTIAL REASON 에 기초하지 않는 것이 명백한 경우에는 분쟁해결 의뢰가 가능토록 할 수 있을것이라고 하여 SWEDLOVE 의장이 이를 TAKE-NOTE 함

0 금융서비스 기구 구성과 관련 SWEDLOVE 의장은 금융전문가(FINANCIAL EXPERT)로 구성한다고만 규정하고 공무원이나 금융 감독자중 누구를 임명할것인가는 각국에맡기도록 하는 것이 타협안이 될수 있을 것이라고 한바 SECEN 도 긍정적 검토의사를표명함.

0 서비스 분야간 보복에 대하여도 SWEDLOVE 의장은 분야간 보복의 허용 또는 금지등 양극단보다는 원칙적으로 같은 분야에 한정하되 불가능한 경우에만 다른 분야에보복을 허용하는 방안이 타협안이 될 수 있을 것이라고 하여 SECEN 이 이를 긍정적으로 검토하기로 함

3. 향후 추진 계획과 관련 SWEDLOVE 의장은 자신과 사무국이 부속서 초안을 새로이 작성하여 배부하겠으며 10월말 회의 기간중에 본격적인 협상이 이루어 질 것이라고 언급하고 동 회의 기간 중 또는 그전에 일련의 비공식협의를 갖겠다고 함.끝

(차석대사 김삼훈-국장)

통상국   2차보   경기원   재무부   상공부

PAGE 1

91.09.24   08:13 DQ

외신 1과 통제관

0070

외 무 부

종 별 :

번 호 : GVW-1810 　　　　　　　　　　일 시 : 91 0923 1230

수 신 : 장 관(통기,경기원,재무부,상공부)

발 신 : 주 제네바 대사대리

제 목 : UR/GNS(금융분야) 회의(3)

　　9.20(금) JARAMILLO 의장과 FRANK SWEDLOVE(캐나다재무부) 공동 주재로 개최된
금융부속서에 대한 표제회의 내용을 하기 보고함.

Top down :
hybrid :
Two-track :

　　1. 일반 논평

　　- 말련은 SEACEN 을 대표하여 다음과 같이 발언함.

　　0 금융서비스 자유화에 기여하기 위하여 타협할 용의가 있음

　　0 TWO TRACK APPROACH와 관련 NEGATIVE LIST방식을 비공식 GUIDELINE 으로
사용하는 방안 수용 가능

　　0 PRUDENTIAL REGULATION 예외 조항에 반영되어서는 안된다는 입장을 확고하나 남
용 가능성을 방지하기 위한 대안을 토의할 용의 있음.

　　- 이에 대하여 캐나다는 TNC/W/50(선진 4개국공동제안) ADD. 1.이 한 체약국이 어
떤 TRACK을 선택하든 불이익을 받지 않는다는 점을 보장한 것이라고 강조하였으며

　　0 미국은 자국의 기본 입장은 본래 모든 국가가 부속서의 의무를 부담하는 것이었
으며 TWO TRACKAPPROACH 자체가 타협안이라고 언급함.

　　2. 쟁점별 토의

　　가. PRUDENTIAL REGULATION

　　1) PRUDENTIAL MEASURE 의 정의(ARBITRAY ORUNJUSTIFIABLE 하지 않고
REASONBLE한 조치에 한정할 것인가 여부)

　　- 스위스는 동 제한 조건들이 없을 경우 너무 광범위하여 LOOPHOLE 이 생긴다고한
반면

　　0 말련은 PRUDENTIAL REGULATION 이 나라마다 다른데 어느나라의 기준을
적용할것이며 또한 PRUDENTIALREASON 의 정의가 무엇인지 문제를 제기함

　　- 미국은 과거 선진국 제안상의 PRUDUNTIALREASON은 한정적인 것 이었으나

통상국　　경기원　　재무부　　상공부

PAGE 1 　　　　　　　　　　　　　　　　　　　　91.09.24　　00:56 FH

외신 1과 통제관

0071

의장비공식 문서의 대안 1에 'INCLUDING' 이라는 용어가 포함되어 개방형이 되었으므로이제는 PRUDENTIALREASON 에 대한 논란이 불필요하며 금융 서비스 기구에 PRUDENTIAL REGULATION 책임자들이 지명되면 충분하다고 하였으며

  O 이씨는 무제한적인 PRUDENTIAL REGULATION 의인정은 곤란하며 시장 접근과 내국민 대우로부터의 일탈과 균형을 이루어야 한다고 지적하였으며 캐나다는 'REASONABLE' 조치에 한정하는 것은 GATT 의 오랜 경험이라고 함

  - 한편 폴란드, 칠레등은 대안 2를 지지하였으며 홍콩 및 유고는 대안 1이 FRAMEWORK 의 SCHEDULING과 부합된다고 함.

  2) 개별 결정의 분쟁해결 의뢰 여부

  - 오지리, 캐나다, 유고, 폴란드등이 대안 3(개별결정 자체는 번복되지 않되 의무 위반 사항은 분쟁 해결 의뢰)을 지지 하였으나

  O 말련은 대륙법 국가의 경우 개별 결정의 정당성을 입증하기 어렵다고 함.

  - 미국은 금융기관 설립인가 신청의 경우 공식신청 이전에 인가 가능성 탐지에 수년을 소비하는 사례를 들어 개별 결정 자체의 검토 보다도 규제 환경(또는 규제 체계)의 검토가 필요하다고 하였으며

  O 캐나다는 개별 결정마다 분쟁 해결을 통하여 번복되는 상황은 상상하기 어려우며 금융 분야의 특성을 고려할때 협정상의 의무나 COMMITMENT 이행 여부를 검토할 기회가 필요하다고 함.

  - 아국은 선진국 제안상의 PRUDENTIAL REGULATION 조항에 의할 경우 대안 2(모든 결정의 분쟁 해결의뢰)가 어떤 결정이 의무 위반 사항은 없음에도 불구하고 자의적이거나 합리적이지 않을경우 분쟁 해결 대상이 된다는 의미인지 문제를 제기한바

  O EC는 의무 위반 사실이 없는한 분쟁 해결 대상이 되지 않는다고 전제하고 대부분의 PRUDENTIAL REGULATION은 국내 규제 조항에 해당하는 것이나 추가 도피 조항으로서 예외 조항에 PRUDENTIAL REGULATION 이 반영되는 것이라 함

  나. TWO TRACK APPROACH

  - 브라질은 봉신.부속서의 경우 시장접근 약속을 한 이후에만 동 부속서가 적용되는바 금융 부속서(3부를 제외한 1,2,5부)도 금융 분야에 시장접근 약속을 전혀 하지 않은 나라에는 적용되지 않는지 문제를 제기한바

  O 스웨덴 및 일본은 적용된다고 답변함.

PAGE 2

0072

- 인도는 대안 2의 GUIDELINE 의 법적 성격에 대하여 의문을 표시하고 FRAMEWORK 제 18조 등에 공식 반영되어야 GUIDELINE으로 기능할 수 있을 것이라고 함.

- 한편 인도, 이집트등은 대안 1(FRAMEWORK적용)을 지지하였으며 EC는 대안 4(모든 국가가 부속서상의 NEGATIVE LIST 방식 적용), 헝가리는 대안 3(TWO-TRACK)을 지지함.

다. 금융서비스 기구

- 브라질은 금융서비스 기구의 필요성에 대하여 합의된바 없다고 지적하는 한편동기구 설치시에도 구성원은 각국이 자유로이 지명할 수 있어야 한다고 언급함.

(기타 발 언국 없음)

라. 분야간 보복

- 발언국 없음

3. 회의 진행 계획

- JARAMILLO 의장은 비공식 협의를 통하여 차기회의 진행 계획을 결정하겠으며금융 부속서가 계속하여 GNS 의제에 포함 될것이라고 언급함.

0 9.21.(토)에는 SWEDLOVE 의장 주재로 그룹별(SEACEN, 선진국등) 비공식 협의가있을 예정임.

4. 건의

- 다음과 같은 이유에서 TWO-TRACK APPROACH에 대한 선진국 안을 긍정적으로 검토할 필요가 있는것으로 판단됨.

0 선진국들이 TRACK 선택의 자유, MFN 적용보장, TRACK 선태과 자유화 약속수준과의 무관등을 명문으로 보장함으로써 이에 대한 반대논리 구사가 어렵게 되었다는점

0 아국의 경우 가까운 장래에 HIGH TRACK 선택을 강요당할 우려가 있으나 HIGH TRACH 선택 그 자체가 높은 수준의 자유화 약속은 강제하는 것은 아니며 한.미 쌍무협상 추이, 아국 금융 산업정책 방향등을 감안할때 큰 문제가 없다는 점. 끝

(차석대사 김삼훈-국장)

기 안 용 지

분류기호 서번호	통기 20644-	기 안 용 지 (전화 : 720 - 2188)	시 행 상 특별취급	
보존기간	영구 . 준영구 10. 5. 3. 1.	장 관		
수 신 처 보존기간		서.		
시행일자	1991. 9.24.			

보조 기관	국 장	전 결	협 조 기 관		문 서 통 제
	심의관				
	과 장				
	기안책임자	조 현			발 송 인

경 유 수 신 참 조	내부결재	발 신 명 의		

제 목	정부대표 임명

UR 금융부속서 공식 회의(9.20)의 정부대표로 임명되어 제네바에

출장중인 재무부 국제금융과 최희남 사무관을 9.21-24간 추가로 개최되는

UR 금융부속서 관련 비공식 회의의 정부대표로 임명하여 주실것을

건의합니다.

  ○ 출장기간 : 9.26까지 연장.   끝.

0074

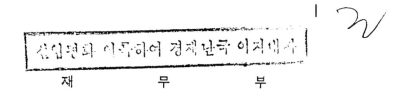

재   무   부

국금 22251-566   (503-9266)   1991. 9. 17.

수신   외무부장관

제목   출장 기간 연장

1. 국금 22251-560 ('91.9.13)와 관련입니다.

2. UR 금융서비스 협상 관련 금융부속서 회의가 당초 9.20에서
9.20-9.24로 연장되었는 바, 아래와 같이 출장기간을 연장하오니 필요한
조치를 취하여 주시기 바랍니다.

아   래

소 속	성 명	기 간	
		당 초	변 경
국제금융과 사무관	최 희 남	9. 18 - 23	9. 18 - 26

첨부 : 관련 문서 1부.   끝.

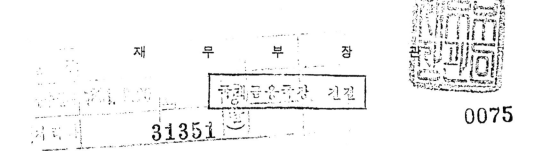

0075

BANK NEGARA MALAYSIA

(CENTRAL BANK OF MALAYSIA)

Telephone: 03-2988044
Telex: MA 30201
Facsimile: 03-2912990
Cable: "BANKMALAYSIA"

P.O. Box 10922
Jalan Dato' Onn
50480 Kuala Lumpur
Malaysia

Our Reference:

September 14, 1991

Mr. Lee Moon-Ho,
Chief of Financial System Division,
The Bank of Korea,
C.P.O. Box 26,
Chung-Ku, Seoul 100,
South Korea.

Dear Mr. Lee,

GATT/MTN Meetings on Financial Services

1. My earlier fax on this issue refers. The next meeting on Financial Services Negotiation is now confirmed, as follows:

   GNS (Finance - formal)   - September 20
   GNS (Informal on Finance)   - September 21 and September 23.

2. If necessary the meeting will be extended for another day, September 24. The Informals will be chaired by the Co-Chairman, Mr. Frank Swedlove. Informals will be based on the attached Chairman's Report.

3. The meeting will discuss all outstanding issues, as follows:

   (i)   Each issue will be treated <u>independently</u>, i.e, <u>no trade-offs</u> between issues e.g. two-track against any other provision.

   (ii) Therefore, if there is no movement on two track, the meeting will proceed to other issues.

   (iii) The purpose of the informals is to attempt to reach a common draft on each provision, (other than Part III) with differences among views to be reflected in square brackets.

0076

— 2 —

(iv) The formal GNS meeting will, therefore, only be a forum for countries to again state positions. The more substantive discussions will take place during the informal meetings.

SEACEN members should attend these meetings to ensure views are aired and hopefully agreed to.

4. The meetings among SEACEN and developing countries suggested earlier, i.e. on September 18 and 19 has been cancelled. Instead, Dato' Basir has tentatively suggested a breakfast meeting among SEACEN countries only on September 20. Please let me know your contact numbers in Geneva so that I could arrange a meeting. I can be contacted at the Noga Hilton (tel no: 022 - 7319381)

Thank you.

Yours sincerely,

(Latifah Merican Cheong)
(for Adviser)

461￦3

기 안 용 지

분류기호 서번호	통기 20644-			(전화: 720 - 2188)	시 행 상 특별취급	
보존기간	영구. 준영구 10. 5. 3. 1.			장 관		
수 신 처 보존기간						
시행일자	1991. 9.24.					
보조 기관	국 장	전 결	협 조 기 관		문 서 통 제	
	심 의 관					
	과 장	대결				
	기안책임자	조 현			발 송 인	
경 유 수 신 참 조	재무부장관		발 신 명 의			
제 목	정부대표 출장기간 연장 허가					

대 : 국금 22251-566

UR 금융서비스 비공식 회의가 9.21-24간 개최됨에 따라

UR 금융부속서 공식 회의(9.20)의 정부대표로 임명된 귀부 국제금융과

최희남 사무관이 동 비공식 회의에도 참석토록 정부대표로 추가 임명

하였음을 통보합니다.

○ 출장기간 : 9.26까지 연장.   끝.

0078

기 안 용 지

분류기호 서번호	통기 20644-	기 안 용 지 (전화 : 720 - 2188)	시 행 상 특별취급	
보존기간	영구. 준영구 10. 5. 3. 1.	차 관	장 관	
수 신 처 보존기간		전 결		
시행일자	1991. 9.24.			
보조 기관	국 장	협 조 기 관	문 서 통 제	
	심의관	제2차관보 :		
	과 장			
기안책임자	조 현		발 송 인	
경 유 수 신 참 조	내부결재	발 신 명 의		

제 목   UR/서비스 협상 정부대표단 임명

     91.9.26-27간 개최되는 UR/서비스 협상 및 동 회의기간중 개최될

서비스 분야 한.미 양자협의에 참가할 정부대표단을 "정부대표 및

특별사절의 임명과 권한에 관한 법률"에 의거, 아래와 같이 임명할 것을

건의하오니 재가하여 주시기 바랍니다.

              - 아   래 -

          - 1 -   0079

1. 회의명 및 개최일시
ㅇ UR/서비스 공식 회의(9.26-27)
ㅇ UR/서비스 협상 관련 한.미 양자협의(9.26-27 예정)
2. 정부대표단
ㅇ 주 제네바 대표부 관계관
ㅇ 경제기획원 대외경제조정실 제2협력관　　이윤재
ㅇ 대외경제정책연구원 연구위원　　　　　성극제 (자문)
3. 출장기간 : 91.9.25-29 (4박5일)
4. 소요경비 : 경제기획원 소관예산
5. 훈　　령 (한.미 양자협의)
ㅇ Framework 분야는 GNS 협상의 기존 입장으로 대처하되
별도의 미측 요구사항이 있을 경우 동 요구사항의 세부
내용을 정확히 파악하고, 이에 대한 아측 입장은 추후
검토, 통보 하겠다는 선에서 답변

0080

- 2 -

o 금번 협상이 최초의 양허협상이므로 각국의 개방 약속에

대한 기대 수준을 적정화하여야 함을 강조하고, 아국의

경우 '86년이래 한.미 쌍무협상에 의해서 이루어진 주요

서비스 업종 개방의 MFN 적용 배제 문제를 검토중임을

설명

o 미측이 Request List를 제시할 경우 이를 접수하고

국내에서 충분한 검토후 아국 입장을 제시할 것이라는

입장 표명.   끝.

- 3 -

0081

경 제 기 획 원

봉조삼 10502 - 669   503-9149   1991. 9. 20

수 신 외무부장관

참 조 통상국장

제 목 UR/서비스협상관련 GNS회의 및 양자협의 참석

  1. 스위스 제네바에서 개최되는 UR/서비스 협상관련 GNS 공식회의 및 한·미 양자협의(7.26~27)에 참석할 본부대표단(자문역포함)을 다음과 같이 송부하니 협조해 주시기 바랍니다.

다   음

가. 출장자

소 속	직 위	성 명
경제기획원 대외경제조정실	제2협력관	이 윤 재
"	~~통상조정2과 사무관~~	~~신 호 현~~
대외경제정책연구원(자문역)	연구위원	성 극 제

9.19
전화통보
삭제

나. 출장기간 : '91. 9.25~29 (4박 5일)

다. 경비부담 : 당원 및 KIEP

첨부 : 1. 출장일정 1부.
      2. 협상대책자료 1부(별도송부).   끝.

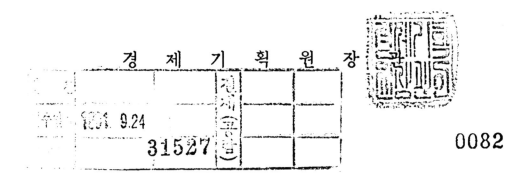

경 제 기 획 원 장

1991. 9.24

31527

0082

출 장 일 정

'91. 9.25(수)   12:40   서울발 (KE 901)

19:10   파리착

21:00   파리발 (SR 729)

22:00   제네바착

9.26(목) ┐
          │ GNS 회의 및 한·미 양자협의 참석
9.27(금) ┘

9.28(토)   10:50   제네바발 (LH 1855)

12:15   프랑크푸르트착

14:20   프랑크푸르트발(KE 916)

9.29(일)   09:50   서울착

0083

46311

기 안 용 지

분류기호 서번호	통기 20644-	(전화: 720 - 2188)	시 행 상 특별취급	
보존기간	영구. 준영구 10. 5. 3. 1.	장 관		
수 신 처 보존기간				
시 행 일 자	1991. 9.24.			

보 조 기 관	국 장	전 결	협 조 기 관		문 서 통 제
	심의관				
	과 장				1.01.9.25
	기안책임자	조 현			발 송 인
경 유 수 신 참 조	경제기획원장관		발 신 명 의		외무부
제 목	UR/서비스 협상 정부대표단 임명 통보				

　

1. 91.9.26-27간 개최되는 UR/서비스 협상 및 동 회의기간중

(한·미양과)

개최될 협의에 참가할 정부대표단이 "정부대표 및 특별사절의 임명과

권한에 관한 법률"에 의거, 아래와 같이 임명 되었음을 통보합니다.

- 아   래 -

- 1 -   0084

가. 회의명 및 개최일시

    o UR/서비스 공식 회의(9.26-27)

    o UR/서비스 협상 관련 한.미 양자협의(9.26-27 예정)

나. 정부대표단

    o 경제기획원 대외경제조정실 제2협력관 이윤재

    o 대외경제정책연구원 연구위원 성극제(자문)

다. 출장기간 : 91.9.25-29 (4박5일)

라. 소요경비 : 경제기획원 소관예산

  2. 출장 결과 보고서는 대표단 귀국후 2주일이내에 당부로

송부하여 주시기 바랍니다. 끝.

- 2 -

0085

발 신 전 보

WGV-1283   910925 1349 FO

번   호 :   종별 :

수   신 : 주   제네바   대사. 총영사 /

발   신 : 장 관 (통 기)

제   목 : UR/GNS 협상

9.27까지 계속되는 UR/GNS 협상 및 동 회의를 전후하여 개최될 서비스 분야 한.미 양자협의에 참가할 본부대표가 아래와 같이 임명 되었으니, 귀관 관계관과 함께 참석 토의 조치바람.

1. 정부대표단 (출장기간 : 9. 25-29)

   ○ 경제기획원 대외경제조정실 제2협력관   이윤재

   ○ 대외경제정책연구원 연구위원   성극제 (자문)

2. 훈   령 (한·미 양자협의)

   ○ Framework 분야는 GNS 협상에서의 기존 입장으로 대처하되 별도의 미측 요구사항이 있을 경우 동 요구사항의 세부내용을 정확히 파악하고, 이에 대한 아측 입장은 추후 검토, 통보 하겠다는 선에서 답변

   ○ 금번 협상이 최초의 양허협상이므로 각국의 개방 약속에 대한 기대 수준을 적정화 하여야 함을 강조하고, 아국의 경우 '86년이래 한.미 쌍무협상에 의해서 이루어진 주요 서비스 업종 개방의 MFN 적용 배제 문제를 검토중임을 설명

   ○ 미측이 Request List를 제시할 경우 이를 접수하고 국내에서 충분한 검토후 아국 입장을 제시할 것이라는 입장 표명.   끝.

(통상국장 대리   최   혁)

보 안	
통 제	

앙 고 재	91년 9월 21일	통기 과	기안자 성명 조현	과 장 [서명]	국 장 전결	차 관	장 관 [서명]	외신과통제

0086

→ 통기

관리 번호	91- 634

외 무 부

종 별 :

번 호 : GVW-1828   일   시 : 91 0925 1000

수 신 : 장관(통이, 경기원, 재무부, 법무부, 농림수산부, 상공부, 건설부, 보사부, 노

발 신 : 주제네바대사   동부, 교통부, 체신부, 문화부, 과기처, 공보처, 항만청)

제 목 : UR/GNS 협상

　　9.23(월) 당관에 전달된 일본의 대 아국 서비스 분야 REAUEST LIST 를 별첨송부함. 다만 사업 서비스중 불분명한 내용은 일본 대표부에 확인후 통보 예정임.

　　첨부: 일본의 REQUEST LIST 1 부 (GVW(F)-368).

　　(대사 박수길-국장)

　　예고: 91.12.31. 까지

　　　　　　　　　　일반문서로 재분류(1981 . 12. 31.)

통상국 건설부	차관	2차보	법무부	보사부	경기원	재무부	농수부	상공부

PAGE 1   91.09.26   06:00

1.　　In accordance with the Procedural Guidelines for Negotiations on Initial Commitments agreed at the Group of Negotiaions on Services of 28 June 1991, Japan presents to the Republic of Korea initial requests for liberalization of restrictions to trade in services in the sectors/sub-sectors and activities as described in the attached list.

This list is of initial and provisional nature in the light of the ongoing negotiations on the General Agreement on Trade in Services and Japan reserves its rights to modify or to make technical changes to this list as necessary and appropriate in the course of the process of initial commitment negotiations.

Japan intends to make additional requests for liberalization in other sectors such as the financial services sector, the maritime transport services sector and the tourism and travel related services sector in the near future.

2.　　"Sector/Sub-sector/Activities" column in the request list is described on the basis of Service Sectoral Classification List prepared by the Secretariat as MTN.GNS/w/120.

3.　　Trade restrictive measures of horizontal nature are described as "Horizontal Measure(s)" in the Sector/Sub-sector/Activities column.

4.　　The terms used in the category column mean as follows:

(1)　MA:　Trade restrictive measures considered to fall under the category of the market access provision (Article XVI) of the General Agreement which is being developed in negotiations in the GNS.

(2)　NT:　Trade restrictive measures considered to fall under the category of the national treatement provision (Article XVII) of the General Agreement which is being developed in negotiations in the GNS.

て～8～

0083

(Country) Korea

Sector/Sub-sector/ Activities	Description	Category
BUSINESS SERVICES Rental/Lesing Services without Operators (non-transport)	(request). Japan requests Korea to make an offer in this sub-sector.	

8-3

0090.

(Country) Korea

Sector/Sub-sector/ Activities	Description	Category
BUSINESS SERVICES Professional Services Engineering Services Plant Engineering Services	1. A joint-venture with the majority foreign capital share (more than 51%) cannot become an exporter of professional services and materials to overseas markets. (request) Japan requests the rollback of such a restriction.	NT
	2. A joint-venture with the majority foreign capital share (more than 51%) is not authorized to own a real estate even for its own office space. (request) Japan requests the rollback of such a restriction.	NT
	(To be continued)	

力一8

0091

(Country) Korea

Sector/Sub-sector/ Activities	Description	Category
	3. There is a Korean law that accords less favourable treatment to the services and service providers of other Parties. The law prohibits foreign companies to sign EPC turn-key contracts. When foreign companies acquire the EPC turn-key contracts, they must form a consortium with Korean companies. In that case, the scope of work for foreign companies will be limited and will make their Korean counterparts more profitable.	NT
	(request)	
	Japan requests Korea to rollback the situation.	
	(clarification)	
	Is it true that there are problems written below?	
	1. Discriminatory limitation is made against import items from Japan as	
	(To be continued)	

ʃ-ʃ

0092

(Country) Korea

Sector/Sub-sector/ Activities	Description	Category
	shown in the No. 89-15 of Korean Commercial and Industrial Advertisement. Authorization of the import items by the Korean authorities takes very long, causing uncertainties and delays in activities under a plant engineering contract. There are some cases where the Korean authorities do not permit such import, making it impossible to fulfill the contract.

2. Foreign companies have to order the equipments to the domestic vendors. | |

9-8

0093

(Country) Korea

Sector/Sub-sector/ Activities	Description	Category
	(clarification)	
COMMUNICATIN SERVICES Audiovisual Services Motion Picture and Video Tape Production and Distribution Services Motion Picture Production and Distribution Services	More informaiton is requested on regulation for "import distribution of motion pictures" Are there any discriminatory measures?

If Korea accords less favourable treatment to the services and service providers of other Parties, Japan requests the rollback of such restrictions. | NT |

ℓ–ℓ

0094

(Country) Korea

Sector/Sub-sector/ Activities	Description	Category
FINANCIAL SERVICES Financial Services Banking and other Financial Services Lending of all Types, incl. inter alia, Consumer Credit, Mortgage Credit, Factoring and Financing of Commercial Transaction Sales Credit	(request and clarification) Japan requests Korea to make an offer in this activity. Are there any restrictions in sales credit? If Korea places quantitative restrictions specified in Artcile XVI:3 or discriminatory measures, Japan requests the rollback of such restrictions or measures.	MA or NT

8~8

0095

(Country) Korea

Sector/Sub-sector/ Activities	Description	Category
FINANCIAL SERVICES Financial Leasing	(request) Japan requests Korea to make an offer in this sub-sector.	

외 무 부

종 별 :

번 호 : GVW-1834

일 시 : 91 0925 1710

수 신 : 장 관(통기, 경기원, 재무부, 과기처)

발 신 : 주 제네바 대사

제 목 : UR/GNS 협상

　　1. 9.24(화) 미국 민간 서비스 자문위원회 위원장 CHARLES P. HEETER (ARTHUR ANDERSEN사 사장)은 당관 이종화 경협관을 방문하여 회계, 세무, 기타 자문서비스 분야의각국 OFFER 분석과 자사의 관심사항을 기술한 문서를 전달하였음.

　　2. 동 문서는 금 파편 송부 예정이니 향후 R/O협상 준비에 참고 바라며, 검토후오류가 있을 경우 당관 또는 ARTHUR ANDERSEN사에 통보 바람. 끝

　　(대사 박수길-국장)

통상국　　2차보　　경기원　　재무부　　과기처

91.09.26　　07:55 WH

외신 1과 통제관

0096

외 무 부

종 별 :

번 호 : GVW-1833　　　　　　　　　　　일 시 : 91 0925 1710

수 신 : 장관(통기, 경기원, 재무부, 농림수산부, 상공부, 보사부, 노동부, 교통부, 체신부,

발 신 : 주 제네바 대사　　　　　　　　　　문화부, 과기처, 공보처, 항만청)

제 목 : UR/GNS 회의(4)

1. 9.24(화) JARAMILLO 의장 주재로 개최된 표제회의 내용을 하기 보고함.

1. 경제통합(9.24.오전, GNS 전체비공식 회의)

- 일본은 TNC/W/50 제 5조 (경제통합) 의 ALTERNATIVE TEXT 를 대체하는 별첨 (FAX 송부)수정안을 배부하였는바 대부분의 나라가 다음사항을 지적함

0 1항 1) B와 관련 일정기간내에 내국민 보다 불리한 대우를 완전 철폐토록 조건을 부과하는 것은 현실적일 뿐만 아니라 인위적임. 한편 내국민 대우 관련 사항뿐만 아니라 시장접근제한 조치 완화 문제도 거론되어야 함.

0 경제통합 협정의 포괄범위와 관련 서비스분야뿐만 아니라 서비스 공급 형태 (MODE OF DELIVERY)도 규정되어야 함.

0 개도국간 경제통합 (2항) 관련 '신축성 부여'만을 언급한 TNC/W/50 상의 대안이 보다 적절함

0 제 5항의 검토 절차는 일반 협정에 반영하기에는 너무 자세함

0 제 8항의 분쟁해결 부분은 어느 체약국이든 당연히 모든 협정규정의 운영과 관련하여 제 22조 23조의 분쟁해결을 의뢰할 수 있기 때문에 불필요함.

- 한편 알젠틴, 헝가리, 유고는 경제통합의 정의규정이 서비스 분야에 한정되어서는 안되고 상품등 다른 분야까지 포괄하는 광범위한 것이어야 한다고 언급함.

2. 인력이동 부속서 (9.24.오후 주요국 비공식 협의)

- 7.25.자 부속서 초안에 대하여 항별로 토의하였는바 주요 내용 다음과 같음.

가. 1항

0 SELF SERVICE PROVIDER 와 체약국 서비스공급기업의 종업원을 대상으로 하되 동종업원의 범위에 비체약국 국민은 제외키로 함

통상국	2차보	보사부	문화부	교통부	체신부	경기원	재무부	농수부
상공부	노동부	과기처	해항청	공보처				

91.09.26　09:06 WG

외신 1과　통제관　0097

O 체약국 국민의 정의에 시민권자뿐만 아니라 영구거주도도 포함하 것을 캐나다가 제의하였으나 EC는 국민의 정의가 나라마다 다르기 때문에 원안대로 'NATIONAL'로 규정하자고 함.

나. 2항

O 괄호부분과 관련 인도는 체재 및 취업에 관한 조치는 경제적 영향을 미칠 수 있는 모든조치를 포함하기 때문에 입국에 관한 조치에 한정하여 규정하여야 한다고한 반면 기타 국가는 입국 체재, 취업 허가 절차가 나라에 따라 일괄처리 또는 구분처리 되기 때문에 세가지 요소를 구분하여 모두 규정하여야 한다고 함.

다. 3항

O 선.개도국간 기존 입장 견지사실만 확인

라. 4항

O 4항은 FRAMEWORK 제 3조 (공개주의)에 의해 COVER 된다고 한바 인도는 자율단체등에 의한 PROFESSIONAL QUALIFICATIONS 에 특별한 관심이 있는바 동 문제가 FRAMEWORK 에서 해결된다면 4항을 삭제할 수 있다고 함.

마. 5,6항

O 일부 자귀 수정이 있었음

바. 7,8항

O 인도는 FRAMEWORK 제 6조 (국내규제)에 의해 COVER 되므로 삭제하자고 한 반면 기타국가는 명문으로 규정할 것을 지지함.

사. 9,10항

O MFN 문제로서 FRAMEWORK 제 2조 (MFN), 5조 (경제통합), 14조 (예외) 와 관계되기 때문에 추후 토의키로 함

아. 11항

O EC는 인력입국에 관한 개별 결정은 투자인가, 설립인가등 다른 개별 결정과 같이 취급되어야 한다는 전제하에 동 조항 존치 입장을 견지하였으며 알젠틴은 단일 입국 VISA결정에 대하여 어떤 체약국이 다자간 분쟁해결을 시도할리 없다는 이유로 동 조항 필요성에 의문을 제기함.

첨부: 경제통합(제 5조)에 대한 일본 제안 1부.

(GVW(F)-0370).끝

(대사 박수길-국장)

PAGE 2

GVW(用)-UB76· /0/25 ,/用ㅇ

Article V

// GVW-1833 첨부„

Economic Integration

1.   (1) Parties to this Agreement may enter into, or be a party to an agreement establishing among the parties thereto a higher degree of liberalisation of trade in services than that set out in their schedules, provided that such an agreement:

    a) covers substantially all services sectors,

    b) provides for a high degree of liberalisation in the respective sectors/sub-sectors, and, in regard to the covered sectors, eliminates within a reasonable period of time* all measures which are inconsistent with the no less favourable conditions set out in Article XVII of this Agreement.

    (2) Parties recognize that such an agreement, when designed to facilitate trade between the parties to the agreement and not to raise barriers to trade with other parties, would contribute to the maintenance and strengthening of the multilateral trading system.

2.   Where developing countries are parties to such an agreement, provided that the agreement has substantial sectoral coverage, a limited number of undeveloped services sectors may be excluded from the agreement in accordance with the level of development of those sectors in the countries concerned.

3.   (1) Any agreement referred to in paragraphs 1 and 2 shall not raise the level of restrictions on trade in services in respective sectors and sub-sectors covered under the agreement in regard to their commitments listed in its national schedules except in accordance with paragraph 6 below, nor raise the overall level of existing barriers to trade with other parties within the respective sectors/sub-sectors.

    Parties to an agreement should seek to implement any common measures with respect to other parties at the least restrictive level existing prior to entering into such an agreement.

    (2) The agreement referred to in paragraphs 1 and 2 shall not be used nor lead to significantly modifying the conditions of competition in disfavour of a party outside the agreement in any of the covered sectors in the agreement.

---

* "The reasonable period of time" shall be agreed to by the parties in (x) years time, on the basis of the experience of the implementation of the Agreement.

0093

- 2 -

4.   Any service provider of another Party that in a
company legally constituted or organized in a country
participating in an agreement referred to in paragraphs
1 and 2 shall be entitled to the full benefit accruing
from the higher degree of liberalisation of trade in
services of such an agreement.

5.   (1) The formation or enlargement of any agreement
under paragraphs 1 and 2, and by significant modification
of such an agreement shall be promply notified to the
PARTIES. The parties to the agreement shall make available
to the PARTIES such relevant information as may be requested
by other parties. The PARTIES shall establish a working
party to examine such agreement or any modification in
the light of the provisions of this Article. The working
party shall submit a report to the PARTIES on its finding
on the consistency of the proposed modification thereof
with this Article. The PARTIES may make recommendation
to the parties or take decisions in accordance with Article
XXIV as they deem appropriate.

       (2) The parties to the agreement shall report
biennially to the PARTIES on the development of such an
agreement until the measures referred to in 1(1)b) are
eliminated. The PARTIES may establish a working party
to examine such reports if they deem it necessary, and
at the conclusion of the reasonable period of time, the
PARTIES may make recommendation to the parties or take
decisions in accordance with Article XXIV as they deem
appropriate.

6.   If a party proposes to take any measure inconsistent
with its commitments under this Agreement in the formation
or enlargement of any agreement under paragraphs 1 and
2, the procedure set forth in Article XXI: 2-4 shall apply.

7.   The members of such an agreement may not seek
compensation from other parties on the basis of any benefits
that may accrue to them by virtue of the agreement.

8.   The dispute settlement provisions of this Agreement
may be invoked with respect to any matters arising from
the application of this Article.

9.   The provisions of this Agreement shall not be so
construed as to prevent any Party from conferring or
according advantages to adjacent countries in order to
facilitate exchanges limited to contiguous frontier zones
of services which are both locally produced and locally
consumed services.

0100

외　무　부

종　별 :

번　호 : GVW-1862　　　　　　　　　　일　시 : 91 0927 2000

수　신 : 장관(봉기, 경기원, 재무부, 법무부, 농산부, 문화부, 상공부, 건설부, 보사부,

발　신 : 주제네바 대사　　　　　노동부, 교통부, 체신부, 과기처, 공보처, 항만청)

제　목 : UR/GNS 회의(5)

9.25(수)-9.26(목) 개최된 표제회의 내용을 하기보고함.

1. 분쟁 해결 (9.25 오전 JARAMILLO 의장 주재 GNS전체 비공식)

- 의장은 11월 초까지 제 2차 서비스 협상 초안을 만들어야 하는 전제 (TNC 의장의 요구 사항)를 고려할때 시간이 축박하므로 협정 발효이후에 다루어도 되는 사항은 유보하고 FRAMEWORK 에 반영할 사항만 토의할 것을 제의

- 한편, 동 회의에 참석한 ROSSLER 법률국장은 의장의 요청에 따라 사무국 비공식문서 (7.9 자)상의 잇슈중 다음 사항들은 협정 발효이후에 다루어도 되는 절차적 사항 이며, 구체적인 절차적 규정은 추후 체약국의 DECISION 형태로하는 것이 향후 개정이 용이한 커다란 잇점이있다고 함.

0 개별 결정: 개별결정의 분쟁해결 의뢰를 금지하는 명문 규정을 두고자 한다면 실질적 잇슈이나 그렇지 않으면 절차적 문제임.

0 국내 구제절차 소진 의무: 추후 결정해도 되는 절차적 문제

0 NON-VIOLATION: 구체적 정의 범위 규정은 추후해도 되나 동 조항의 존치 여부는 실질적 문제

0 전문가의 역할: 절차적 문제

0 서비스 분야간 보복: 토의 연기 가능

0 서비스 상품간 보복: 법률적 의미에서 매우 복잡한 문제이며 이에 대해 언급할 입장에 있지 아니함.

0 기득권 보호: 구체적 사례 발생시 고려 가능

0 결론적으로 현재의 22조 23조로 모두 COVER 할수있으며, 오직 NON-VIOLATION 조항의 반영 여부만 결정하면 됨.

- EC 는 이에 대하여 법률적으로는 맞는 논평이지만 서비스 협상 결과의 전체적

통상국	2차보	법무부	보사부	문화부	교통부	체신부	경기원	재무부
농수부	상공부	건설부	노동부	과기처	해항청	공보처		

외신 1과　통제관

0101

균형을 맞춘다는 관점에서 지금 결정을 요하는 사항이 많다고 지적하였으며

　　0 다른 나라들도 쟁점별로 자국 입장을 밝힘으로써 선.개도국간 기존 입장이 반복되었음.

　　- 각국의 발언이후 의장은 NON-VIOLATION 조항만추후 재토의하고 기타 사항은 현재의 22조, 23조 그대로 토의를 완료할 것을 제의하였으나 EC 가강력한 이의를 제기함으로써 전체를 재협의키로함.

　　2. SCHEDULING (9.25 오후 및 9.26 오전 HAWES 호주대사 주재 주요국 비공식 협의)

　　- 무차별적 질적 규제는 합법적인 국내규제로서 SCHEDULING 대상이 아니라는 것은 기합의된바 있으나, 이러한 무차별적 질적 규제 (인가기준,자격기준, 기술적 표준)들중 합법적 국내규제로의 판별 기준 (7.25 자 의장 COMMENTARY 16조4항) 적용에 불확실한 요인들이 많기 때문에 무차별적 질적 규제 자체에 대한 규율은 마련하지 않은채 동 규제의 운영 (ADMINISTRATION)에 대하여 규율하는 접근 방법이 논의되고 있음.

　　- 이와 같은 맥락에서 EC 는 별첨 (FAX송부)와 같은 2단계 접근 방법을 제시하였는바

　　0 UR 에서 체결되는 서비스협정에는 무차별적 질적 규제를 REASONABLE, OBJECTIVE AND INPARTIAL MANNER 하에 운영하여야 한다는 의무를 제 6조 (국내 규제)에 규정하고

　　0 무차별적 질적 규제 자체가 합법적 국내 규제가 되기 위한 조건 또는 기준은 UR 이후에 설정한다는 작업 계획만 규정하는 접근방법으로서 많은 나라의 지지를 받고 있음.

　　- 한편, 스위스, 북구, 호주, 뉴질랜드 등 4개국은보다 적극적인 대안 (별첨 FAX 송부)을 제시하고있는바

　　0 무차별적 질적 규제의 운영을 봉하여 시장접근 약속을 무효화 또는 침해하지 않도록 의무 규정을 명문화 하고

　　0 이에 관한 변경이 있을 경우 즉각 봉지토록의 무화 하자는 것이나

　　- 다음과 같은 이유에서 많은 나라가 비판적 입장을 견지하고 있음.

　　0 시장접근 약속의 무효화 또는 침해 금지는 NON-VIOLATION 규정으로 해결 가능

　　0 NATIONAL SCHEDULE 에 기재하는 무차별적 질적규제의 법률적 지위가 애매함.

PAGE 2

0102

0 국내 규제의 변경시 즉각 통지는 과도한 부담을 초래하며, 일반적인 TRANSPARENCY (제3조) 규정으로 충분함.

3. 양허 협상의 실질적 기준 (9.26 오전 JARAMILLO의장 주재 주요국 비공식 협의)

- 양허 협상의 실질적 기준은 미국의 요청에 따라 토의를 연기하였으며, 다만 제18조 (양허 협상)의 일부 괄호로 된 사항들에 대하여 합의를 도출하였음.

첨부: 1. EC 제안 1부

2. 4개국 공동제안 1부. 끝

(GVW(F)-377)

(대사 박수길-국장)

DRAFT

25.9.91/2

Guw(71)-377 10P27 2000

Guw-1862 礼)

ARTICLE VI - DOMESTIC REGULATION

Points for Discussion

In the light of ongoing consultations, it is my impression that possibilities for progressing work on Article VI are more likely to be found in the text proposed by the EC. There seems to be growing acceptance that matters discussed under paragraphs 4, 5 and 6 of Article XVI should be dealt with in paragraph 2 of Article VI. Discussion has identified a number of issues requiring resolution, of which the main ones seem to be the following:

Issues for Discussion/Resolution

1. [In sectors or sub-sectors where specific commitments are undertaken]:

    - The issue to be settled is whether paragraph 1 should relate to "good administration" of regulations in <u>all</u> service sectors (general obligation) or whether it should be limited to sectors or sub-sectors where specific commitments have been undertaken. (Many insist that this should be confined to the latter.)

2. ... reasonable, objective and impartial manner:

    - What will these terms mean in practice? (It would seem useful to obtain a legal viewpoint.)

8—1

O-HAW   0104

- 2 -

3. **With a view to ... unnecessary barriers to trade:**

    - Is it necessary to spell out the purpose of this exercise or can this phrase be dispensed with?

4. **[in sectors or sub-sectors where a party has undertaken specific commitments]:**

    - Would it be preferable to say "in sectors or sub-sectors <u>subject to</u> or <u>covered by</u> commitments"?

5. **... through appropriate bodies ...:**

    - The question has been raised as to whether it is necessary to be as specific at this stage.

6. **Work programme objective:**

    - It has been pointed out that inserting "<u>shall aim to</u> ensure that such requirements are ..." would constitute a more realistic objective for the work programme aimed at developing the criteria.

7. <u>**Inter-alia:**</u>

    - This phrase implies the existence of other criteria; if so, which ones?

- 3 -

8. **not more burdensome than necessary to ... [achieve national policy objectives]:**

    - It has been suggested that "the quality of the service" is but one example of a policy objective.

9. **licensing requirements:**

    - It has been pointed out that the restriction on the supply of the service relates not so much to the licensing requirement, but to the licensing procedure (outlined in paragraph 2 of the 23 September text by the SNANZ countries).

10. **Criterion (2d)?:**

    - It has been proposed that as a further criterion, technical standards should be based on relevant international standards where these exist.

8-3

C-HAW   0106

REVISED TEXT REPLACING PARAGRAPH 2 OF ARTICLE VI

[1.] In sectors or sub-sectors where specific commitments are undertaken, ① each party shall administer all measures in a reasonable, objective and impartial manner. ②

[2.] With a view to ensuring that measures relating to qualification requirements, technical standards and ③ licensing requirements do not constitute unnecessary barriers to trade in sectors or sub-sectors where a party has undertaken specific commitments ④ the PARTIES shall, through appropriate bodies ⑤ they may establish, develop any necessary disciplines. Such disciplines shall ⑥ ensure that such requirements are, inter alia : ⑦

    (a) based on objective and transparent criteria, such as competence and the ability to provide the service;

    (b) not more burdensome than necessary to ⑧ maintain the quality of the service.

    (c) In the case of licensing requirements, ⑨ not in themselves a~ ~~additional~~ restriction on the supply of the service.

(.) ⑩

8 — 4

0107

DRAFT
25.9.91

ARTICLE XVI - MARKET ACCESS

Points for Discussion

An addition to Article XVI has been suggested by Switzerland, the Nordics, Australia and New Zealand. The main concern underlying this proposal is to ensure that market access commitments are not nullified or impaired by the application of measures which relate to qualifications, standards or licensing matters and which, being of a qualitative non-discriminatory measure, would not require scheduling under the approach being developed.

Consideration of the proposal has given rise to questions regarding the need for additional transparency, the purpose and legal implications of notification and implications for Article XX.

Issues for Discussion/Resolution

1. Identification of requirements relating to licensing, standards and qualifications:

- Is the intended obligation ("shall indicate") already covered by the general transparency requirements in Article III, or is it better dealt with in terms of a scheduling instruction with regard to Article XX?

- If the latter, how much information is required for such an indication, e.g. title of or reference to legislation, or stipulation of the nature of the requirement?

- What is the legal status of such information as there seems to be no implication that the legislation as such is to be bound?

P-RAW   0108

- 2 -

2.   4(d) Consumer protection legislation ?

- It has been proposed that measures constituting <u>consumer protection legislation</u> should be added to the list.

- One question that arises is whether this is not really a motivation or objective of licensing or qualification requirements, i.e. is of a different category.

3.   Undertaking on application of measures to ensure that such measures do not nullify or impair concessions:

- Several participants have responded sympathetically to the proposal that access commitments be accompanied by an undertaking not to frustrate intended benefits of concessions through the application of domestic regulations. Even though such regulations would not be bound, modification to regulations or adverse changes in the means of their application could give rise to nullification and impairment cases.

- A question has been raised as to whether this would find expression in a new Article XVI:4 or whether it could be accommodated by amending the chapeau of Article XVI.

4.   Addition to Article XX, Schedules of Commitments:

- It has been suggested that there should be an obligation to notify the introduction of new measures which are consistent with the criteria specified in Article VI:4. This is an area requiring further consideration including the implications for modification of schedules where such measures would be inconsistent with the obligation proposed under note 3 above.

P.HAW

8 - 6

0103

- 3 -

Additional commitments

A further proposal has been made by Canada in relation to the possibility of negotiating additional commitments with respect to measures not subject to scheduling under Articles XVI or XVII. If this is accepted a decision is needed as to whether this would constitute a new Article XVIII and how it could be appropriately reflected in amendments to Article XX.

8 - 7

P-HAW   0110

ADDITION TO ARTICLE XVI MARKET ACCESS

(4)   In sectors or subsectors where market access commitments
      are undertaken, a Party shall indicate where measures are
      maintained which constitute

         (a)   licencing requirements
         (b)   technical standards
         (c)   qualification requirements
         ( )

Such measures shall not be applied in a manner which
nullifies or impairs access available under the terms of
the market access commitments in the relevant sector.

ADDITION TO ARTICLE XX SCHEDULES OF COMMITMENTS

( )   Where a Party maintains measures which fall under Article
      XVI (4) it shall indicate the existence of such measures
      by an inscription in Column ( ).

( )   A Party shall promptly notify other Parties of the
      introduction of new measures on standards, licencing
      requirements and qualification requirements which are
      consistent with the provisions of Article VI(5) in sectors
      or subsectors in which the Party has made a specific
      commitment.

(9186G)

0111

8 — 8

외 무 부

종 별 :

번 호 : GVW-1863   일 시 : 91 0927 2000

수 신 : 장 관(봉기, 경기원, 재무부, 법무부, 농수부, 문화부, 상공부, 건설부, 보사부,

발 신 : 주 제네바 대사   노동부, 교통부, 체신부, 과기처, 공보처, 항만청)

제 목 : UR/GNS 회의(6)

9.27(금) 종료된 표제회의 결과를 하기 보고함.

1. MFN 에 관한 GNS 전체비공식회의(9.27.오전)

- 캐나다만이 인력이동 협정과 영화 공동생산협정 관련 구체적인 MFN 일탈요청사항을 비밀 유지 조건하에 사무국에 제출하였음을 밝혔으며 기타 발언국 없음.

0 이는 지난 7월 각국이 MFN 일탈을 원하는 구체적 정부조치를 제출하고 암실작업을 통하여 MFN 일탈대상을 확정하기로 함에 따라 정책적 토의의 필요성이 약화된 때문인 것으로 사료됨.

2. GNS 공식 회의(9.27.오후)

가. OFFER 제안 설명

- 헝가리 (GNS/W/135), 남아프리카 (GNS/W/136), 이집트 (GNS/W/137)가 자국 OFFER 제안 설명을 하였으며

0 코스타리카 및 베네주엘라도 분야별 구체적 약속내용을 담은 수정 OFFER 를 제출하였음.

나. 향후 협상 진행 계획

- 10.16주: JARAMILO 의장 및 HAWES 호주 대사주재로 SCHEDULING, 협정 제 4조 및 양허협상의 실질적 기준, MFN 및 관련 이슈, 기타 조문에 대하여 비공식 협의

- 10.21.주 : 서비스 분야별 토의

0 10.21(월): GNS 공식회의, 10.16주 비공식 협의결과 보고

0 10.22(화): 해운분야

0 10.23(수): 금융분야

0 10.24(목) : AUDIO VISUAL

통상국 상공부	2차보 상공부	법무부 건설부	보사부 노동부	문화부 과기처	교통부 해항청	체신부 공보처	경기원	농수부

PAGE 1   91.09.28   08:46 WG

외신 1과 통제관

0112

O 10.25(금) : 봉신

- 10.21-25 : 10.16.주 비공식 협의사항에 대한 협의계속, 서비스 분야별 토의와 병행

O 10.26(토) : 비공식 협의 결과 보고

- 10.26 이후 : 갓트사무국 법률전문가와 각국법률전문가 (희망국 참가) 공동으로 법적 조문화

- 10.28주 : 양자 또는 복수국간 REQUEST/OFFER협상 (일본만이 REQUEST LIST 를 배부하였는 바타국가도 REQUEST 를 조속히 배부하도록 촉구)

JARAMILLO 의장과 HAWES 대사 주재로 협정의 모든 조문에 대한 비공식 협의 계속

- 11.1 : 작업 완료를 위한 GNS 공식 회의

다. 기타

- 호주는 다음주중에 각국에 REQUEST-LIST 를 배부하겠다고 하였으며 캐나다 역시 모든 참가국에 대한 COMMON REQUEST 와 일부 국가에 대한 구체적 REQUEST 를 제출하겠다고 함.

- JARAMILLO 의장은 주요국 비공식 협의를 거쳐 재작성된 제 4조 및 18조와 인력 이동 부속서초안 (본부대표 지참)을 배부함

- HAWES 대사는 SCHEDULING 에 대한 비공식협의 경과를 설명함 (기보고 전문 참조)

- 갓트사무국은 원산지 규정에 대한 배경문서를 배부함. (본부대표 지참)

3. 건의

- 10.16.부터 3개 협상과제 (FRAMEWORK, 분야별부속서, INITIAL COMMITMENT)에 대한 집중적 협상이 진행될 예정인바

O 10.21.주에는 각분야별 전문가의 회의참석이 필요한 것으로 사료됨.

(금융, 봉신분야는 10.21.주 이전에는 비공식 협의개최 가능성이 있음)

- 10.28 주 부터의 양허협상에 대비, 아국 OFFER 의 정밀한 보완작업뿐만 아니라 주요 선진국에대한 REQUEST-LIST 준비가 시급한 것으로 판단됨.끝

(대사 박수길-국장)

PAGE 2

0113

외교문서 비밀해제: 우루과이라운드2 20

우루과이라운드 서비스 협상 2

초판인쇄 2024년 03월 15일
초판발행 2024년 03월 15일

지은이 한국학술정보(주)
펴낸이 채종준
펴낸곳 한국학술정보(주)
주 소 경기도 파주시 회동길 230(문발동)
전 화 031-908-3181(대표)
팩 스 031-908-3189
홈페이지 http://ebook.kstudy.com
E-mail 출판사업부 publish@kstudy.com
등 록 제일산-115호(2000. 6. 19)

ISBN 979-11-7217-122-3 94340
      979-11-7217-102-5 94340 (set)